CORNISH SHIPWRECKS

The wreck of the frigate *Anson* on Loe Bar in 1807.

CORNISH SHIPWRECKS

The South Coast

by

RICHARD LARN and CLIVE CARTER

TAPLINGER PUBLISHING COMPANY
NEW YORK

First published in the United States, 1969

TAPLINGER PUBLISHING CO., INC.
29 East Tenth Street
New York, N.Y. 10003

© Richard Larn and Clive Carter 1969

Library of Congress Catalogue Card Number: 69 - 17400

In Memory of

the late F. E. STRIKE BEM

to whose enthusiasm and encouragement
this work owes so much

Made and printed in Great Britain by
Clarke Doble & Brendon Limited, Plymouth

CONTENTS

LIST OF ILLUSTRATIONS

*The map sections on pages 37, 43, 67, 80, 99, 143,
145, 161, 162, 190, 216 and 234 are based on
Ordnance Survey maps by permission of the
Controller of Her Majesty's Stationery Office.
Crown copyright reserved.*

'—that I take away God's grace from them, their English meaning is that they now shall have nor receive no benefit from shipwreck. They have been so long used to reap purchase by the calamity of the ruin of shipping as they claim it hereditary.'

—Sir John Killigrew, December 1619

CHAPTER ONE

NO FRIENDLY COAST

THE view from one of Cornwall's prominent headlands on a fine summer's day suggests little of violence or death. With a gentle breeze coming from the sea, the air full of crying gulls, and the swell lapping quietly at the cliff base and over rocky outcrops, it is difficult to believe that this coast could completely destroy a ship and its crew; though, if the headland is one such as Rame Head, Dodman or the Lizard, the remains of a dozen or more ships lie hidden at its very foot. But visit that same scene during a full gale from the south-west and there can be no doubt why seamen have held this coast in fear and respect since time immemorial. The wind comes howling unhindered from the open wastes of the Atlantic and seems to clutch at the sea, to pick it up and hurl it against the cliffs. The rock shudders under the impact, the waves are thrown back against the wind, and the air is filled with a fury of sound and spray. Small wonder that the crews of the old Lizard lifeboat at Polpeor used to reach their boat by crawling down the approach road on hands and knees for fear of being blown clear over the cliff edge. In these conditions, there was little chance of survival for any ship in distress caught close in to this relentless coastline.

There have been so many wrecks, known and unknown, on the coast of Cornwall, that to attempt an estimate of their number would be futile. The records go back to about AD 1300 but the claims to 'rights of wreck' by various lords of the manors are of even greater antiquity, and, apart from wrecks of which some record exists, untold numbers of ships have sunk without trace. When there was evidence of a wreck it was often only timber or cargo found on some lonely beach, days or even weeks after a storm or period of dense fog, sometimes accompanied by shapeless bundles of flesh and clothing, the pathetic remnants of seamen or passengers. They usually had no means of identification on them, and none knew from whence they came. No ceremony and little respect was given to their interment, and the cliffs of Cornwall hold the remains of thousands of men, women and children, washed ashore and buried almost where they were found, in anonymous graves marked sometimes with a rock from the beach, soon overgrown. On the clifftops overlooking Loe Bar and to the west of Porthleven, where these stones can still be seen, memorial crosses were erected in 1949.

It was not until July 1808 that an Act of Parliament was passed requiring that bodies cast ashore were to be given Christian burial in consecrated ground. The chief sponsors were Thomas Grylle, a Helston solicitor, and Davies Gilbert, a local Member of Parliament, and with enforcement of the Grylles Act came a five-shilling reward for reporting the finding of a corpse—and a fine of at least five pounds for failing to do so. It then became the responsibility of the local authorities—the police, the church or the lord of the manor—to ensure that bodies were properly buried. The business of transporting the bodies from the beach to the graveyard was often unpleasant, in which case the finder was awarded an extra payment of one shilling and sixpence, and if the corpse was in a particularly advanced state of decomposition, there was a further payment of 'beer money' on completion of the gruesome task. Prior to 1808 it was not uncommon for corpses washed ashore to be conveniently moved to another part of the beach or foreshore to avoid responsibility for disposing of them, and seldom were bodies found with clothing on them—the dead had no use for clothing.

Once the Act had become law, local parish registers began to record such burials in order to substantiate their claim for reimbursement and these early records give some idea of the numbers in which bodies came ashore. The parish records of Mullion, for example, show that between 1808 and 1874, a total of 132 corpses were washed ashore. Sixty-seven of these were buried in Mullion churchyard, and it must be presumed that either the remainder were identified and buried by relatives, or that Mullion churchyard became full and they were interred elsewhere. The same records also show that at least twenty-nine vessels sank in Mullion roads alone during the same period, and Mullion's toll is not to be compared with other parts of the Cornish coast far more notorious for wrecks, such as the Lizard or the Manacles.

The reasons for the vast numbers of shipwrecks on the Cornish

NO FRIENDLY COAST 13

coast are not difficult to understand. The first and most obvious is the position of Cornwall, a long, narrow wedge which juts sixty miles out into the busy Atlantic approaches to the British Isles, appearing on the map rather like a seabooted leg and foot striding out into the shipping lanes. Not only the ships inward bound to English ports, but also those for the North Sea and the Baltic made landfall at Land's End or the Lizard, the 'toe and heel' of the boot and the south-western extremity of England. Here the shipping routes divide, vessels bound for Wales, Liverpool and the Irish Sea passing the north coast of Cornwall, those for the English Channel and beyond passing the south coast.

Apart from the great flow of ordinary shipping relatively close to the coast, Cornwall's geographical location also accounts for its own extensive seaborne trade, which has meant that from earliest times many ships have regularly approached or left its dangerous shores. Long before Christianity reached the rest of Britain, Irish and Breton saints had landed on its western shore, and both Romans and Phoenicians beached their galleys to trade for tin and gold. The Plantagenet kings hired its fleets to transport soldiers to the French wars or the Holy Land, where they rubbed shoulders with pilgrims who had embarked from Cornwall. From mediaeval times to the nineteenth century, trade flourished with Ireland, Spain, the Low Countries and the Baltic, while the fisheries rose from tiny 'porths' with few boats and men, until during their heyday in the decades before the First World War they employed hundreds of men, women and children, and it was possible to walk from one side to the other of harbours like Polperro, Mevagissey and Newlyn on the decks of moored luggers. Every Cornish port once boasted a fleet of sailing ships, many of them launched by its own shipyard. These ships traded far and wide; some took casks of pilchards to Spain and the Latin countries, returning with fruit, wine or brimstone from the Mediterranean. Others plied the North American emigrant trade, bringing back timber, cod or furs, but most of the smaller schooners, smacks and ketches plied the humbler coasting trade. During the great copper and tin-mining booms, scores of these small ships sailed on every tide, loaded with ore for Swansea or Newport, and returned with coals to feed the boiler fires of the pumps and whims of hundreds of mines which once worked all over the county. There was also a busy trade in culm and limestone

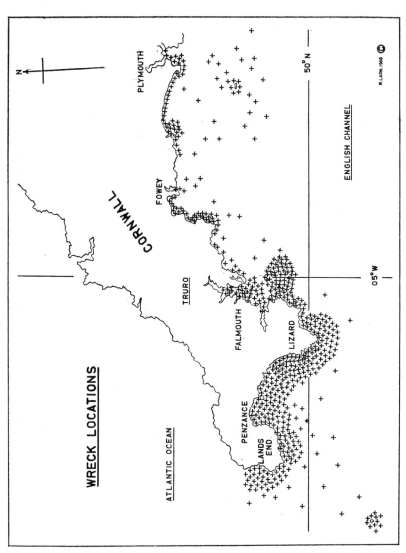

Wreck concentrations off the South Cornish coast between Land's End and Rame Head.

for agricultural purposes, firebrick and clay from Bridgwater, and roofing slate from North Wales. Even when mining began to decline there was still the china clay industry of east Cornwall, and until the modern motor-coaster arrived on the scene, the ports of St Austell Bay saw the coming and going of dozens of small schooners and ketches.

The coast of Cornwall was never a pleasant one for any ship to be near in bad weather; there was virtually no shelter from the Atlantic gales along the north coast, but a vessel between Land's End and Rame Head had a chance of reaching shelter in Mount's Bay, Falmouth—Cornwall's major port where '500 of sail' could ride safely—Fowey or Plymouth Sound. On the other hand, a gale from south or east turned all these into a dreaded lee shore. Then sailing ships blown off course or caught inshore with an on-shore wind were often incapable of sailing clear of the land and, becoming embayed between two headlands, would be driven ashore and wrecked. When a sailing ship was thus caught in a bay, people from far and near would crowd the clifftops to watch the unfortun-ate vessel beat back and forth, attempting to claw its way seaward to safety. It was not uncommon for a ship to sail back and forth in this manner for days at a time, the spectators ashore moving along the coast in sympathy; men staying away from work to watch, the children from school. Sometimes, in a desperate attempt to avert disaster, the master of a ship would anchor, take in all sail and 'strike' or lower the topmasts to reduce resistance to the wind. But early sailing ships did not have the advantage of heavy studded chain or cable attached to their anchors. They used, instead, huge ropes, often ten inches in diameter and when, as often happened, these snapped under the strain of a ship at anchor the vessel would drive ashore. The seabed of Mount's Bay, especially in the Loe Bar area, bears witness to the number of ships which lost their anchors in this manner. Once the master of a ship accepted going ashore as inevitable, he would try to pick a safe stretch of shoaling beach in the hope of saving life and possibly reducing damage to his vessel. But there was always the danger that he would strike rock before reaching the shallows, or swing broadside on to the shore and capsize. This is what happened when HMS *Anson,* beached deliberately in Mount's Bay after losing three anchors, capsized, drowning nearly 100 officers and men.

Apart from the necessity for taking a ship close in to land so that its master could establish his position, vessels were also required to pass close to the Lizard in order to exchange signals with Lloyd's station near Bass Point. Sailing ships might be several months on passage and the duration of a voyage was so uncertain that owners could seldom establish markets for a cargo in advance. It therefore became the practice for ships to leave foreign ports with no idea as to their eventual destination. They sailed with the simple instruction to proceed to 'Falmouth for orders'. As the anticipated date of arrival drew near, the ship's owners would find the most profitable market for its cargo and pass instructions to Lloyd's signal station, which would relay them to the ship when eventually she appeared. If no market was readily available the vessel would be instructed to enter Falmouth and lie at anchor until its final port of discharge had been decided. The earliest method of signalling was by means of flag hoists, and ships often had to take considerable risks when standing close in to read the little squares of bunting fluttering from the yard-arm of the signal station. The wrecks of many ships that came too near to the Lizard still lie amongst the Stags reef or the inner and outer Cledges rocks, part of the huge reef that extends seawards for a quarter mile from the headland.

Falmouth was in its prime as a seaport 150 years ago, and dozens of ships entered and left harbour every day. In the late 1850s, a local newspaper, *The Falmouth Packet*, reported that 'the town had recently witnessed 320 vessels at anchor at one time', and this vast exchange of shipping at Falmouth accounts to some extent for the large number of wrecks that occurred on the Manacles reef, which lies across the approach to the harbour.

By far the greatest number of shipwrecks, however, were due, in Cornwall as elsewhere, to the inadequacies of navigational aids in those early days. The first reliable ship's chronometer did not appear until 1772; sextants, or their earlier equivalents, were seldom part of a ship's standard equipment, and navigational charts were for the most part unreliable and sometimes dangerously misleading. A survey of the Isles of Scilly, instituted in 1680 by the newly-formed Trinity Brethren, showed that the Scillies were, in fact, ten miles south of their previously designated position. Some thirty years later, in 1707, when Sir Cloudesley Shovel's fleet was returning from the Mediterranean, four of his ships struck the western

Page 17: Penzance lifeboat returning from the brigantine *Jeune Hortense*, stranded at Long Rock on 17 May 1888. The lifeboat carriage is in the foreground.

Page 18: The 798-ton costal tanker *Allegrity* wrecked at Caerhays near the Dodman on 13 December 1961, during a hard SSE gale.

rocks of the Scillies—drowning the admiral and 2,000 officers and men. (The wreck of one of these ships was located by naval divers in 1967.) When in the course of recent research into navigational standards of the time, the log-book positions of the surviving ships were plotted for a specific time, there was found to be a discrepancy of as much as forty miles between their calculated positions.

Sailing ships carried few officers and it was not uncommon for a merchant ship to cross the world with only one man on board capable of establishing the ship's position. Other officers may have had some basic training in navigation but were often denied opportunity for practice by masters who liked to keep the ship's navigation a 'closed shop'—even to the extent of keeping the charts under lock and key.

Because the standard of navigation was so poor, a visual sighting of land was the only guarantee of a ship's position. In the days of sail, a lookout would be posted as high as possible in the fore or mainmast rigging as a vessel approached land. There, 100 feet or more above sea level, the lookout had a visual range of ten to twelve miles in clear weather, though a steep and prominent headland could be sighted from as far as thirty miles off. But in bad weather, fog or driving rain, visibility at sea can be instantly reduced to only a few yards, and approaching land under such conditions, and especially a rock-girt coast such as Cornwall, was an infinitely more hazardous undertaking then than it is today with such modern aids to position-finding as radar and electronic depth-sounders.

Another popularly cherished but quite unsubstantiated cause of shipwrecks on this part of the coast has been the alleged activities of 'Cornish wreckers' who were said to mislead ships by displaying false lights, or extinguishing recognised land beacons in the hope of luring a vessel ashore. In fact, there is little evidence that 'wrecking' in this sense ever took place in Cornwall, and no recorded convictions, but there are grounds in abundance for applying the term, more accurately, to the age-old Cornish practice of wholesale plundering of any wreck that came ashore. The nearest approach to evidence of a deliberate wrecking is probably an incident in December 1680 when a Virginian trader was wrecked near St Agnes, Isles of Scilly, and the lighthouse keeper was sacked for having failed to light the fire in the lighthouse until after the ship

B

had struck, and for later looting the wreck's cargo. As a result of this incident, the Trinity Brethren issued instructions barring any Cornishman from employment at St Agnes lighthouse.

Helping yourself to what the sea brought to your doorstep, however, was an altogether different matter and certain districts, such as Breage and Germoe, Porthleven and the Scillies were particularly notorious for the scale and efficiency of their plundering. When a wooden ship came ashore it quickly went to pieces and its scattered cargo would often travel down the coast to come ashore in some lonely cove miles away from the wreck itself. To the Cornishman of those days, such offerings were no less than his birthright. The standard of living, especially for the tinners, labourers and fishermen, was desperately low, luxuries were few and far between and a rumour of goods for the taking was enough to bring people from all walks of life hurrying to a wreck. As if by magic, donkey carts, hand carts, even wheelbarrows would appear, be loaded to overflowing, and then as quickly disappear. Goods were buried on the clifftops for subsequent recovery, hidden in millponds and under water-wheels, beneath cottage flagstones or in the thatch, or—a favourite place—in mine shafts. During the demolition of an old cottage at the Lizard some years ago, the collapse of the ceiling brought with it a quantity of gold and silver foreign coins and some jewellery, no doubt the proceeds from some long-forgotten wreck.

But there was another side to the picture and for every instance of looting wrecks there are a dozen accounts in the records of self-less bravery in rescuing and succouring victims of shipwreck. No coast in England has a finer record of achievement by its lifeboat service than Cornwall and, volunteers to a man, successive generations of families have always been proud of their positions in the local lifeboat. In the fishing villages, too, the inhabitants have traditionally rallied every resource available to them in their efforts to save life at the scene of a wreck, swimming out to a ship with a line, throwing open their homes to survivors and spending entire nights on a gale-swept beach to help as best they could. Only when the lives of all on board had been saved did the age-old instincts assert themselves, remembering as one old Sennen Cove fisherman once put it, 'there's nothing like a good wreck'.

Disagreement over the ownership of wrecks between the Crown

authorities and local lords of manors were frequent occurrences. The area considered most valuable belonged to the lord of Connerton, who owned from Cudden Point on the south coast to Gwithian beach, the other side of Land's End. The lord of Methleigh owned all wreck between Cudden Point and Loe Bar, the lord of Winnianton from Loe Bar to Polurrian, and the manor of Predannack Wartha—the entire Lizard area. Such rights were enforced by armed retainers who would seize anything they considered the property of their master, and often a great deal more if they could get away with it. When the reputed 'treasure ship' of Gunwalloe came ashore in 1526, three local lords banded together and carried off goods to the value of £10,000. But the retainers and lords did not have things all their own way. In 1340 a vessel went ashore at Porthleven, near Helston, and before the watchdogs could arrive the villagers descended on the wreck and removed not only every scrap of its cargo but the entire structure of the ship itself.

Two other 'treasure ships' are also known to have gone ashore at Gunwalloe, one carrying a quantity of bullion, silver plate, church ornaments, gold cloth and armour, all of which spilled out on the sand in the shallows below the old cliff fortress. The other wreck contained silver coins, which have been found in varying numbers ever since. At least four full-scale salvage attempts have been made on the wrecks, but each has left the promoters out of pocket. The last known finding of a coin occurred in late 1966, when a holiday visitor from Germany found one amongst the rocks.

Mount's Bay is another area reputed to be rich in treasure. A Flemish ship described as being 'exceptionally rich' was wrecked there in 1566 and another, the rich prize of the Earl of Cumberland, lost in the same area in 1589, was looted by Penares, 'a gentleman of great and good authority'. But the best authenticated treasure ship went ashore at the Lizard with over £100,000 worth of silver bars on board. Sir John Killigrew set about its recovery, and 'threatened death to anyone who tried to stop him'. The area became a recognised site for testing new diving apparatus, and numerous inventions have been tried out there. During a search of the wreck of the *Jonkheer Meester Van de Wall Putteshock*, sunk at Poldhu Cove in 1867, the searchers found a metal box containing £13,000 in Dutch currency, sovereigns and jewellery. Meantime, the local fishermen were busy with tongs and glass-bottomed buckets, recovering ingots of pure tin from the same wreck and selling them for the princely sum of £15 a ton! At Loe Bar, an area is still known as 'the gold mine' because of the numerous gold sovereigns which have been picked up there in the past. It has been said that they came from the wreck of HMS *Anson* and that the frigate was a pay ship, but in fact she was on blockade duty off Brest and was not carrying bullion, although she no doubt carried a small quantity of coin. Ships carrying tin from Cornish mines have also been frequent victims over the years and as recently as the summer of 1966 one such wreck found off the north coast of Cornwall contained two piles of ingots worth a small fortune.

There can be no doubt at all that wrecks exist around Cornwall, as they do elsewhere, worth a king's ransom, and only await finding by a lucky or determined diver. The wide and unrestricted use of the aqualung and sport-diving equipment has opened up the sea to everyone and of the thousands of holiday-makers who come to the West Country each year an ever increasing proportion come to dive. Conditions in Cornwall for sport diving are excellent and compare with anything to be found in the world, despite the low temperatures and vicious tides. Some of these visitors discover old wrecks for themselves and take the trouble to research into their histories, but all too many have neither the interest nor the time to discover what it is they have located. If they find an object of interest, it is usually carried away to adorn a wall or serve as a door-stop for a while, finally finishing up in the dustbin.

In an attempt to discourage such indiscriminate 'looting' of wreck sites, the University of London's Institute of Archaeology has recently formed the Committee of Nautical Research. This committee has already started on the immense task of compiling notes on every known wreck around the British Isles, and is interested in each and every wreck 'find'. Elsewhere, notably at Helston in Cornwall and Brixham in Devon, maritime museums have been formed with the object of compiling records which will be of assistance to divers, both local and visiting, and providing centres at which their more interesting finds can be housed and exhibited for the benefit of all.

The collection of wreck information, photographs and charts which follows this chapter represents but a fraction of the total wreck information of Cornwall. It would need many such volumes to encompass it all, but it is hoped that it will inspire and encourage others with similar interests. It is an indescribable thrill to research into a wreck, often for months on end, and eventually to use that information to locate the actual vessel on the sea bed. To touch a ship's wheel, unmoved since the day the ship sank, to run one's hand over the engraved name on a ship's bell—silent for perhaps a hundred years—only those who have experienced this sensation for themselves can know just what it means.

CHAPTER TWO

RAME HEAD TO ST ANTHONY
LIGHT

O N the western side of the ancient haven of Plymouth Sound rises the first of the tall cliffs of Cornwall. Rugged, but without the desolation of the far west, they run southwards from the mouth of the Tamar, beneath the wooded slopes of Mount Edgcumbe into Cawsand Bay, the last great stronghold of Cornish smuggling, and rise steadily to Penlee Point, and the high bluff headland of Rame. Here they swing sharply westwards and begin their long march to the Dodman, the Lizard, and at last Land's End and the open Atlantic. History in the making has been seen by every creek and inlet. Barbary corsairs, Breton pirates and Dutch privateers have swept past Rame Head on their unlawful occasions; the remains of a watchtower, where a keeper was once paid eightpence a year to keep a lookout for them, can still be seen there. In August 1588, the great Armada passed only a few miles seawards, and perhaps its commander, the unhappy Don Medina Sidonia, glimpsed the trees of Mount Edgcumbe in the morning sunshine, his promised reward for conquering heretic England. Sixty years later the cliffs echoed to the roar of cannon as Parliamentary Plymouth lay besieged by the Royalist army. The Dutch wars followed, and Plymouth developed into an important naval yard, where English men-of-war could refit, victual and press crews.

But Plymouth Sound had a grave disadvantage; when the wind blew from the south or south-east it became the dreaded lee shore. Men-of-war so caught were often wrecked, and the remains of the *Coronation*, of 90 guns, and the *Harwich*, of 70 guns, still lie where the gale flung them in 1691, drowning most of their crews. Another serious hazard was the Eddystone reef, nine miles south of Rame Head, hard in the path of ships making for the Sound. One of the early wrecks on the reef was the 350-ton ship *Half Moon* of

Danzig, which struck on 6 February 1673 and sank instantly, though her crew rowed ashore at Looe. It took the tenacity and peculiar genius of Henry Winstanley to erect the first lighthouse on the Eddystone. He lost one of his own ships there in August 1695, and when another, the *Constant*, followed it that winter, he decided to build the lighthouse. It was completed in 1700 after four years of work under almost impossible conditions, only to be swept away, together with Winstanley and its keepers, in a hurricane which struck the British Isles in November 1703.

Other lighthouses were subsequently built, but Plymouth Sound still remained as dangerous in a gale as the coast around Rame and beyond to the west, where ships were often embayed and wrecked in the wide sweep of Whitesand Bay. On 12 December 1720 the trader *Josiah and Betty* was lost off Rame, though her crew escaped. On 3 March 1750 the *Endeavour*, bound from Exeter to Cadiz, was wrecked at Downderry, not far from Looe, the fishing village astride the river at the western end of Whitesand Bay. A contemporary newspaper reported that 'the customs staff from East and West Looe saved the wreck from the wreckers, who came armed with rugged short bludgeons'.

Ten years later the loss of another warship, the *Conqueror*, wrecked on Drake's Island at the mouth of the Tamar, bore witness to the continuing dangers of the Sound, and in January 1762 six merchantmen were lost and as many men-of-war dismasted during a southerly gale. There was a fairly common disaster, though perhaps from an unusual cause, when the frigate *Kent* suddenly blew up while at anchor off Cawsand in 1769; a careless gunner had knocked out his pipe near the powder magazine. A French frigate fell victim to Rame Head on 11 November 1787, and many other merchantmen and warships were wrecked or stranded, both inside and west of the Sound.

In 1788 a scheme was put forward by the master-attendant of the naval dockyard to build a breakwater across the mouth of the Sound, and so provide the fleet with a sheltered and well-protected anchorage. Warships would then no longer have to anchor in Torbay when the weather made the Sound impossible, but nothing was done, even though Torbay was little safer than the Sound. In January 1796 there could have been a major disaster when the large East Indiaman *Dutton*, carrying 400 soldiers and their

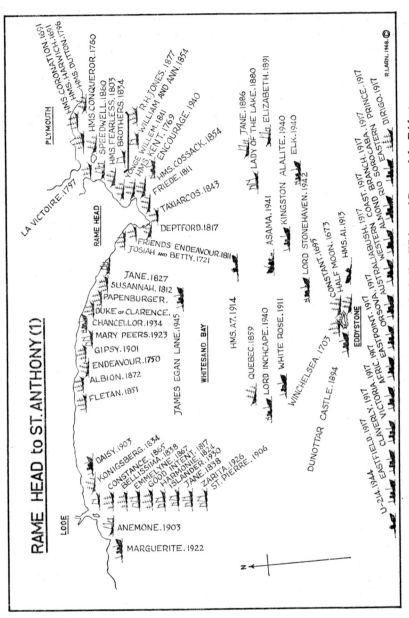

RAME HEAD to ST. ANTHONY (1)

PLYMOUTH

HMS CORONATION.1691
HMS. HARWICH.1691
HMS. DUTTON.1796
HMS. CONQUEROR. 1760
SPEEDWELL. 1860
HMS. FEARLESS. 1803
BROTHERS. 1834
R. H. JONES. 1877
WILLIAM AND ANN. 1854
YONGE WILLEM. 1841
HMS. KENT. 1769
ENCOURAGE. 1940
FRIEDE. 1811
HMS. COSSACK. 1854

LA VICTOIRE. 1797

RAME HEAD

TAXIARCOS. 1843

DEPTFORD. 1817

FRIENDS ENDEAVOUR. 1811
JOSIAH AND BETTY. 1721

JANE. 1827
SUSANNAH. 1812
PAPENBURGER.
DUKE OF CLARENCE.
CHANCELLOR. 1934
MARY PEERS. 1923
GIPSY. 1901
ENDEAVOUR. 1750
ALBION. 1872
FLETAN. 1851

JAMES EGAN LANE. 1945

WHITESAND BAY

HMS. A7. 1914

QUEBEC. 1859
LORD INCHCAPE. 1940
WHITE ROSE. 1911

WINCHELSEA. 1703

DUNOTTAR CASTLE. 1894

DAISY. 1903
KONIGSBERG. 1834
CONSTANCE. 1865
BELLISSIMA. 1838
EMMELYNE. 1867
GOOD INTENT. 1817
HARMONIE. 1824
ISLANDER. 1930
JANE. 1838
ZARITA. 1926
ST. PIERRE. 1906

LOOE

ANEMONE. 1903

MARGUERITE. 1922

JANE. 1886
LADY OF THE LAKE. 1880
ELIZABETH. 1891

ASAMA. 1941
KINGSTON ALALITE. 1940
ELK. 1940

LORD STONEHAVEN. 1942

CONSTANT. 1695
HALF MOON. 1673
HMS. AI. 1913

EDDYSTONE

AUSTRALIA BUSH. 1917
WESTERN COAST. 1917
ALMOND BRANCH. 1917
RIO SOROCABA. 1917
EASTERN PRINCE. 1917
DIRIGO. 1917

ORSOVA. 1917
AFRIC. 1917
EASTPOINT. 1917

VICTORIA. 1917
CLAVERLY. 1917
EASTFIELD. 1917
U-214. 1944

R. LARN. 1968.

N

Wreck locations between Rame Head and Looe, including Whitesand Bay and the Eddystone.

families, struck below the Hoe foreshore at Plymouth. Captain Edward Pellew, later Lord Exmouth, organised the rescue, and through his efforts only a dozen or so lives were lost. A breakwater would probably have saved the *Dutton*, but the scheme lay dormant during the French revolutionary wars, and there were more wrecks. On 23 March 1799 the French brig *La Victoire*, bound from Bordeaux to Malta with wine and cordage, which had been captured a few days earlier by HMS *Triumph*, entered the Sound in a hard southerly gale. She missed stays, struck a ledge beneath Mount Edgcumbe, and sank in deep water, lost with her valuable cargo. One of the big Cawsand smuggling luggers was caught deep laden with contraband by a severe gale on 14 November 1800, and disappeared off Rame with all on board. In February 1803 the brig-o'-war *Fearless*, of 12 guns, Captain George Williams, drove on to Redding Point near Cawsand and broke up, her crew surviving. A Papenburger from Hanover, another prize to HMS *Triumph*, drove from her anchors on 29 January 1806 and was battered to fragments in Whitesand Bay, drowning a midshipman and five others of the crew.

By this time the Admiralty was in charge of the redoubtable Lord St Vincent, who knew well the dangers of the Sound and remembered Lord Howe's prophecy that Torbay would one day be 'the grave of the British Fleet'. The scheme for a breakwater was revived in 1806, and plans were drawn up by John Rennie, the celebrated Scots engineer, and Mr Whidby, the master-attendant of Woolwich dockyard. The breakwater was to be a mile long, situated two miles out from the Hoe foreshore, and enclosing about five square miles of open water. But again the plan was shelved while others were discussed, and more ships were lost. During the great easterly gale of 22 January 1809, the Plymouth packet-brig *Rose* disappeared between Rame Head and Looe, while bound for Falmouth. Her stern was washed in next morning, but Captain Knight and twenty-six passengers and crew had perished. In November 1810 the London ship *Mary Ann*, a week out of the Downs for Malta with bale goods and coffee worth £60,000, was bearing up for Plymouth, crippled aloft and leaking, when her master made the common mistake of confusing Whitesand Bay with the Sound. The ship struck a few hours before midnight, in a hard ESE gale. The mate tried to take a line ashore and was never seen again, but the rest of the crew got off when the wind and seas moderated. Even before dawn the *Mary Ann* was breaking up, and most of her cargo was lost, either to the sea or to the wreckers.

Early the following year, while final deliberations were taking place over Rennie's plans, there were two more wrecks. On 3 February the Fowey sloop *Friends Endeavour*, Will Pearce master, sank on the western side of Rame, shortly after leaving Plymouth for Falmouth. Ten days later the master of the Danish brig *Friede*, laden with oil for London and but lately parted from a Gibraltar convoy, made the same mistake as the captain of the *Mary Ann* and put her on the rocks. Six of the crew were saved by Cawsand fishermen. A few months later a decision to build the breakwater was finally reached and twenty-five acres of land near Oreston were purchased for quarrying; further supplies of stone were to be brought in from Dartmoor. On 11 April 1812 the Plymouth ship *Susannah* was wrecked with all hands outside Portwrinkle, but on 12 August that year the first great block for the foundations of the breakwater was dropped into the Sound. Work went ahead fast for the first year, and by March 1813 some of the stone showed at low water springs, although gales frequently hampered the labourers and engineers and kept barges and lighters away. In January 1817 a severe SSW gale swept the coast and played havoc within the Sound. The Falmouth packet *Princess Mary*, which had overrun her reckoning and put in for shelter, was wrecked with few survivors. The schooner *Telegraph* and the sloop-o'-war *Jasper* suffered the same fate, the brig *Farmer's Delight* of Polperro struck and capsized on the Devon shore, and the Sunderland brig *Deptford* ran into the surf near Rame, with the loss of all on board. Heavy seas almost levelled the breakwater, but work slowly went ahead in spite of the storms. During a tremendous blow in the autumn of 1823 seven ships were lost, and on 22 November 1824 twenty-five ships were driven ashore in the Sound, while the brig *Harmonie* was wrecked further down the coast at Looe and her crew of six were lost. On 14 October 1825 the Penzance sloop *Good Intent* put to sea from the Sound to avoid being wrecked, but had hardly cleared Rame Head when she capsized in heavy seas. A woman, her child and the ship's boy were drowned in the cabin, but the rest of the crew clung to the hull until picked up by the sloop *Heed*, which landed them at Helford.

On 13 December 1827 the crew of another Cornish vessel suffered, not so much from the stormy seas as from their own unsympathetic countrymen. The Fowey schooner *Jane* was heading up Channel laden with oranges and lemons from Lisbon to London, when a south-easterly gale drove her into Whitesand Bay, where, as usual, a number of local men had gathered with booty in mind. Captain Rowett spent several hours on an offshore rock shivering in his underwear before rescue, but the others, including two passengers, a Spanish officer and his wife, scrambled ashore unaided. In an attempt to save some of his possessions the Spaniard had filled his pockets with his silver spoons and coins, but his bulging pockets were quickly spotted as he stumbled from the waves and the skirts of his coat hacked off by a cutlass. By the time the preventives arrived from Looe the wreckers had disappeared up the cliffs, and little of the *Jane*'s cargo and gear was left.

A January gale in 1828 drove another fifteen ships ashore in the Sound, and the half-finished breakwater was itself proving something of a hazard in foggy weather, though it might have been the contempt bred of familiarity that wrecked the Cawsand smuggling boat *Brothers* on 4 March 1834. She was running for home with contraband when she crashed on to the stonework near the western end. Her crew of five were rescued from the rigging by a longboat from the nearby lightship and soon disappeared ashore, leaving the *Brothers* and her illicit cargo to be seized by the customs men. Later that month the ship *Konigsberg*, bound from Memel to Bristol with timber, was wrecked westwards of Rame, though no lives were lost.

The breakwater was completed in 1841 at the cost of £1½ million, after 4½ million tons of limestone and granite had gone into its construction. The Sound was at last sheltered, but Cawsand Bay was too far to the south to be protected and easterly gales still caused shipping casualties there. In February 1841 the Dutch East Indiaman *Yonge Willem*, bound from Surinam to Rotterdam with coffee, spices and sugar, struck near Cawsand village during a hard ESE gale, but the pilots got her safely into Plymouth. By contrast, the Greek brig *Taxiarcos*, Vafrapola master, was lost beneath Rame Head on 27 January 1843 in perfect weather. She was standing up Channel under a full press of sail, bound for Hull with grain from the Danube, when the duty helmsman mistook the course and steered north-east instead of south-east. The brig ebbed dry, but a heavy ground swell broke her up on the evening's tide. Tragedy followed on 25 January 1846 when the little Fowey smack *William and Amelia*, homeward bound with limestone from Plymouth, was lost with all hands in the same place. On 17 November that year the London barque *Duke of Clarence*, Davidson master, in ballast from the Thames to Newport, was wrecked in Whitesand Bay. The coastguards and customs men took charge of her before the local people could begin wrecking, but a few weeks later a young fisherman was hauled before the magistrates for stealing an iron chain, and sentenced, with the severity then usual, to a long term of hard labour.

Another large barque was lost on 6 December 1849. Early in the morning two Falmouth pilots met the *Shepherdess* of London, an East Indiaman inward bound for Plymouth with teak logs, off the coast, but though she was leaking badly the wind was fair and Captain Stainbank refused their help. He stood in towards Plymouth, but off Rame Head that evening the wind flew around to south-east and freshened into a gale. There was no hope of getting into the Sound and the *Shepherdess* drove to leeward until, at almost midnight, she struck three miles west of Looe under the tall cliffs of Talland and broke in half. The cargo washed out of her tier by tier, forming a bridge over which the crew, the captain's wife and a passenger escaped ashore, but two men who tried to swim were drowned. During the same night's gale the Plymouth sloop *Caroline*, Atwell master, fighting to round Rame Head with a heavy cargo of granite for the new dockyard works at Devonport, drove ashore at Seaton, just east of Looe. Her wreckage was found at dawn, with the bodies of her crew lying on the rocks. Two years later there was almost another tragedy at Seaton, when the French brig *Flétan*, in ballast for Wales, crippled and with her mainmast gone, drove ashore there on the morning of 15 January 1851 during a fierce SSW gale. Her owner had already been lost overboard, but the captain, his son and six men were rescued by rocket line just before the brig broke up.

Men-of-war still occasionally ran foul of the cliffs about Rame. On 28 October 1854 the big ironclad HMS *Cossack* of 29 guns was inward bound from Sheerness to Devonport, where she was to undergo minor engine repairs before going out to the Crimea and

then to the North American station. In a thick fog, Captain Fanshawe was bringing her in under easy steam when both he and the
master lost sight of the breakwater lights, and at 4 am the *Cossack*
struck the Draystone rock off Penlee Point, a mile inside Rame.
She backed clear, but the impact had knocked off her forefoot and
broken the false keel, and at a court martial a few weeks later
Captain Fanshawe and the master were severely reprimanded. Only
a month later, the Looe smack *William and Ann*, homeward bound
with limestone, was run down off the western end of the breakwater
by the Liverpool packet *Nile*. The smack was sunk and her captain
drowned but the *Nile* escaped, only to be wrecked on the north
coast of Cornwall on her next voyage.

The coastguards at Looe were greeted with an unusual sight on
11 October 1859, when dawn revealed the topsails of a large barque
standing out of the sea, a mile south-west of Downderry. They put
off to investigate, and a search of floating debris produced a packet
of letters which identified her as the American barque *Quebec*, of
Maine. There was no sign of survivors, but when the coastguards
later returned ashore, they learned that Captain Alexander Ruark
and his crew had landed at Plymouth. The 700-ton *Quebec* was in
sand ballast for Newcastle from Bordeaux, where she had just
unloaded staves, when at 5 am on 10 October she struck the Eddystone in calm hazy weather and a light south-easterly breeze. She
was so close to the lighthouse that her bowsprit cap was less than
ten feet from the kitchen window when she ground to a halt. The
steam frigate *Topaz* appeared, bound for Vancouver, but on being
told that no lives were in danger she continued on her voyage and
the Plymouth cutter *Heroine* arrived to help. It was after dark when
the tide finally lifted the *Quebec* clear and Captain Ruark steered
for Plymouth. Leaking badly, and with the sand ballast choking
her pumps, she rapidly became waterlogged, and at 3 am was
abandoned in Whitesand Bay, where she sank in six fathoms.

The winter of 1860 brought a tragic reminder of the danger of
Cawsand Bay in a hard southerly gale. The 135-ton Looe schooner
Speedwell was one of the many Cornish coasters then engaged in
the copper trade to South Wales. She regularly took copper ore from
Looe to Newport and returned with coal for Calstock, or one of
the ports on the St Germans river. On the evening of 28 December
1860 she was towed down river as usual, and hove-to under Mount

Edgcumbe to await high water, when she would return to Looe to load for Wales. The weather was threatening, and during the night the wind shifted from SSE to SW, and dawn found the *Speedwell* dangerously close to Redding Point, rolling heavily to two anchors. At 10 am the tug *Wellington* put a hawser aboard, but it parted and the schooner dragged slowly shorewards. The coastguards were waiting on the rocks with rocket apparatus, but Captain Hoskin and his crew preferred to launch their boat which capsized within seconds, drowning the captain, mate James Thomas, able seaman David Libby, 18-year-old Thomas Clapp and Walter Hoskin the captain's young nephew.

The *Speedwell* was one of the many small sailing ships, both British and foreign, which once plied the coast of east Cornwall and provided most of the wrecks between Rame Head and the Dodman. Her home port of Looe, with the rocky bulk of St George's Island a mile south of the pierhead, was an awkward place in a gale. Fowey harbour, a dozen miles down the coast, could also be difficult, its roadstead flanked by the high land of Gribben Head, a dead lee shore to any ship running for shelter in a hard south-easterly. To the west of Gribbin lay St Austell Bay and the thriving china clay ports of Par and Charlestown. The bay is exposed from south and east, and many small schooners, ketches and dandies were lost on the sands of Polkerris, Par and Crinnis after anchoring to await the discharge of their cargoes of coal, culm, firebrick or limestone. Further west, between Black Head and Chapel Point, another clay port, Pentewan, with its narrow sand-flanked entrance, and the fishing port of Mevagissey, could be equally inhospitable in a southerly gale.

On 30 October 1953 the Falmouth sloop *Active,* homeward bound with general cargo from Plymouth, failed to clear the Dodman in a hard SSW gale. Captain Southward ran for the shelter of Fowey, but mistook the high land above Mevagissey for Gribben Head and ended up on the beach at Pentewan. The sloop ebbed dry, and her cargo was unloaded by horse and cart before she broke up. A similar accident befell Captain Gastin of the French schooner *Rochellaise*, Dunkirk to Cette with wine and salt, who tried to get into Mevagissey at the height of a SSE gale on 10 June 1857. A few weeks before the *Speedwell* tragedy in 1860, a French lugger had also been wrecked; the *Jeune Algue* sailed from Ply-

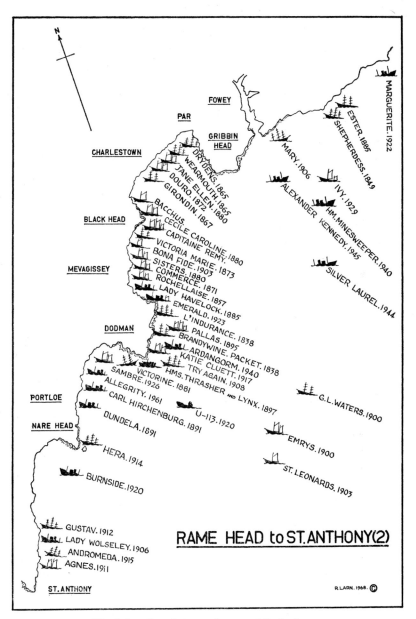

N

MARGUERITE. 1922

FOWEY

ESTER. 1885

SHEPHERDESS. 1849

PAR

GRIBBIN
HEAD

CHARLESTOWN

MARY. 1906

DRY DENS. 1865
WEARMOUTH. 1865
JANE ELLEN. 1865
DOURO. 1872. 1880
GIRONDIN. 1867

IVY. 1929

ALEXANDER KENNEDY. 1945

HM. MINESWEEPER. 1940

BLACK HEAD

BACCHUS. 1880
CECILE CAROLINE. 1880
CAPITAINE REMY.
VICTORIA MARIE. 1873
BONA FIDE. 1903
SISTERS. 1880
COMMERCE. 1871
ROCHELLAISE. 1857
LADY HAVELOCK. 1885

SILVER LAUREL. 1944

MEVAGISSEY

EMERALD. 1923
L'INDURANCE. 1838
PALLAS. 1895
BRANDYWINE. PACKET. 1838
ARDANGORM. 1940
KATIE CLUETT. 1917
TRY AGAIN. 1908
HMS. THRASHER and LYNX. 1897

DODMAN

VICTORINE. 1881

SAMBRE. 1926
ALLEGRITY. 1961
CARL HIRCHENBURG. 1891

G.L. WATERS. 1900

PORTLOE

U-113. 1920

NARE HEAD

DUNDELA. 1891

EMRYS. 1900

HERA. 1914

ST. LEONARDS. 1903

BURNSIDE. 1920

GUSTAV. 1912
LADY WOLSELEY. 1906
ANDROMEDA. 1915
AGNES. 1911

RAME HEAD to ST. ANTHONY (2)

ST. ANTHONY

R. LARN. 1968. ©

Wreck locations between Looe and St Anthony.

mouth on 30 November, under charter to a St Austell merchant, in limestone ballast for Par where she was to load for Rouen. Off Rame Head, the wind increased to gale force and she was blown right down the coast to Pentewan. There she was boarded by a pilot from Gorran Haven who headed for his home port, a tiny fishing hamlet snugged into the high cliffs between Mevagissey Bay and the Dodman. Unfortunately it was low water, and the lugger struck the sand off the pierhead. While the pilot was ashore seeking help, the *Jeune Algue* was blown in under the cliffs and filled up, her captain and crew having to be rescued by the coastguards.

A mile eastward of Gorran Haven are the Gwineas rocks, one of the most dangerous reefs on this part of the coast. As early as 26 January 1838, the brig *Brandywine Packet*, Captain Almond, Charente for Sunderland with an obvious cargo, was embayed off the reef at the height of an ESE gale. Captain Almond failed to wear ship, and the brig struck heavily, fell on her beam ends and went to pieces in mountainous seas. The crew were all drowned save for one James Gilchrist, an 'honest young sailor' as the local newspaper termed him, who jumped on to the Gwineas and was later rescued by the longboat from the Revenue cutter *Fox*. The *Brandywin Packet*'s cargo was washed ashore and the local people made ready for an orgy, but the coastguards and customs men who had been protecting the French ship *L'Indurance*, wrecked near Mevagissey the previous day, were too quickly on the scene. The thirsty crowds were kept at bay, and some three to four hundred casks were placed in store under guard, together with valuables from both wrecks.

The largest sailing ship lost on the Gwineas was the 1,350-ton Russian barque *Pallas*, Weser master, also wrecked in an easterly gale and snow, on 26 November 1895, while on voyage to Bristol with Baltic timber. Unlike the *Brandywine Packet*, she was strong enough to take the impact; her mainmast went overboard and she drove on to Perhaver beach, where sixty years before the brandy barrels had been stacked. Falmouth lifeboat came up to assist, but the Russian crew scrambled ashore and, aided by the Gorran fishermen, scaled the cliffs, hauling up Captain Weser, a big stout man, on the end of a rope.

The latest wreck on the Gwineas was also one of the largest ships lost east of Falmouth: the 5,200-ton steamer *Ardangorm* of

Page 35: The four-masted steel barque *Andromeda*, wrecked near Falmouth on 13 February 1915, inward bound from Oregon with wheat.

Page 36: (above) The schooner *J B Wood* ablaze in Carrick Roads, gutted and beached on 17 April 1903; (below) one of the German submarines blown ashore in a gale at Falmouth after the First World War.

Glasgow which struck the reef on 4 January 1940. As it was wartime, all navigational and shore lights were extinguished, and the
night was pitch dark with a hard ESE gale. Though badly holed,
the *Ardangorm* remained afloat and at daylight eleven men were
taken ashore by the Fowey lifeboat. Heavy seas continued to sweep
the steamer, and towards dusk, soon after a naval tug had arrived, she
had to be abandoned. Owned by the Ardan Steamship Co of

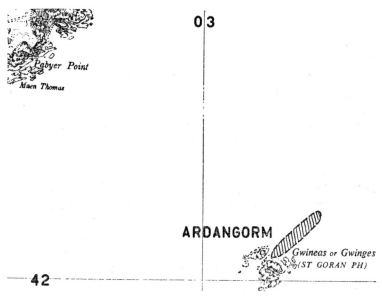

Location of the 5,200-ton steamer *Ardangorm*, wrecked on the Gwineas
rocks in 1940.

Glasgow, where she was launched in 1930 by Connell & Co, the
Ardangorm was heavily salvaged in later years, but much of her
wreckage, including her propeller, still lies below the reef.

Lifeboats were established at Polkerris in 1859, Looe in 1866
and Mevagissey in 1869, and they soon distinguished themselves by
daring rescues of ships and men. The Polkerris boat saved the combined crews of the Shields barque *Drydens* and the brig *Wearmouth*,
wrecked outside Par in a SSW gale on 2 November 1865. The same
storm also wrecked the French lugger *Constance* near Fowey, after
she had been blown off her course for St Malo from Cardiff. The

c

Looe boat failed to reach the Plymouth sailing trawler *Emmelyne* which sank off the harbour on 5 January 1867 without survivors, but in December that year saved the polacca brig *St Brannock* from destruction on the rocks at Maymean. The Mevagissey boat performed a gallant rescue only a few weeks after she arrived, when she saved the crew of the brigantine *Girondin*, wrecked in a SSW gale on 29 December 1869, while bound from Bordeaux to Belfast with maize.

During the next fifty years there were many brave rescues, but ships and lives were still lost between Rame and the Dodman. The St Ives schooner *Commerce* was lost outside Pentewan during a November gale in 1871; the Dutch galliot *Douro* was wrecked at Par on 27 March 1872, while waiting to enter with Welsh coal; the schoooner *Albion* was driven ashore just east of Looe on 22 November 1872, while in ballast from Penzance to Par, with the loss of four lives; the French brig *Victoria Marie*, bound for Gloucester with maize, drove ashore below Black Head on 25 February 1873 and broke up, her crew escaping over the bowsprit. The Padstow schooner *Ariel* struck the Callyvarder Rock in April 1878 while entering Par for clay, and lay capsized off the pierhead until locomotives from the small mineral line connecting the port and the clay pits were used to haul her upright. But there was no salvage for the little Scots smack *Christian* of Fraserburgh, wrecked at Black Head in a SSE gale on 19 January 1879, while in ballast from Falmouth to Charlestown, or for the 43-ton coasting smack *Lady of the Lake*, of Bideford, which foundered off Rame Head on 30 January 1880. She was well known on the north Cornish coast, and a survivor of several strandings at Bude. She was bound from Falmouth to Devonport with a load of granite blocks when she sprang a serious leak and sank just after her crew had rowed off to a nearby Plymouth trawler.

Occasionally there would be a wreck with serious loss of life. On 30 October 1877, at the height of the worst south-westerly gale for a decade, the Newport barque *R H Jones* shaved past Rame Head and crashed into Plymouth breakwater, leaving only one survivor out of a crew of twenty. She was the sister ship of the *G I Jones*, which was lost in Mount's Bay six years later with only two survivors. There was a double disaster in St Austell Bay on 9 February 1880. During the afternoon, four coasters left Fowey for Charlestown, but as they passed Gribbin Head the fresh north-west gale backed south-west, and two were forced to put back damaged. The schooners *Jane Ellen* and *Sisters*, both coal-laden from Cardiff, stood down the coast, and the gale raged on through the dark hours. The *Jane Ellen* was discovered at dawn on the rocks just east of Charlestown. Captain Williams and his crew had perished while trying to row ashore. The *Sisters* lay embedded in the sand a hundred yards from Pentewan harbour. Her sole survivor, a young Scots sailor named Daniel Fraser, related that the schooner had been blown right down the coast and then, bearing up again, had failed to weather Black Head. Captain Pappin tried to wear ship but failed, and she ran into the breakers. The mate and an able seaman disappeared almost at once, and although the captain hung on for an hour he grew exhausted and was swept away, leaving Fraser alone to scramble ashore at dawn.

There was another tragic wreck on 3 March 1881. The French schooner *Cecile Caroline* of Croisex left Charlestown in the evening and hove-to under Appletree Point, half a mile to the east. During the night the stiff SSE breeze freshened to a gale, and at dawn her wreckage and the bodies of her crew lay on the rocks, or floated in the clay-whitened waters. Two more French sailors died that night when the brigantine *Victorine*, laden with pitwood for Wales, struck below the Dodman. On 1 September 1883 another French crew narrowly escaped drowning when the lugger *Bacchus* of Nantes was wrecked at Porthpean while in ballast for Charlestown. So did the crew of the Austrian brig *Ester*, which was wrecked in Talland Bay on 10 March 1885 during a fresh easterly gale while bound from Cyprus to London. But when the schooner *Jane*, of and from Llanelly for St Vaast with coal, disappeared off Rame on 25 April 1886, there were no survivors. Five years later the Welsh ketch *Elizabeth*, Penryn for Devonport dockyard with granite blocks, foundered in the same place on 9 December 1891, but her crew were rescued. In May 1900 there were two fatal collisions off the Dodman. On the 16th the Cardiff steamed *Warsfield* cut down the 142-ton Welsh schooner *Emrys*, Griffiths master, Port Madoc for the Baltic with slates. The crew jumped on to the *Warsfield*, except for the fourteen-year-old cabin boy who, because he was wearing his seaboots for the first time, could not make it and went down with the schooner. On 30 May the Dublin brigantine *G L Waters*,

London to Swansea with scrap iron, was run down by the Norwegian ship *Sterling*, the captain and his wife being either killed by the falling masts or drowned.

There was tragedy of a different kind in the loss of a fine ship when, on 7 December 1901, the French windjammer *Gipsy* was blown past Falmouth and wrecked in Whitesand Bay. Originally Devitt & Moore's famous colonial flyer *Rodney*, she had been launched as an iron full-rigger of 1,447 tons net by W Pile & Co of Sunderland in 1874, and although an uncomfortable ship in bad weather, she was by no means the 'half-tide rock' that so many clippers were. Her passenger accommodation was well-known for its luxury, including such rare amenities as piped water in the cabins and a bathroom with continuous hot water, while supplies of fresh meat, milk and eggs from the miniature farmyard carried on board raised the menu far above that of many of the emigrant ships to America and Australia. Most of her life had been spent plying between London and Melbourne or Sydney and in 1888, when taking part in the annual wool race, when clippers laden with the new season's wool raced each other home to London, the *Rodney* arrived second off Gravesend after a passage of seventy-eight days, only an hour behind the immortal *Cutty Sark*.

A strange coincidence about the fate of the *Rodney* was that just six years before her wreck, while outward bound for Sydney in November 1895, her figurehead of a lion had been smashed off by a gale in the Channel. Six months later it came ashore in Whitesand Bay where, as the *Gipsy*, she was destined to meet her end.

In 1897, when the wool clippers were being gradually ousted by the faster steamers, Devitt & Moore sold the *Rodney* to French interests. She was re-registered at Nantes in the name of *Gipsy*, and her next four years were without incident. Then, late in the summer of 1901 she left Iquique, Chile, for Falmouth for orders with a full cargo of nitrates. She had a fair passage until about 5 December when, nearing the Scillies, the weather grew thick and squally with a freshening south-west wind. The *Gipsy* thrashed on before the storm until the Dodman was sighted early on the 7th. Realising that he had overshot Falmouth, her master decided to run for Plymouth, but as the day wore on the wind backed and increased, until by dusk it was blowing a hard gale and driving the ship ever nearer to the land. Rolling in the heavy seas, she was seen from Looe, still making headway up the coast, frequently hidden by violent rainstorms. At six o'clock hopes that she had made Plymouth were dashed when distress rockets flared up from Downderry, and soon the lifeboat *Boy's Own No 1* was away through the surf on the last service of her fifteen-year career at Looe. She found the *Gipsy* on the rocks and stood by while the French crew tried to pump her dry and get clear; they were unsuccessful, and after a couple of hours they had to abandon her. The captain admitted that they would have made Plymouth safely if he had not mistaken the lights of Whitesand Bay for those of the Sound; it was a common enough error, but it was the end of the beautiful *Gipsy*.

Eighteen months later there was another wreck in Whitesand Bay, on 1 March 1903, when the 600-ton Liverpool coaster *Daisy*, Dieppe for Penarth in ballast, left the shelter of Plymouth Sound only to be wrecked in a southerly gale at Polhawn, the second of the many wrecks and strandings between Rame Head and the Dodman in the decade before the First World War. Already in February the Penzance schooner *Margaret* had been lost at Pentewan. On 17 May the French ketch *St Leonards*, bound from Morlaix to Llanelly, foundered off the Dodman; the lugger *Anemone* of Looe was wrecked near the village on 10 September, and on 12 December the *Bona Fide*, the largest mackerel driver in the Mevagissey fleet, was badly damaged by stranding outside her own pierhead.

New Year's Day 1906 saw the wreck of the Milford brigantine *Mary*, London to Newport with scrap and old cannon. She had tried to enter Fowey at the height of a SSE gale, but struck beneath the battery on St Catherine's Point, leaving only her captain to get ashore. An old cannon discovered by divers off St Catherine's Point in 1967 may well have formed part of her cargo. The French schooner *St Pierre* of Nantes escaped serious damage a month later, on 22 February 1906 when, running before a hard southerly gale, she drove ashore at Looe. Her crew were rescued by the lifeboat, and the schooner, which was almost new and in ballast from Cherbourg to Charlestown, was refloated after extensive salvage work and towed to Falmouth for repairs.

At midnight on 5 October 1908 the Padstow barquentine *Try Again*, Captain J H Carbines of St Ives, struck a rock off the Dodman while standing down Channel from Antwerp for Dublin

with a cargo of superphosphates. A fresh ESE gale sent heavy seas
rolling over her decks, and as the captain followed his men down
a ladder on to the rocks, he was caught by a breaker and so badly
injured that they had to leave him and climb the cliffs to fetch help.
The coastguards brought him to the clifftop just as dawn was
breaking. There was an almost identical wreck nearby on 27 December 1917, when the 126-ton Fowey schooner *Katie Cluett* missed
stays and drove ashore on the Dodman while bound from Falmouth
to Pentewan in ballast. She also broke up in heavy seas, but on
this occasion the captain was drowned before he could reach the
rocks.

Occasionally a large sailing ship would 'get away with it', like
the German training barque *Gustav*, which stranded on Gowan
Sands near Portscatho on 16 January 1912 in a south-easterly
gale. She had been in tow from London to Swansea when the
hawser broke off the Eddystone, and she went ashore while trying
to get into Falmouth, but was refloated by tugs next day. But for
the German steel barque *Hera* there was a tragic end in Veryan
Bay, on the rugged stretch of coast between the Dodman and Falmouth. Originally the British *Richard Wagner*, she was owned by
Rhederei Aktien of Hamburg, who had lost their square-rigger
Pindos on the Manacles in 1912. On 1 February 1914, ninety-one
days out from Pisagua with Chilean nitrates, the 1,994-ton *Hera*
was nearing the Lizard. The weather was thick and rough with a
hard WSW gale blowing, and as Captain Lorentz had been relying
on dead reckoning for three days her actual position was in doubt.
After some deliberation he decided to stand slowly in towards
Falmouth Bay, hoping to pick up the flash of the Lizard or St
Anthony lights. As dusk fell the weather became steadily worse,
and hours passed without sight of a single shore light. Then
suddenly, at about midnight, second mate Petersen reported land
ahead. Captain Lorentz ordered the *Hera* to be put about, but she
was slow in answering her helm and seconds later she struck
violently on the tall, jagged Gull Rock, a quarter of a mile off Nare
Head, the western tip of Veryan Bay.

Distress rockets were fired and the boats manned, but the *Hera*
rolled forward and settled fast by the head. The port boat capsized
alongside, and Captain Lorentz and three men disappeared. The
others, including helmsman Alfred Johannsen, scrambled back on

to the wave-swept decks. After an abortive attempt to free the starboard boat, chief officer Muhliesen led them up the jigger mast to escape the seas. As the *Hera* sank deeper they were forced higher; cold and exhaustion soon carried off the chief mate, and in a short while second mate Petersen also slipped into the sea. Before he went he passed his whistle up to able seaman Meyer above, who

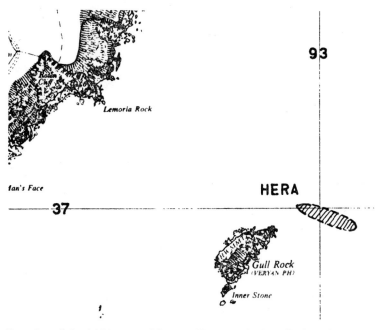

Location of the 1,994-ton steel barque *Hera*, wrecked on Gull Rock in 1914.

in his turn gave it to Johannsen. By this time he and the four others, third mate Hoffman, able seamen Larsen and Cauci, and cadet Bersier, had been nearly two hours on the mast top. But rescue was at hand; soon after 2 am Falmouth lifeboat appeared around Gull Rock. Johannsen, barely able to hold the whistle in his frozen fingers, blew harder, until at last the shrill piping, barely audible above the gale, was heard by the coxswain and the five exhausted men were pulled aboard the *Bob Newbons*.

Nineteen men had died in the wreck. Eight bodies were soon

recovered, and were buried the following day in Veryan church-yard. Captain Lorentz's body was found at nearby Portloe. The *Hera*, with only her foretopsail showing above the water, was sold by auction a fortnight later to Harris Bros of Falmouth for £205. Although she was in an exposed position much of her gear was recovered, but quantities of her plating and ribs still lie below the surface under Gull Rock.

Just over a year after the loss of the *Hera* another large barque, the 1,762-ton, four-master *Andromeda*, was wrecked in almost identical conditions, a few miles away on Killygerran Head. She had arrived off Falmouth 116 days out from Portland, Oregon, with 3,000 tons of wheat, but due to war regulations Captain Deeks was not allowed to come in without a pilot. Neither cutters nor tugs could reach him in the heavy ssw gale, and the *Andromeda* dragged her anchors on to the rocks at four o'clock next morning. An able seaman survived coming ashore on a capsized lifeboat, but an apprentice was lost overboard. Captain Deeks, his wife, her young sister and the rest of the crew went up the rigging, where the captain's little daughter perched asleep on the knees of a sailor until they were all rescued by Portscatho rocket brigade at dawn. The *Andromeda* was auctioned for breaking up, on 3 March 1915, for a mere £170. She had been launched in 1890 by Duncans of Glasgow for G F Smith, but in later years had been sold to Black & More of London, who had also owned the beautiful *Queen Margaret*, lost at the Lizard in 1913.

Compared with the number of sailing ships, few steamers have been wrecked between Rame Head and Falmouth Bay. There was little need for them to come anywhere near this part of the coast; most of the steamer traffic passed up the north coast of Cornwall, to and from the Welsh coal ports, while those passing up or down the English Channel gave the Eddystone and the Dodman a wide berth. Even when one inadvertently came too close inshore, there were no deadly ship traps like the Manacles, Lizard or Runnelstone lying in wait. Occasionally a liner entering Plymouth might miss her way in the fog and run into danger, as did the Union Castle's famous *Dunottar Castle*, which almost wrecked herself on the Eddystone in thick fog on 24 August 1894 while outward bound for the Cape, via Plymouth. Similar weather caused Atlantic Transport's *Philadelphia* to strand near Rame Head on 9 January

1914 while inward bound from New York with 300 passengers and mails. Better known as the *Paris* of Manacles fame, she was refloated on the flood tide and reached Plymouth with only a few dented plates to show for her second encounter with the Cornish coast.

Steamers making for Falmouth also occasionally overran their destination in fog or rough weather. The 500-ton *Lady Havelock* of Cardiff, bound from Huelva to Swansea with copper ore and coming in to bunker, lost her bearings and grounded at Portmellon, near Mevagissey, but was refloated on the next tide. The 566-ton schooner-rigged *Dundela*, of Belfast, ten days out from the Azores to London with fruit, was also running for Falmouth to bunker when she was caught by the great blizzard of 9 March 1891. Blinded by driving snow and helpless against the severe ENE gale, she struck near Portloe village, a few miles from the Dodman. Only a short while later the 900-ton *Carl Hirschberg*, of and from Hamburg for Cardiff, drove ashore close by. Both crews got ashore in the early hours, but by dawn the *Dundela*, owned by Harland and Wolff and built by them in 1883, had broken in half. The *Carl Hirschberg* survived the gales, and was refloated a month later after a channel had been hewn through the rocks to enable her to reach deep water.

The Dodman was perhaps the greatest hazard to vessels which overran Falmouth while coming up Channel. The afternoon of 29 September 1897 found the town alive with rumours that two warships had gone ashore in thick fog beneath the great headland. The mystery was solved early in the evening when the destroyer *Thrasher* limped into Carrick Roads, supported by two naval tugs. The *Thrasher*, a four-funnelled thirty-knotter launched by Cammell Laird of Birkenhead only the previous year, had left St Ives Bay at three o'clock that morning with the destroyers *Lynx* and *Sunfish*, on a stokers' training cruise. Off Longships they became separated in the fog, and at 11.30 am the *Sunfish*, creeping along under easy steam, suddenly found herself under tall cliffs. She went astern with alacrity and her commander, recognising the Dodman and realising that he had overshot Falmouth, put about and arrived in Carrick Roads at 1.30 pm.

The *Thrasher* and the *Lynx* had not been so lucky. Hardly had their lookouts seen the cliffs than they struck below the Dodman. The impact buckled the *Thrasher*'s frame, and her deck plating rippled from stem to stern. Worse still, her main steam pipe fractured and clouds of scalding steam blasted into the boiler room. Three men escaped up the ladders, but three others were trapped, until an Irish stoker named Lynch gallantly fought his way below and dragged out stoker Paul. Both were badly burnt and Lynch died that evening in the house of a Mevagissey coastguard. The other two stokers were beyond aid, and the watertight doors leading to the stokehold were closed to stop the flooding.

The *Lynx*, much less damaged, managed to kedge herself off, and eventually limped into Devonport. Meanwhile the naval tug *Trusty* and the destroyers *Ferret* and *Spider* had been dispatched to the Dodman, where the Falmouth tug *Triton* had already arrived. The *Thrasher* was hauled afloat at high tide, and two naval tugs brought her, decks awash and listing heavily to starboard, into Carrick Roads where she was temporarily repaired before being towed up to Devonport to join the *Lynx* in dry-dock. The *Lynx*, which had also almost been wrecked at Sennen Cove, near Land's End, on Christmas Day 1894, was at sea again within a month and remained in service until 1912; the *Thrasher* survived the First World War and went to the breakers in 1921.

A happier note was struck when the 729-ton British & Irish Co's *Lady Wolseley* stranded in Gerrans Bay on 21 August 1906, while making for Falmouth in dense fog on her regular run from London to Dublin via south coast ports. The sea was flat calm and realising that, with a falling tide, she was going to be stuck for some time, her captain ordered lunch to be served early, while a piano was brought on deck and an impromptu concert party organised. For the rest of the afternoon music floated across the fog-shrouded bay, and though several passengers later went to Falmouth in a tug, most stayed on board until the *Lady Wolseley* was refloated next morning.

Mystery marked one of two disasters off the coast during the winter of 1911. In one, the captain and his young son were drowned when the Appledore schooner *Agnes*, Charlestown to Runcorn with clay, was wrecked at Killygerran on 7 December 1911 in a southerly gale. The other concerned the Liverpool coaster *White Rose*, owned by Hughes & Co, which had sailed from La Pallice for the Mersey with grain on 9 December 1911. Two days later a severe gale blew up, and nothing more was heard of her until 17

January 1912, when two Cawsand fishermen found her broken lifeboat on the rocks near Mount Edgcumbe. No trace was ever found of her crew of ten, or of her master, Captain W Smith, a Cornishman from Polruan, near Fowey.

The First World War saw German submarines operating in the approaches to Plymouth and a large number of ships fell to their torpedoes. In the first few months of 1917 alone they sank the White Star liner *Afric*, the steamers *East Point* and *Rio Sorocaba*, and the four-masted barque *Dirigo*, southwards of the Eddystone. The steamer *Claverly* and the Prince liner *Eastern Prince* were torpedoed in August, and the steamers *Australiabush*, *Western Coast*, *Victoria*, *Almond Branch* and *Eastfield* during a fortnight in November.

Derelict ships are not unusual off the Cornish coast, and in November 1920 there were three adrift off the Dodman almost at the same time. The first was the all too aptly-named American wooden steamer *Burnside*, which was three days out from the Azores on voyage from Philadelphia to Rouen with coal when she caught fire west of Scilly on 15 October. In answer to Captain Knudson's 'SOS' the tanker *Safitha* took the *Burnside* in tow, but the flames soon drove the engineers on deck. To make matters worse, a westerly gale was rising fast, and when the hawser parted there was nothing the crew could do but wait for the US Shipping Board's tug *Goliath,* which was steaming fast from Falmouth. Even when she reached the heavily listing steamer it was too rough for a rescue, and the *Burnside*'s crew had to wait until dawn before ferrying themselves across to her in their only serviceable boat. The *Burnside* was left still blazing fiercely, with one funnel gone and decks collapsing, and it seemed she would not last another couple of hours. But heavy seas put out the fire and a week later the Admiralty sent a destroyer to find and, if necessary, sink her. The search took some time and it was not until 12 November that her battered and capsized hulk was towed into Falmouth Bay. Rather than risk her sinking and blocking the roadstead, she was taken up into Gerrans Bay, where she stuck in shallow water and had eventually to be blown up, a task that took a month's hard work, depth charges and many sticks of dynamite.

Only two days after the *Burnside* was dragged into Falmouth Bay, the ex-German submarine, *UB-113*, under tow from Harwich via Devonport to Falmouth, where she was to be used as a naval target, broke her hawser and settled down in heavy seas four miles off the Dodman. Anticipating the purpose for which she was intended, the sloop *Kennet* destroyed her with gunfire and removed a potential danger to navigation. She was the third submarine to go down off the coast. In October 1913 the elderly *A-1* had sunk off the Eddystone while under tow to the breakers, and in January 1914 the *A-7* had failed to surface while on exercise off Rame Head, with the loss of her nine crew.

The last of the three derelicts was the 1,853-ton, five-masted wooden auxiliary schooner *Capitaine Remy* of Bordeaux, launched in 1918 for the French government by the Foundation Co of Portland, Oregon. She was bound from Barry to Nantes with 2,500 tons of coal when she was crippled by a south-east gale fourteen miles south of the Lizard, in the early hours of 29 November 1920. Every mast was smashed or carried away and when it was apparent that the auxiliary steam engine could not hold her against the storm, the crew got into their boats, securing their painters to the poop rails. They drifted for several hours until at last the Brixham fishing smack *Gratitude* sighted them and by skilful manœuvring managed to take them all on board. The *Capitaine Remy* was only four miles from the land when the master of the *Gratitude* bore away up Channel to land the Frenchmen at Brixham that evening.

A few hours after the rescue the coaster *Marena* encountered the big derelict and, unable to take her in tow, salvaged her papers from one of the boats still drifting nearby. The *Capitaine Remy* then disappeared and was thought sunk until coastguards sighted her drifting keel upwards two miles of Pentewan forty-eight hours later. A steamer reported having nearly rammed her eight miles south-east of the Lizard at midnight on 2 December, and next morning the collier *Oakton*, Swansea for Rouen, arrived at Plymouth down by the head and decks awash, having hit the capsized hulk five miles east by south of the Lizard. For another week the *Capitaine Remy* played hide-and-seek with her searchers but on 10 December the Fowey tugs *Cruden Bay* and *Gallant* at last picked her up between the Dodman and Gribbin Head and she was finally beached 300 yards off Polkerris, where the hull was stripped of its fittings, the brass rudder work alone fetching £2,000.

The decline of the great sailing coaster fleets during the twenties and thirties saw the ketches, schooners and barges fast disappearing, and those that were left being fitted with auxiliary engines so they were less vulnerable to the gales. But still the occasional old coaster got into difficulties; on 7 December 1923 the 250-ton schooner *Mary Peers* of Chester, a forty-eight-year-old veteran of Clemens' famous Gannel yard at Newquay, was driven ashore in Whitesand Bay during a strong south-easterly gale while in ballast from Torquay to Fowey. Her crew were saved by the Tregantle LSA company, but the old schooner was left jammed on her side on the rocks, a total loss.

Thick fog on 21 May 1926 put the 720-ton steel auxiliary schooner *Sambre*, of Antwerp, ashore near Dodman Head as she made for Fowey with cased spirit from Bordeaux, but she got off unaided on the flood tide. A week later Looe lifeboat performed her last service before the station was closed when she rescued the crew of the 90-ton ketch *Zarita*, John Trewin master, wrecked on the Magmain rocks while running for shelter from a south-west gale on a voyage from Plymouth to Genoa with bricks and clay. The ketch, formerly a yacht owned by Lord Brassey, soon broke up. One of the last Falmouth schooners, the *Ivy,* dating from 1878, vanished during a February gale in 1929 after leaving the Downs loaded with cement for Penryn, and a broken boat recovered off Fowey gave no clue to her fate. On 4 July 1930 another elderly schooner, the 145-ton *Tarragona* of Dublin, launched back in 1863 by Kennedy of Whitehaven, struck the Yawl Rock off Dodman, while coal-laden for Polperro, but escaped with only a few chafed planks. Less fortunate was the 22-ton wooden cutter yacht *Islander*, built by Kitto's of Porthleven in 1911 as the *Gertrude Irene*, which was wrecked in Lanivet Bay on 20 August 1930, drowning a crew of high-ranking naval officers.

A few trawlers were also lost, like the 220-ton *Marguerite* of Boulogne which got off course in fog while running for Plymouth on 3 May 1922 and was wrecked in Talland Bay, the crew being rescued by Looe lifeboat. On 9 September the following year the *Emerald*, another Boulogne trawler, was lost at Mevagissey in similar circumstances. Thick weather and a strong south-westerly gale also accounted for the Plymouth steam trawler *Chancellor*, lost under Withnoe Point in Whitesand Bay on 17 January 1934, and the rescue of her crew won the Tregantle LSA company the award for the best wreck service of the year.

The Second World War added many more ships to those sunk in the first. Most were deep-water casualties like the London collier *Alexander Kennedy* or the steamer *Silver Laurel*, torpedoed south of the Eddystone, but a number of trawlers were lost close in on minesweeping duties. The little motor-fishing-vessel *Encourage* was mined 600 yards off Plymouth breakwater on 25 October 1940, and the trawler *Lord Inchcape* was blown up further down the coast on the same day. The *Kingston Alalite* was lost on 10 November 1940, the *Elk* on 27 November 1940, the *Asama* on 21 March, 1941, and the *Lord Stonehaven* on 2 October 1942. A German submarine, *U-214*, was sunk in the old hunting ground south of the Eddystone on 26 July, 1944, but probably the best-known casualty was the American Liberty ship *James Egan Lane*, which was torpedoed in convoy near the Eddystone in March 1945 and stayed afloat just long enough to be run ashore in Whitesand Bay. Her valuable cargo of tank parts, jeeps, lorries and other general cargo for the Allied war effort was salvaged during the post-war years, but the wreck still remains upright on a sandy bottom in eighty feet of water, her holds still stacked with railway rolling stock and pickaxes, and her entire port side a carpet of sea anemones.

Since the war, there have been few wrecks between Rame Head and Falmouth; an occasional motor-coaster has run on to a sand-bar off Par, or a small fishing-boat, yacht or pleasure craft has gone on to the rocks. The last major wreck was the 798-ton coastal tanker *Allegrity*, which struck Grebe Point, drifted off and came ashore at Caerhays, near the Dodman, on 13 December 1961 while bound from Havre to Stanilow with lubricating oil. Despite the hard SSE gale, her crew were rescued by Falmouth lifeboat, but the tanker, launched in 1945 by the Grangemouth Dockyard Co as the *Empire Tavistock*, defied all efforts to refloat her, capsized a week later and became a total wreck.

CHAPTER THREE

FALMOUTH BAY

AN expression once common in the West Country claimed that, 'Truro might have the honour, but Falmouth has gotten the trade'; meaning that although Truro was the capital city of the county, Falmouth, due to its location and excellent harbour, was attracting all the trade of Cornwall. Certainly, a century ago it was not uncommon to see two or three hundred ships lying at anchor in Carrick Roads and in the channel leading to Penryn, all of which brought considerable business to the town as well as benefiting the nearby villages of Flushing, Mylor and St Mawes.

Although Falmouth had nothing more than a few stone quays and jetties until 1860, when the present harbour complex was started, there had been a settlement and anchorage at Penryn, or Penmerryn to use its older name, as early as 1246. For many years the majority of tin shipments were made from Penryn, and to protect both the settlement and ships from surprise attack a huge 'chain boom', made from wrought-iron links, was stretched across the creek from bank to bank at night or in times of danger.

As the years went by and silting began to affect the upper reaches of the Fal and its many creeks and outlets, the settlement at Falmouth, favoured with deep-water anchorages, steadily expanded until it eclipsed Penryn and became the most important seaport in the west. Forts were erected on either bank at the entrance to the outer reaches of the harbour, at St Mawes to the north-west, and Pendennis to the south-west, both being started in 1542. At about the same time Mylor became a royal dockyard, building and repairing ships for the royal fleets. In 1661 the first stone quay was authorised at Falmouth so that ships could come alongside to load or discharge, and in 1688 the famous Falmouth 'packet' service to Lisbon started, later to be extended to the West Indies and America.

One of the earliest wrecks around Falmouth occurred on 18

November 1720, when 'a Dutch ship from Nantes ran on a shoal
near that port laden with brandy and saffron, she might have been
got off but the country people came so thick that they were obliged
to leave her. But some of the plunderers having drunk too much
brandy, and being busy in the hold with a candle, they set fire to
the brandy, by which means the ship and cargo were destroyed and
twelve of the ruffians perished in the flames'. Seven or eight of the
gang were arrested, and ' 'tis thought examples will be made of them
according to the Act of Parliament'. The Yarmouth snow *Squirrel*,
Henry Williams master, which drove ashore near Falmouth while
bound for Boulogne with brandy, met a similar fiery end. She, too,
was plundered, and burnt out after her cargo had accidentally been
set alight.

Other early wrecks were the frigate *Spencer* and the *Olive Branch*
of Ramsgate, lost with all hands off Falmouth on 19 December
1754, and another man-o'-war, the fireship *Firebrand*, which caught
fire and blew up in Carrick Roads on 13 October 1781. Her crew
escaped unharmed, including Captain Hill, who had only just been
given command of her for gallantry while serving with Admiral
Hyde Parker. In January 1792 the Dutch frigate *Briel* struck the
Minstral rock, among the Manacles, and grounded between there
and Falmouth. Her story was given in the home news appendix of
the *Ladies Magazine*, dated 6 June, 1792:

> 'Arrived at Plymouth HM cutter *Sunflower*, Lieutenant
> Webber, who has been sent to Falmouth to inspect the loss of
> the *Briel*, a Dutch frigate of thirty-six guns with 350 soldiers
> and sailors, in a heavy gale of wind. On her first voyage, bound
> for Lisbon and thence to Demerara in South America, all on
> board were saved except six. She went ashore between the
> Manacles and Falmouth, and as soon as she was perceived
> by the country people they came down with all kinds of
> weapons they could procure, and plundered the ship and
> people of everything they could lay hold of—they even stript
> the crew of the clothes off their backs.'

One of the worst disasters in the Falmouth area occurred in
1811, when HMS *Franchise* ran down and sank another vessel in
convoy. The 36-gun frigate *Franchise* and the 18-gun *Primrose* were
escorting a fleet of transports and merchant vessels to Lisbon. At
3 am on 21 February, whilst off Falmouth in a gale, the *Franchise*
struck the transport *John and Jane* which was carrying 272 men

and seven officers of the 11th Regiment, fifteen women, six children and an unspecified number of crew. Of the 300 or so persons on board, most of whom were asleep when the collision occurred, 269 drowned. This was not the only incident that night; in the same convoy the American *Industrious* rammed and sank another transport, the *Wellington*, laden with stores. The captain and five of the *Wellington*'s crew were lost. The *Industrious* put back into Plymouth with her fore and main mast missing, the *Franchise* to Falmouth to report the incident and land bodies.

Although Falmouth is an excellent haven for ships during westerly or south-westerly gales, the anchorage is very exposed to easterly winds. Sailing vessels lying in Carrick Roads would be obliged to take the full brunt of easterly gales which drive straight in between the headlands. A dragging anchor or a broken cable meant that the unfortunate vessel would be blown on to the jagged rocks of Trefusis Point, and one of many ships lost here was the government-hired transport *Queen*, returning from the Peninsular wars and carrying the bulk of a British regiment of the line together with their families and ten French prisoners of war. Under the command of Captain Carr, the *Queen* left Lisbon just after Christmas 1813 with over 300 people on board and joined a small Portsmouth-bound convoy of eight ships—the *Latham, Inclination, Henry, Ocean, Fame, Burton, Ceres* and *Apollo*—all under the charge of the 36-gun frigate *Melpomene*. The homeward journey was rough and uncomfortable and it was with some relief that the convoy anchored at Falmouth on 10 January 1814. Despite a strong easterly wind and unsettled weather, Captain Carr considered it sufficient to lay out the port anchor with only thirty-five fathoms of cable, considerably less than the length generally deemed necessary to hold such a vessel in a deep anchorage. However, for three days she lay at anchor without incident and then on the afternoon of Thursday 13 January she began to drag. For some time this went unnoticed by the lookout on deck, and when at last the captain was informed it was too late to take action. The starboard anchor, although 'catted', had no cable attached and while this was being brought up from below the port anchor cable parted and the vessel was adrift. The wind bore her rapidly down on Trefusis Point and at 4.30 am, with the crew still struggling with the cable of the starboard anchor and panic reigning among the passengers

D

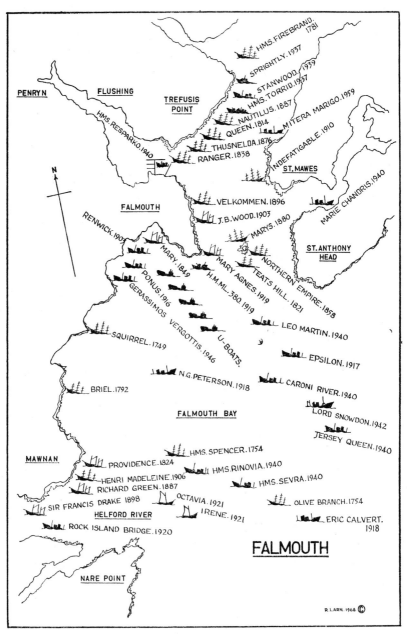

PENRYN   FLUSHING

TREFUSIS POINT

HMS.FIREBRAND.
1781

SPRIGHTLY.1937

STANWOOD.1939

HMS.TORRID.1937

NAUTILUS.1887

QUEEN.1814

MITERA MARIGO.1959

HMS.RESPARKO.1940

INDEFATIGABLE.1910

THUSNELDA.1876

RANGER.1838

ST. MAWES

N

FALMOUTH

VELKOMMEN.1896

MARIE CHANDRIS.1940

J.B.WOOD.1903

MARYS.1880

RENWICK.190

MARY.1849

NORTHERN EMPIRE.1858

ST.ANTHONY HEAD

PONUS.1916

MARY AGNES.1919

H.M.ML.380.1919

TEATS HILL.1821

GERASSIMOS VERGOTTIS.1946

U-BOATS.

LEO MARTIN.1940

SQUIRREL.1749

EPSILON.1917

N.G.PETERSON.1918

CARONI RIVER.1940

BRIEL.1792

LORD SNOWDON.1942

FALMOUTH BAY

JERSEY QUEEN.1940

HMS.SPENCER.1754

MAWNAN

PROVIDENCE.1824

HMS.RINOVIA.1940

HENRI MADELEINE.1906

HMS.SEVRA.1940

RICHARD GREEN.1887

SIR FRANCIS DRAKE 1898

OCTAVIA.1921

OLIVE BRANCH.1754

HELFORD RIVER

IRENE.1921

ERIC CALVERT.
1918

ROCK ISLAND BRIDGE.1920

FALMOUTH

NARE POINT

R.LARN.1968 ©

Wreck locations in Falmouth Bay and Carrick Roads.

on deck and below, the *Queen* drove onto the Trefusis rocks and broached-to. Huge waves crashed down on the deck carrying all before them and the sea poured down hatchways and ladders, adding to the chaos below. Attempts were made to fire a cannon as a signal of distress but the sea had swamped the guns and now heavy snow was falling, making it impossible to see the wreck from the shore.

Captain Carr ordered the masts to be cut away and as they fell under the onslaught of axes the ship lurched heavily, guns broke adrift, bulwarks were smashed, the hull gave way and most of those below were either crushed to death or instantly drowned. Less than twenty minutes after striking, the *Queen* was no more than a broken, half-submerged hulk. Some of the troops managed to scramble ashore and daylight revealed a sight never forgotten by those who witnessed it. Scores of bodies washed about in the shallows or lay draped across the rocks and entangled in rigging. Only eighty-five soldiers, nine women, one child and four prisoners survived; the captain and his entire crew, apart from the bosun and a cabin boy, lost their lives. Some 250 bodies were eventually recovered, but not before looting had commenced, and a number of troopers were later tried by court martial for robbing corpses.

A total of 136 dead were laid to rest in a mass grave in Mylor churchyard, the villagers erecting a memorial tablet which, although eroded by weather, is still decipherable and reads:

'To the memory of the warriors, women and children who, returning from the coast of Spain unhappily perished in the wreck of the *Queen*, transport, on Trefusis Point, January 14th 1814. This stone is erected as a testimony of regret by the inhabitants of this parish.'

But the tragedy is perhaps better expressed in the simple epitaph composed by one of the surviving officers:

'In memory of Catherine, wife of Lieutenant Robert Daniell, 3rd Regiment; also his children, Margaret, Eleanor, William, Robert and Edward Alexander who unhappily perished in the wreck of the *Queen*, transport, on the awful morning of January 14th 1814, leaving an unfortunate husband and father to lament their loss to the end of his existence.'

Trefusis Point claimed another victim on 14 February 1838 when the packet brig *Ranger*, at anchor in Carrick Roads, was caught by a south-easterly blizzard with most of her crew ashore. Without manpower enough to strike her yards and topmasts to reduce wind resistance, she dragged steadily shorewards during the night and at seven o'clock next morning drove stern first on to the Point, quickly swinging broadside on. Blue lights were burned, guns fired and the longboat was launched to take a line ashore but very soon it capsized, drowning an able seaman named Andrews, from St Mawes, and injuring five others. Salvage proved a difficult task as later gales had driven the *Ranger* high up on the rocks, but with the aid of lighters from Devonport and a naval salvage party under the direction of Captain Plumridge, Superintendent of Packets, she was hauled off on 15 March and towed up to Mylor. At a subsequent court martial held on board HMS *Royal Adelaide* in Plymouth, her acting master Hunter was found guilty of gross negligence and dismissed the Service.

There were no casualties when the large Norwegian brigantine *Thusnelda* dragged her anchors in a south-westerly gale and was driven ashore on the same point during the night of 31 October 1887. Though her decks were quickly awash, all her crew were able to clamber into the rigging, from which they were rescued in daylight by the Falmouth tug *Briton*. Later the ship, which had been launched at Faaborg in 1876 and was laden with hides and bones from Pelatus, was salvaged by Leans of Falmouth and was still afloat in the 1920s as the schooner *Elsie* of Swansea. Less fortunate was the Dutch brig *Nautilus*, Kortner master, which became a total loss when driven ashore the same night close by the *Thusnelda*. Bound from Antwerp to Cadiz in ballast and sheltering in the Roads, her cable parted in the gale and she was quickly carried on to the rocks. The only casualty was her cook, Jan Schmidt, whose body was not recovered until a month later.

More recent victims of Trefusis Point include the customs launch *Sprightly*, after breaking loose in Falmouth harbour on 15 December 1936 and, three months later, on 15 March 1937, the old 'R'-class destroyer *Torrid*. The *Torrid*, of 1,000 tons displacement and launched in 1917, had been towed into Falmouth the previous day en route to the scrapyard of Thomas Ward at Hayle. Caught out in the Roads by a sudden south-westerly gale and with only a watchman on board, she dragged her anchor on to the Mylor side of Trefusis, was left high and dry as the tide fell and was eventually broken up where she lay.

Returning to earlier events in Falmouth Bay, on 17 April 1903 the tug *Marian* had no sooner cleared St Anthony Head with the Danish schooner *Edmond* in tow for Par than she sighted, some distance off, a sailing ship on fire, the 126-ton Prince Edward Isle-built wooden schooner *J B Wood* of Newport, bound from Dublin to Dunkirk with a cargo of slate. Temporarily abandoning the *Edmond*, the *Marian* took the burning vessel in tow and brought her into Falmouth where, almost completely gutted, she was scuttled at Foundry beach. At a salvage court held on 25 May, the tug *Marian* was awarded £200 for her services, but the master of the tug *Carbon*, who claimed to have helped in getting the vessel ashore, had to be content with only £20.

Across from Foundry Beach, at St Mawes Castle, a long reef of rock projects into the shipping channel and was the site of the stranding of the Russian barque *Indefatigable* in 1910. After being weather-bound at Falmouth for a week, she left harbour on 22 January for Cardiff in tow of the tug *Challenge*. Off Land's End the sea was too rough to continue, so both returned and anchored in the Carrick Roads. That night the barque dragged her anchors, went ashore close to the old castle and was high and dry at low water. The tugs *Dragon*, *Marian* and *Briton* managed to pull her clear and get her into dry-dock but as her owners were unable to pay the costs of the salvage and docking she was sold by order of a local court.

Two comparatively modern wrecks still lie within the confines of Falmouth harbour. The earlier of the two was the 4,155-ton steamer *Stanwood* which had been launched as the *Hesione* in 1915 by Lank Retheritg of Hamburg. Owned by the Shipping Controller for the rest of the First World War, she then passed into the hands of the Elder Dempster Line and finally to the Stanhope Line in 1937. On 10 December 1939 the *Stanwood*, bound from Leith to Dakar, was lying at anchor near the North Bank with her coal cargo on fire. The fire had been discovered earlier when she was alongside Falmouth docks and she had been towed out clear of other shipping. It was decided to flood her holds in an attempt to put out the fire but either it was overdone or mismanaged for she sank so suddenly that the tugs *Fairnlee* and *Northgate Scott*, tied up alongside, had to cut their mooring lines and fire hoses to avoid being dragged down. Even then the suction of the sinking vessel drew both tugs across her deck, one ramming the bridge the other the ship's foremast. All the crew of the *Stanwood* escaped, except for the radio operator who drowned in his bunk. As the *Stanwood* went down, she slipped off the shallow edge of the bank into deep water and sank in about ninety feet on the Mylor side of Trefusis. Extensive salvage was carried out on the wreck over the years but a quantity of wreckage remains.

The other vessel, the *MV Mitera Marigo*, and the most recent wreck of any size in the Falmouth area, had been in collision with the German-owned steamer *Fritz Rhysen* during the early hours of Friday 29 May 1959. Greek-owned and Liberian-registered, the 9,200-ton *Mitera Marigo* collided with the 10,900-ton German vessel in dense fog off Ushant and was so extensively damaged that Falmouth tugs raced out and brought her into Carrick Roads at 8 pm the same day. She had a huge hole in her bows, No 1 hold was flooded, and her forepart looked as if she had struck a mine. In danger of foundering, she was towed a little way up the estuary and secured to a buoy, just across the channel from where the *Stanwood* had sunk. The tug *Englishman* stood by her all night but the *Mitera Marigo was* settling fast and, about midnight, the Falmouth lifeboat was called out. When she did go she went very quickly, the crew abandoning ship in their own boats and a local customs officer literally stepping off the ship's rail into a boat as the rail disappeared underwater. After finding the bottom, the wreck remained perfectly upright with masts protruding from the sea. As her bunkers still contained fuel oil, which might escape and contaminate the oyster fisheries and harbour, a local firm, with the assistance of the Navy, managed to pump the oil into lighters after a floating screen had been placed around the wreck. Considerable salvage work was carried out on the wreck, which was then flattened by explosives to remove a navigational hazard. Now covered deeply in places by fine silt, a great deal of the wreck remains in ninety feet of dark, muddy and turbulent water and the site is marked on Admiralty charts.

During the two World Wars the majority of losses occurred outside the harbour, in Falmouth Bay, a veritable graveyard of sunken ships. Most were sunk by mines, although German aircraft claimed ships both inside and outside the harbour, and several ships sank after being towed in from the Channel. In a raid on the harbour on 10 July 1940 three ships alongside the north arm— the steamer *Marie Chandris*, the tanker *British Chancellor* and the Greek tanker *Tuscalusa*—were all set on fire. The *British Chancellor* was not badly damaged but the *Marie Chandris*'s cargo of raw cotton burnt like tinder and, still ablaze, she was towed to a small bay near St Mawes and sunk by gunfire. Later, the shell-holes were patched, the ship refloated and beached at Place Hole where, after salving what was left of the cotton, the vessel was cut up for scrap. Much the same fate befell the *Tuscalusa*, which was towed and sunk at St Just Pool. After her superstructure had been cut away, the vessel was carved up into sections and floated down to Freeman's yard at Penryn to be reduced to scrap. A few weeks later, on 24 August, HMS *Resparko*, a 248-ton trawler converted to a minesweeper, was also bombed and sank at her berth inside the basin.

At the entrance to Falmouth harbour, almost exactly in the centre of the fairway, lies a rocky shoal known as Black Rock. It has claimed many victims over the years, one of the earliest having been the sloop *Teats Hill* of Plymouth, wrecked on it while entering the harbour on 24 April 1821 during a heavy squall. The 1,515-ton wooden ship *Northern Empire* of Oldenburg, built at Maine in 1854, was on passage from Callao to London with a cargo of guano when she broke adrift from her tug while shifting berth in the harbour on 3 March 1858. She broke her back when she struck Black Rock but was later beached on Trefusis Point for salvage. The Whitby brig *Marys*, Dundee-built in 1849 and bound from Liverpool to London with salt, was also wrecked on Black Rock, on 22 October 1880.

Falmouth Bay holds the remains of at least ten steamships, most of which are still marked on Admiralty charts though all at various times have been flattened by salvage companies to reduce their hazard to shipping. The largest is the *Caroni River*, a 7,807-ton oil tanker which struck a mine on 20 January 1940 just after she had left Falmouth harbour to carry out engine trials and sank within an hour. As the entire area had recently been swept for conventional 'contact' or 'horned' mines and there had been no reports of enemy aircraft over the bay which might have laid mines by parachute, magnetic mines from a mine-laying submarine seemed the most likely answer. A German coastal submarine of 300 tons was known to be capable of carrying nine such mines, which meant, if the naval experts had guessed correctly, that eight more could still be lying on the bottom of the bay. A magnetic 'sweep' was improvised and a minesweeper left Falmouth harbour on the same course and speed as the *Caroni River*. Very soon, eight big explosions in succession, each followed by towering columns of water, proved the experts right. It remained to discover how the Germans had managed to navigate close inshore with such accuracy at night, and an after-dark cruise round the bay soon supplied the solution. St Anthony Head clearly silhouetted against the night sky was one good bearing; the other was the Manacles light buoy, flashing out its warning to friend and foe alike. The Manacles buoy was speedily extinguished and did not flash again for the rest of the war. The *Caroni River* sank right in the middle of the bay and though marked as three separate 'wrecks', they are, in fact, three parts of the same ship.

Other marked wrecks in the bay are the steamers *Epsilon*, 3,211 tons, sunk 31 January 1917; the Danish *N G Peterson*, 1,282 tons, sunk 13 March 1918 with a cargo of iron ore; *Eric Calvert*, sunk 22 April 1918; *Jersey Queen*, 901 tons, mined on 6 October 1940, and the *Leo Martin*, 1,951 tons, sunk 13 November 1940. All these ships, as well as a number of others, lie in less than 100ft of water. Unmarked wrecks include those of two minesweepers, HMS *Rinovia* and *Sevra* which blew up and sank in November 1940. *Rinovia* was launched at Berkeley in 1931 for the Rinovia Steam Fishing Co of Grimsby; *Sevra*, 253 tons, a converted whaling vessel belonging to the South Georgia Co of Capetown, was launched at Teeside in 1929.

On the western side of the seaward approach to Falmouth, and south of the town, lies Pendennis Point. Originally known as Pendinas, Celtic for 'headland fortress', it is dominated by the old castle which has looked out over the bay for the past four and a half centuries. A considerable number of vessels have been stranded or wrecked here, or further west in Gyllyngvase and Swanpool bays. The Norwegian barque *Velkommen* finished her days on the rocks beneath the walls of Pendennis on 28 November 1896. Launched at Stavanger in 1883 as a wooden three-master of 360

Page 61 : (above) The Liverpool full-rigger *Andola*, wrecked on the Manacles in an easterly gale on 31 January 1895; (below) all that was visible of the liner *Mohegan* on the Manacles at dawn on 14 October 1898; 104 lives were lost.

Page 62: The great blizzard of March 1891 wrecked the Liverpool ship *Bay of Panama* at Nare Head.

Page 63: The Greek freighter *Archangelos* being towed clear of Dolor Point, Coverack, where she grounded on 17 April 1929.

Page 64: (above) The German barque *Pindos* broadside on to the rocks near Coverack on 11 February 1912; (below) motor transport of the 1920s, with the French collier *Maurice Bernard* in the background, at Kennack Sands on 25 May 1925.

tons, she left Le Havre in ballast for Newport on 27 November under tow from the *Sir W T Lewis*. An easterly gale forced the ships to seek shelter at Falmouth but as they approached Black Rock the tow parted and the sailing ship went ashore, despite dropping both anchors. The crew of eight and the captain's wife were rescued by breeches-buoy and Leans of Falmouth later attempted her salvage. But her keel was washed away before work commenced, and after being dragged and towed into dry-dock she was sold for scrap, fetching £145.

The 83-ton schooner *Mary Agnes* of Wexford, Morlaix to Cardiff in ballast, missed stays whilst entering Falmouth in a north-easterly gale at 8 pm on 4 January 1919 and went ashore on the rocks beneath the present coastguard lookout. The Falmouth lifeboat was launched, but three local men, John Snell, William Lewty and Reggie Tonkin, reached the wreck first in a small boat and saved the crew of four. The *Mary Agnes*, which had been built at Wexford by Devereux in 1865, went to pieces where she lay. Amongst the same rocks lie the rusting engines and remains of ML *No 380*, a fast coastal patrol boat of the First World War. She had sailed from Queenstown, southern Ireland, on 29 November 1919 for Portsmouth but was forced to accept a tow from another launch after an engine breakdown, finally being brought into the Helford estuary by the destroyer, HMS *Ursula*. That night a freshening south-west gale forced the commanding officer of the launch to seek the shelter of Falmouth, but once out in the bay ML *380* rolled and pitched heavily. Without warning, her galley exploded and a sheet of flame set the vessel on fire. An accompanying launch, ML *No 524*, took off the crew, leaving the burning launch to drift down on Pendennis where her tanks exploded and she sank.

Another minor naval incident in the vicinity was the collision between HM torpedo-boat *Speedy* and the Admiralty collier *Stokesay*. The steamer was rammed by the torpedo-boat while on exercises on 18 June 1906, and shortly after sank in the shallows of Swanpool beach. Naval divers patched up the hull and she was re-floated and towed to Devonport for docking. The 800-ton Newcastle collier *Renwick*, in ballast from Devonport to Burryport, dragged ashore at Gyllyngvase during a south-westerly gale on 26 February 1903 and, by morning, her stem had been torn off and the hull flooded. Captain Anderson of the Western Marine Salvage

Co undertook to salvage her and within fifteen days had the *Renwick* safely in dry-dock. Of the many sailing ships which have gone ashore at Swanpool and Gyllyngvase in the past 100 years, the 123-ton Dartmouth schooner *Mary* was a typical example. She was 105 days out from Accra with a cargo of palm oil for London when a Falmouth pilot, boarding her at dawn on 7 December 1849, found the crew had been without food for fourteen days and were about to kill and eat the ship's dog. In the course of an argument over pilotage fees, the vessel drove ashore near Gyllyngvase House, then a vicarage, and when a line was thrown ashore the vicar himself secured it to a small stone archway and the crew were able to drag themselves ashore. The ship's cargo was saved through the vigilance of a coastguard who had to use his pistol to hold off the wreckers, and the pilot had his licence suspended.

Of all the vessels sunk in Falmouth Bay, the most improbable were the six German U-boats wrecked in 1921. Nine captured submarines were allocated to Falmouth for gunnery practice and experiments, and eight of these duly arrived and were anchored at Gyllyngvase. Two were intentionally sunk during trials but the remaining six were swept on to the rocks along Castle Drive during a winter gale and for many years could be seen lying in the shallows, where they could easily be boarded. One sank close inshore near the bathing beach and part of its rusting hull still shows at low water; the others sank along the line of rocks and their remains lie scattered over a wide area. Over the years their ownership has changed hands several times and they are still being salvaged.

The most dramatic wreck at Falmouth was, without doubt, the 5,077-ton tanker *Ponus* which, laden with crude oil, went ashore on 3 November 1916, caught fire and burnt like a torch for almost three days. At the time, a number of so-called tankers were either converted cargo ships or had been built on the lines of a conventional cargo-carrying ship, with accommodation and bridge amidships. The 405ft-long *Ponus* was just such a 'tanker' and had been built in 1902 by Russels of Port Glasgow, where she was launched as the *Kennebec*. She arrived at Falmouth at 7 pm on 2 November from Trinidad and as no pilot was available she anchored three-quarters of a mile off-shore. During the night the wind increased almost to gale force and though a second anchor

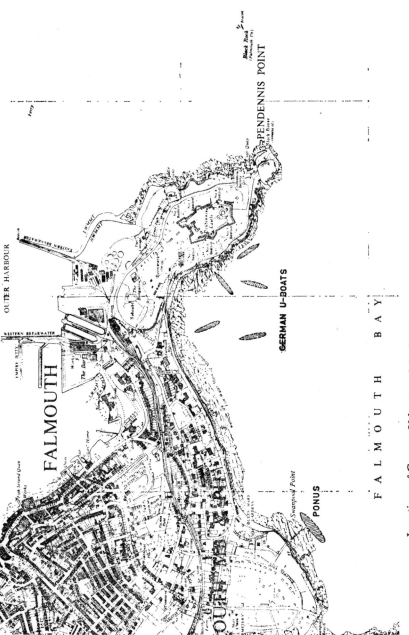

Locations of German U-boats and the 5,077-ton steamer *Ponus*, wrecked off Falmouth.

was dropped it fouled the first and the *Ponus* dragged ashore on the spit of rock between Swanpool and Gyllyngvase. Blasts on her siren and distress rockets roused most of Falmouth and hundreds flocked to the beach to watch the tug *Victor* trying to tow the Falmouth lifeboat round Pendennis to the rescue. But heavy seas forced them to turn back and at 10 am Captain Collins, master of the *Ponus*, risked lowering two of the ship's boats, both of which managed to reach the shore. The master himself and the rest of his crew were rescued by the lifeboat on a second attempt.

An hour later a thin trickle of smoke was seen to be rising from the ship and quickly became a thick plume. The onlookers were first amused, then alarmed to see a man appear on deck wearing nothing but a very short vest. Soon discovering that he was the only man left on board, he quickly assembled a primitive raft, threw it overboard and jumped in after it. Raft and man were swept under the stem and pinned against it and only a timely rescue by a dinghy which put off from the beach saved the life of the man in the vest.

By evening, the entire midships section of the *Ponus* was ablaze and when the funnel collapsed the entire sky was lit by the flames. At 5.30 am on 4 November a terrific explosion sent burning oil pouring out over the sea to spread along the beach in an unbroken line. Further explosions occurred as the day wore on and soon the fire had become a very real hazard to property on shore. A boat from the *Ponus*, somehow full of blazing oil, broke adrift and floated down to Pendennis, spreading the fire. By 7 pm the ship's sides were glowing red-hot and the rising tide caused the sea around the wreck to boil and spit. The fire burnt all that night and all the next day, finally dying down on 6 November. Yet despite its severity the ship remained on the rocks, its structure virtually intact, for two years until November 1918 when a large section of the stern was cut away and taken into Falmouth docks for scrapping. The remainder was demolished by successive salvage firms and gales, but a great deal of her iron plating remains in the shallows. On some charts the wreck of the *Ponus* is still marked, with the inscription, 'being demolished, 1923'.

One final incident in the area, before Falmouth is left behind, should be the Greek-owned, 6,243-ton *Gerassimos Vergottis*, which collided with the Dutch steamer *Van Ostade* on 3 July 1946 eleven miles south of Land's End, suffering serious damage. Tugs brought her into Falmouth Bay and beached her 100 yards off Gyllyngvase. Naval divers patched her up and the following day, assisted by the salvage ship *Lifeline*, she was safely docked at Falmouth.

The few miles of coastline between Falmouth and the Helford estuary consist mostly of high cliffs and shallow water close inshore. The Brixham schooner *Providence* went ashore here, near Maen Porth, on 15 April 1824, while in ballast from her home port to Newport.

In the Helford river itself, a southerly gale, accompanied by pouring rain and heavy seas, put the pilot cutter *Richard Green* ashore at 1 pm on 2 September 1887. The four pilots and three apprentices on board were saved, but the cutter was a complete loss on Paul's Point, near Mawnan church. Other small wrecks locally were the Bideford schooner *Sir Francis Drake*, which had discharged coal at Port Navas when she was blown ashore and smashed up on 1 May 1898. The *Henri Madeleine*, a French ketch on passage from Southampton to Brest with nitrates, sprang a leak and had to be put ashore on 11 November 1906. The wreck was sold to a Mr Chard but broke up before salvage could be started. The yacht *Irene* struck Nare Point on 17 September 1921 during a gale, and another yacht, the *Octavia*, sank off the mouth of the river the same day.

The last wreck to be recorded in this chapter is that of the American steamer *Rock Island Bridge* and her story begins in the early hours of 22 March 1920, when she was in collision with the American steamer *Kenosha*, both homeward bound in ballast, ten miles east of the Lizard in fog. Damage to the 3,545-ton *Rock Island Bridge* was so extensive that her crew promptly abandoned ship, but when, two hours later, she showed no signs of sinking, they re-boarded her and sent out radio distress signals. By the time the tug *Triton* arrived the *Kenosha* had the damaged vessel in tow and both captains refused to change the tow until they were clear of the Manacles. Soon afterwards a bulkhead in the *Rock Island Bridge* collapsed under the weight of water in the hull and the crew again abandoned ship, leaving the tug to take over the tow.

After spending the night at anchor off Porthallow, the *Rock Island Bridge*, now dangerously low in the water, was towed into the Helford river where she sank in nine fathoms, falling over onto her starboard side. On Tuesday, 18 May, she was put up to auction at the Baltic Exchange by order of her owners, the US Shipping Board, the auctioneers claiming that she was worth £200,000 afloat and that salvage would not be difficult. Bidding started at £5,000 and she was finally sold to the All Seas Marine and Salvage Co for £15,000. The new owners, a recently-formed salvage concern, carried out extensive repairs to the hull and, using several tugs, tried to pull her upright on 12 September 1920 but failed. Operations continued but without success and the salvage tug *Gundreda* was almost wrecked herself at Helford on 22 October 1922. Huge concrete blocks were then sunk into the cliff face and used as anchorages for wires in the hope that she could be pulled upright. Iron frames were built on to the hull to increase the leverage, but still she refused to move and, in the end, she had to be declared a total loss. For years the wreck lay awash in the Helford river, a constant hazard to navigation until, eventually, she was reduced to scrap by explosives. Built in 1920 by the Submarine Boat Co, Newark, NJ, the *Rock Island Bridge* was of 324ft overall length and fitted with a geared turbine engine, her original boilers having been adapted for oil burning. The remains of the wreck, now partially covered by sand and silt, still lie on the bottom of the Helford river, a popular fishing mark for the local residents but no longer a danger to navigation.

CHAPTER FOUR

THE MANACLES

THE coastline between Nare Point and Cadgwith centres natur-
ally on the Manacles, a reef with a sinister name and a
particularly evil reputation. Well over a hundred ships have
been wrecked here and nearly a thousand people have drowned,
and though the worst disasters occurred many years ago, the reef
still commands healthy respect and a wide berth.

The name probably derives from the Cornish 'maen eglos', meaning church rocks, a possible reference to the church of St Keverne
whose tower serves as a landmark visible for many miles around.
A collection of rocks covering about one and a half square miles
and almost submerged at high tide, the Manacles stretch nearly
a mile out to sea to the east of St Keverne. South-east from
Manacle Point, a large red buoy is held in place by a huge anchor
cable reaching 200 feet down to the seabed, marking the limit of
the danger presented by this reef which lies across the southern
approach to Falmouth. Ships entering or leaving the harbour can
safely pass close on the seaward side of the buoy but most continue
to give it a wide berth, too many fine ships having been lost through
cutting the corner.

A study of the chart shows that there are only two safe channels
for negotiating the Manacles. The widest leads into Porthoustock
Bay and is still used by the coasters of 5-700 tons which load stone
alongside the quay. The other, which runs parallel to the coast
past Manacle Point and Godrevy beach to Lowland Point, is
normally used only by fishermen. In the early 1800s, the Falmouth
packet *Marlborough*, returning from the United States, was intercepted by a French privateer off the Lizard. Having known the
coast since his youth, Captain Bull took his ship close inshore and
through this inner channel while the privateer, attempting to
follow, struck a rock near Carn Du and sank. It was this same
channel that saved the Greek motor-ship *Alkon* of Meihan when

she found herself among the Manacles in bad visibility on 15 September 1966 and was able to anchor before striking a reef.

The respect shown to the reef is understandable for it has caused some appalling tragedies. The loss of the Admiralty transport *Dispatch* and the brig HMS *Primrose* during the same night in 1809 brought 110 bodies ashore and many more were unaccounted for. When the emigrant barque *John* went down in 1855, 120 bodies were recovered, and in 1898 106 people were drowned in the wreck of the liner *Mohegan*.

North of the Manacles lies the Helford estuary, its southern bank beyond Gillan creek rising to the headland at Nare Point. The Cardiff steamer *Northfield*, Sulina to Falmouth, went ashore here on 28 May 1913 but was towed clear and beached alongside the eastern breakwater at Falmouth, her hull badly damaged and her cargo of barley ruined by the sea. From Nare Point, the high cliffs turn south into Porthallow Bay, and less than 250 yards from this headland lies the remains of a wreck which is legend in Cornwall, the *Bay of Panama*.

She was a 2,282-ton, four-masted, square-rigged steel ship, launched by Harland & Wolff at Belfast in 1883 and described as one of the finest sailing vessels ever built. She left Calcutta on 18 November 1890 with 13,000 bales of jute between decks, destined for the mills at Dundee. The homeward voyage was uneventful, and by the early days of March 1891 the *Bay of Panama* was nearing Cornwall. The weather was deteriorating fast and Captain David Wright hove-to in order to take deep soundings. The results led him to believe he was close to the Lizard. Dawn on 9 March came with all the signs of an approaching blizzard. At 4 pm, when the deck watch was relieved, a strong north-easterly gale was blowing accompanied by driving snow. For the best part of the day the ship had been under fore and main topsails only, but now all sail was furled. This storm became known as the 'blizzard of '91', the worst the West Country had known for 200 years. Animals died in the fields of Cornwall and Devon in their hundreds, and four ships were wrecked on the Manacles alone.

At 11.30 pm a white light, thought to be that of a steamship, was sighted from the *Bay of Panama* but there was no answer to their blue distress flare. A little after 1.30 am on 10 March a huge wave pooped the ship, sweeping her from end to end and smashing

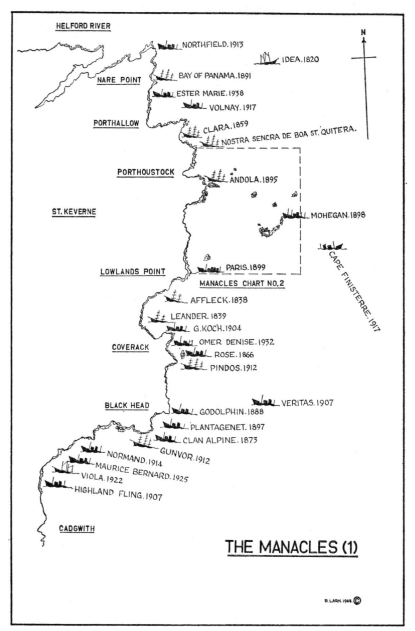

Wreck locations between Nare Point and Cadgwith.

THE MANACLES (1)

R. LARN. 1968. ©

E

every boat on deck. Soon afterwards, still in driving snow and with
visibility almost nil, the ship went headlong into the cliffs south
of Nare Point, less than seven miles from the safety of Falmouth.
As the vessel struck, she swung round until her bows pointed east,
listing heavily to starboard. One mast came down, and both fore
and main topmasts broke off and fell into the sea. The second mate
managed to fire a distress rocket before a wave swept along the deck
and washed him overboard. The same wave swamped the cabin,
carrying the captain, his wife, the cook, steward and four apprentices over the side to drown.

Meanwhile the mate ordered the rest of the crew into the rigging
to get above the freezing water which swirled over the deck. The
bosun, carpenter and sailmaker took shelter behind the deckhouse,
but two were swept overboard to die in the darkness. The bosun
managed to reach the mizzen rigging, but during the night went
out of his mind and jumped into the sea. Extreme cold and
exposure took its toll of the others in the rigging, all soaked by
spray which turned to ice on their clothing and on the ropes to
which they clung. At least six seamen froze to death, others lost
their grip and fell into the sea.

Daybreak revealed the *Bay of Panama* hard and fast under the
cliff, broadside on to the sea, her bowsprit less than fifty feet
from the rocks. Her rigging and deck were in ruins, with a mass
of cordage attached to the masts trailing alongside. A few pitiful
figures still hung in the rigging, some alive, some dead; it was
impossible to tell the difference from ashore. A local farmer searching the clifftops for his sheep was the first to find the wreck and
promptly made for Porthallow to inform the coastguards, who set
out from St Keverne with rocket apparatus.

By 9 am a breeches line had been rigged and seventeen survivors
from the crew of forty were brought ashore. Quite incapable of
helping themselves, they had to be lifted from the rigging and
placed in the breeches-buoy with limbs in the position in which
they were found. Several bodies were floating alongside or lying
in the scuppers of the wreck, the first to be recovered being that
of the captain's wife. The survivors were taken to St Keverne where
they were thawed out, fed and put to bed. Next day, a local carrier's
horse-drawn bus took them to Gweek on the first stage of their
journey to Falmouth, but snowdrifts blocking the road forced them

to abandon it and for the second time in twenty-four hours they were exposed to near-Arctic conditions. Some without shoes, they struggled along the road and eventually reached the outskirts of Falmouth, having as *The Falmouth Packet* reported, 'endured as much privation in that walk as they did in the actual shipwreck'.

Two days later the steamer *Hermes*, belonging to the Neptune Salvage Company of Cowes, Isle of Wight, arrived to inspect the wreck, but the actual work of salvage was carried out by two Liverpool divers who set up a steam donkey-engine and boiler on deck to operate a winch and tranship the cargo of bagged jute into barges alongside. The work was interrupted in August when the donkey boiler burst, killing one man and sending pieces of metal as high as the clifftop. Sightseers came in their hundreds to see the wreck and hear the story of the crew's ordeal. Timber from her deck was cut into small pieces and sold as souvenirs, and her bell was donated to a small chapel at Helford, where it can still be seen high up in the pointed tower, weather-beaten and green.

Over the years, winter gales have reduced the wreck of the *Bay of Panama* almost to the level of the sand upon which she lies, but in the spring, before the new weed covers her keel and ribs, a great deal can be seen, even from a boat, as her remains lie in less than thirty feet. A prominent marker for the site is a cluster of white rocks on the side of the cliff, almost level with the wreck which lies in an indentation on the coast. A bronze hawse plate from the wreck, set into a piece of her original timber, can be seen in the 'Five Pilchards' inn at Porthallow, along with a fine model of her in full sail and some photographs of the wreck.

On 5 August 1938, the 1,865-ton Danish steamer *Ester Marie* went ashore at Penare beach in dense fog, only yards from the wreck of the *Bay of Panama*. She was in ballast, bound from Caen to Gydynia, and after laying out a kedge anchor managed to pull herself off with the aid of tugs.

Of all the ships sunk around the Manacles, the *Volnay* perhaps brought more benefit to the local population than any other. A British steamer of 4,610-tons, owned by Gow Harrison & Co, she was homeward bound from Canada with luxury goods and ammunition for troops in France when, off the Manacles, there was an explosion under her bows and it was assumed she had struck a mine. Two tugs brought her into Porthallow Bay on 14 December

1917. For some reason she was not beached—perhaps her captain thought she would not sink—but sink she did, settling down in seventy feet of water with only her masts and the top of her super-structure above the surface. An obliging easterly wind got up during the day, and soon her cargo was coming ashore by the ton. An inhabitant of Porthallow who still remembers it said that at one time it was impossible to walk on the beach itself; every square foot was piled with crates, boxes, sacks, barrels and cases, four and five feet high in places. No boat was launched for days, as there was no room to get one down to the sea. There were sealed boxes of coffee and tea, butter and potato crisps, cigarettes and matches, biscuits and jam, peanuts and tinned meat—all the luxury items which had been rarely seen since the country tightened its belt two years before. Early in 1918 the Admiralty carried out diving operations on the wreck using a local diver, Harry Carter, and his assistant, Arthur Cox. After the war, Mr Chard of Fal-mouth, diver and mayor of his home town, worked the *Volnay* for a while, after which it remained untouched for years. Ownership then passed into the hands of a local salvage company who are currently engaged in removing ammunition from the wreck, and amateur divers are advised to keep well clear.

In 1859 there was a stranding on the fringe of the Manacles reef that might have proved a major disaster had the weather not been calm. It was foggy with a light south-westerly wind when the *Clara*, a 938-ton wooden ship under charter as a transport, went aground on the Porthkerris side of Pencra Head on 3 October. Owned by Teighe & Smith Ltd, of London, she had left Plymouth for Calcutta the previous day with the families of troops stationed in India. There were 412 people on board, including 197 women and 198 children. The *Clara* went ashore at 3 am, but was towed off the same day and returned to Plymouth, where divers found extensive damage to her bows.

Not far from where the *Clara* went aground lie the remains of a vessel with the second longest name of all the ships known to have been lost in Cornwall. The *Nostra Sencra de Boa Nova St Quitera* sank between Porthoustock and Porthkerris at 3 am on 20 May 1807 during fog, on voyage from Hamburg to Oporto with staves and tar, and two of her crew were drowned. Several large copper nails of the kind used in sailing-ship construction at that time have since been found by divers less than 200 yards off Pencra Head and may be from this wreck.

The small bay at the old fishing village of Porthoustock has seen a number of wrecks, but with the decline of the port's fishing and stone trade no ships have been lost there for some forty years. One of the last occasions was when the Plymouth sailing-barge *Sweet May* was caught alongside the quarry jetty by a sudden gale on 15 December 1927. A motor-boat which tried to tow her clear was wrecked and the barge, abandoned on the rocks, soon sank and went to pieces. A small steamer, the *Liffey* of Waterford, from Lynn to Cardiff in ballast, stranded at the same place on 2 February 1896 but was towed clear. Also close at hand is the wreck of the 158-ton wooden schooner *Georgina*, which caught fire and sank on the Leveller rocks on 22 February 1881, whilst bound from London to Cork with a cargo of railway sleepers.

At the northern limit of the Manacles and close inshore is the Shark's Fin Rock which wrecked the 2,093-ton full-rigged steel ship *Andola* in 1895. Registered at Liverpool and built there by T Royden & Sons she left Barry Docks on 7 September 1893 under the command of Captain Passmore bound for Santa Rosalia with a cargo of coke destined for the copper mines of Rue de Balio, California. Arriving there in February 1894, her cargo was discharged into boats manned by Yaki Indians, who then ferried out tons of small boulders which were trimmed down into her hold as ballast. In May she sailed for Seattle and, after discharging her ballast off Port Townsend, was towed down Puget Sound to Elliott Bay, where she loaded 2,000 tons of grain, topping up with a further 100 tons at Tacoma before leaving for Falmouth in August 1894.

She took a long time to get home, encountering gale after gale, and on one occasion was under bare poles for fifty-six hours, relying on an old tarpaulin lashed to the mizzen mast to give her steerage way. During the evening of 21 January 1895, at the height of a gale, a huge wave swept the length of the ship carrying away the dinghy and creating havoc on deck. The captain called for volunteers to clear the wreckage but the four seamen who came forward had no sooner left the shelter of the forecastle than another great wave hurled them into the scuppers. Three were left injured, but the fourth, able seaman Dillon, was washed overboard and drowned. Eventually, on 29 January 1895, one hundred and eighty days out and more than two months overdue, the *Andola* limped into Falmouth. Tugs brought out much-needed fresh water and food, but on the same day a message came from the owners instructing her to sail at once for Hull to discharge, a harsh order after the privations of six months at sea. Within an hour of leaving Falmouth on the evening tide she had passed the Eddystone, but a change of wind then forced the *Andola* to tack right across the Channel until her crew saw the lights of France, then back again to sight the Lizard light on the port beam several hours later.

With the ship being driven steadily backwards by wind and tide, sail was shortened to lower topsails and at 7.30 pm that night, when a snow storm had reduced visibility to a few yards, the sharp ears of an apprentice heard a bell clanging to seawards. By then they were inside the Manacles buoy and Captain Passmore at once ordered the topsails furled and tried to stand off. Some fifteen minutes later the crew were thrown off their feet as the ship crunched into the northern side of the Shark's Fin Rock, only yards from the Manacles beach. Apprentice Alfred Hunt, who had heard the warning bell, was told to bring flares from the chartroom while paraffin was poured on the mizzen sail and set alight as a distress signal. The flares were either damp or defective, for the lad was sent below to fetch 'bomb rockets' from the magazine. As he raised the lid of the locker, sparks from the flare he carried fell amongst the explosives and, panic-stricken, he fled back on deck. No sooner had he reached the open than a bomb rocket burst through the deck, burying a large piece of metal in his thigh and flinging him unconscious into the scuppers. Further explosions which blew the roof off the charthouse and injured the helmsman and an able seaman were so loud that they could be heard in Falmouth, where the lifeboat was launched on the rumour that a liner was ashore.

The crew of the *Andola* launched a boat into which the injured were lowered, but the Porthoustock lifeboat, alerted by a coastguard who had seen the *Andola* strike, was soon alongside to take off the twenty-eight remaining members of the crew. By daylight the wind had moderated and the wreck was broadside to the sea, bows pointing south and waves breaking over the deck. There was no sign of damage, but it was obvious she was grinding her bottom out on the rocks as she bumped and rolled in the swell. Later, her cargo swelled, bursting her plates, and she became a total loss. The owners, Messrs E F & W Roberts, put her in the hands of William Broad of Falmouth for auction and she is reported to have fetched a good price. Although salvage was carried out on the wreck, a great deal remains lying just outside the entrance to Porthoustock on the southern side in about thirty feet of water. Broken plates and ribs are scattered amongst the boulders and in places whole sections of double bottom remain intact, and many items of interest can still be recognised. But, as with the *Bay of Panama*, a carpet of summer weed cloaks the wreck. Several fathoms of anchor cable lie near the bows, and it is here that a number of brass letters from her name have been found, each weighing about four pounds and standing ten inches high.

Rough weather forced the 144 tons net steamer *Medina* to shelter in Hayle between 4-6 November 1883, before resuming her voyage from Newport to Devoran, near Falmouth. Captain Faull was pleased with his ship; she was almost new and on her second voyage. She passed the Lizard at 9 am on 7 November and, to save time, he took her through the inner channel of the Manacles. As it was a calm day and the tide full, he did not consider it was taking any risk but at 3.30 pm the *Medina* struck a rock on the edge of the channel. A fishing-boat took off the crew of eight, but the captain refused to leave until 9 pm when there was obviously no hope of saving his ship. The *Medina*, owned by James Weir of Cardiff, broke her back, and hull and stores were sold by public auction the following week.

The following year a large steamer belonging to the Lady Dalhousie Steamship Co was wrecked on the Manacles in clear, calm weather. Bound from London to Newport in ballast, the *Lady Dalhousie* arrived off Falmouth on 13 April 1884 and appeared to be making a normal approach into the bay when she suddenly sheered off and ran at full speed on to the Manacles. A submerged rock tore a hole in her bottom plates, and whilst trying to reach the shallows of Porthoustock she went on to hit the Maen Chynoweth or Morah Rock, where she stuck fast. She quickly began to fill and although tugs and the lifeboat were soon on the scene it was obvious that she could not be saved and the crew were taken off. Next morning everything of value was collected and a salvage party began unloading the stores. This work continued for two days, until the wreck gave a sudden lurch, slipped off the rock and sank in fifty feet, leaving only her masts showing. On 23 April, the wreck was sold to Leans of Falmouth for £175, but has since changed hands. The *Lady Dalhousie*, of 1,982 tons gross, was

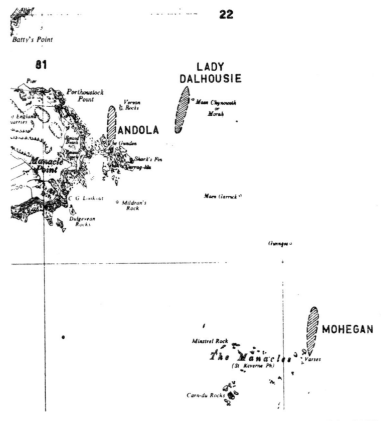

Locations of the wrecks of the *Lady Dalhousie* (1884), the *Andola* (1895) and the *Mohegan* (1898).

launched at Newcastle by the Wallsend Slipway Co in 1881, and was registered at Lloyd's as an iron-built, single screw, schooner-rigged steamer, with two decks and five bulkheads. She was 285ft in length overall, with a beam of 36.1ft and a draught of 23ft. She was one of eight ships in the line, all of which had names prefixed by the word 'Lady'. Although her upperworks, boiler and engines were removed, as was the common practice of salvage at the time, most of the hull remains on the bottom and still fouls the occasional fishing line or lobster pot.

Of the hundreds of vessels which have sunk in the area, most were lost in the outer Manacles, a group of rocks in a semicircle dominated by Carn Du. The earliest recorded wreck was the *Star Cross*, which foundered on the outer rocks on 28 February 1787. Commanded by a Captain Walters, she carried a cargo of iron. The full-rigged ship *Sarah* was also wrecked here on 10 October 1799, while outward bound for the West Indies with horses and mules, all the crew being saved.

Among so many shipwrecks on those notorious rocks, the loss of the *Primrose* and the *Dispatch* were perhaps the most tragic of all. January 1809 found a small British army under the command of Sir John Moore retreating across the mountains of northern Spain, pursued by a vastly superior French force commanded by Napoleon Bonaparte himself. Men and animals were in an appalling condition, more from the bitter cold and continuous rain than actual combat. The retreat continued, day after day, until, exhausted, barefooted and ragged, they reached Corunna. Whilst a fierce rearguard action was being fought on the heights above the town, most of the army embarked in Admiralty-hired transports. The 7th Dragoons, sorely depleted in men and horses, went aboard the *Dispatch,* commanded by Captain Barclay. They were but a shadow of the fine regiment that had left England, having only three officers, seventy-two men and thirty-six horses.

On 14 January 1809 the *Dispatch*, dodging heavy fire from French batteries overlooking the harbour, sailed for home. The following Sunday she encountered snow and an easterly gale; by the early hours of Sunday 22 January, it had reached hurricane force. She was swept towards the coast and at 3.30 am drove ashore on Lowland Point, between Coverack and Porthoustock, where she broke up in the heavy seas. The villagers tried their best to save as many as possible, but no boat could be launched, either from ship or shore. News then reached the would-be rescuers that another ship had been wrecked at the northern end of the Manacles. Six fishermen from Porthoustock—George Tonkin, Stephen Old, Edward Tonkin, Bartholomew Tripp, William Matthews and his brother Joseph—manned the largest boat in the village and rowed out to her. They returned hours later, soaked and exhausted, bringing with them the sole survivor of the wreck, a lad named John Meaghen. He told his rescuers that the ship had struck at about 5.0 am and sank within minutes. A number of papers were washed ashore from which it was deduced that the ship was HMS *Triumph*, but the lad assured them she had been the brig-o'-war, HMS *Primrose*, bound for Spain. And indeed it was the *Primrose* of eighteen guns, Commander James Mein, launched at Fowey only the previous year, and carrying 126 officers and men and six passengers.

Daybreak revealed the bodies of men and horses washing about in the shallows, and cast up on the rocks in dozens. Only seven survived the *Dispatch* and, apart from the boy, the entire company of the *Primrose* were lost. The number of seamen aboard these two ships was never disclosed, but would not be less than eighty, so at least 270 people were drowned. Among the dead from the *Dispatch* were Major Cavendish, the twenty-five-year-old son of Lord Cavendish of Eastbourne, and Lieutenant the Hon Edward Waldgrove, third son of the fourth earl of Waldgrove. Their bodies were identified by fellow officers who should have been aboard the *Dispatch*, but who, at the last moment, had accepted an invitation from Captain Lindsay to take passage in the *Barfleur*.

Only 110 bodies were recovered, of which 104 were buried in St Keverne churchyard between 24 January and 2 April. A large memorial tablet was placed on the wall of St Keverne church, donated by fellow members of the regiment. This tablet was removed in later years, and finally found its way into a private house near Helston. Still in the church is another relic, a brass gudgeon or rudder fitting from the *Primrose*, found many years later by fishermen engaged in the salvage of the *Le Marne*. The *Primrose* is thought to have sunk in the vicinity of Carn Du, where, in 1965, a small brass cannon was found on the bottom, some 400 yards to the west of the Varses rocks. It is well preserved and bears the date '1809'; it may have been one of the *Primrose*'s saluting guns, or possibly an army gun and nothing to do with the ship's armament. As for the *Dispatch*, there is little chance of her wreck being found as she was close inshore and must have broken up completely. There is, however, a record of a salvage attempt being made late in May 1848 using a diving bell, when several large brass and iron cannon were recovered.

Forty-five years passed before there was another wreck with a heavy loss of life, although the Manacles continued to take its toll of ships and men. Among them were the *Providence*, 27 March 1811, bound for Liverpool; the sloops *Expedition* on 1 August 1811, bound for Swansea in ballast, and *Island* of 75 tons, which sank half a mile off Porthoustock in April 1813 while bound from Dartmouth to Dublin with cinders and pipeclay. There were a score of other wrecks between 1813 and 1840, among them the brig *Commerce*, 28 June 1813; the ketch *Dolphin*, 27 November 1815; the barque *William*, 17 October 1818; two luggers, laden with contraband, which sank with the loss of all hands on 21 April 1822; the *Venus*, May 1826; the schooner *Auspicious*, 1 May 1828; the brig *Rose*, 24 April 1838; the brig *Affleck*, 21 September 1838; *Osiris*, 6 May 1838; the brig *Leander*, 18 January 1939 and the brig *Pictou*, 24 September 1939.

During the early 1850s, the 486-ton Plymouth barque *John* was engaged in transporting emigrants to Canada and the United States. Early in 1855 she underwent a complete overhaul on which her owners spent £200, which may sound a paltry sum today but was then sufficient for the ship to be docked, scraped and re-painted and to have her rigging renewed. She was scheduled to sail for Quebec on 3 May, but men were still putting the finishing touches to their work even as the passengers came up the gangway. When finally the *John* did sail she had on board 279 people; 149 adults, 98 children, sixteen infants in arms and sixteen crew under the command of Captain Edward Rawle.

At 4 pm the barque left Plymouth with her passengers, mostly Devon folk, waving a brave good-bye to friends and relations. The weather was fine and, looking forward to settling down in a new land, they were eager to set out on their great adventure. With the wind from the north-west the *John* soon cleared the Sound and headed down Channel under full sail. At 9.30 pm the lights at St Anthony and Falmouth were sighted and the captain pointed them out to several passengers on deck, having, they thought, their last look at England. By this time the Lizard light should have appeared to the south-west and the mate was so worried by its absence that he even asked passengers whether they could see it. Captain Rawle was less concerned. 'You'll see it fast enough when we get there,' he said, and soon after retired to his cabin, leaving

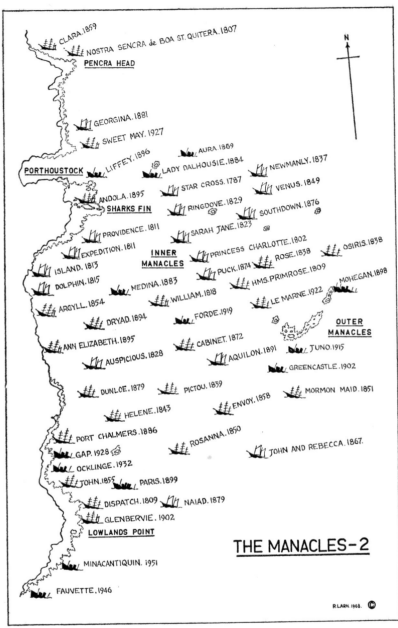

CLARA.1859
NOSTRA SENCRA de BOA ST.QUITERA.1807
PENCRA HEAD

N

GEORGINA.1881
SWEET MAY.1927
AURA.1869
LIFFEY.1896   LADY DALHOUSIE.1884   NEWMANLY.1837
PORTHOUSTOCK   STAR CROSS.1787   VENUS.1849
ANDOLA.1895   RINGDOVE.1829   SOUTHDOWN.1876
SHARKS FIN
PROVIDENCE.1811   SARAH JANE.1823
EXPEDITION.1811   **INNER**   PRINCESS CHARLOTTE.1802   OSIRIS.1838
ISLAND.1813   **MANACLES**   PUCK.1874   ROSE.1838
DOLPHIN.1815   MEDINA.1883   HMS.PRIMROSE.1809   MOHEGAN.1898
ARGYLL.1854   WILLIAM.1818   LE MARNE.1922
DRYAD.1894   FORDE.1919
ANN ELIZABETH.1895   CABINET.1872   **OUTER**
AUSPICIOUS.1828   AQUILON.1891   JUNO.1915   **MANACLES**
GREENCASTLE.1902
DUNLOE.1879   PICTOU.1839   MORMON MAID.1851
HELENE.1843   ENVOY.1858
PORT CHALMERS.1886
GAP.1928   ROSANNA.1850
OCKLINGE.1932   JOHN AND REBECCA.1867.
JOHN.1855   PARIS.1899
DISPATCH.1809   NAIAD.1879
GLENBERVIE.1902
LOWLANDS POINT

THE MANACLES-2

MINACANTIQUIN.1951

FAUVETTE.1946

R.LARN.1968.

Wreck locations between Pencra Head and Lowlands Point, and on the
Outer and Inner Manacles.

the second mate on watch. Still worried, the mate came on deck again at 10.0 pm, took a look round and then roused the captain to tell him that the ship was too close to land. By this time the fine weather of the afternoon had given way to a strong southerly wind which whipped up the sea, causing the ship to roll heavily. Captain Rawle came up at the mate's insistence, but after sizing up the situation, blandly dismissed his chief officer's fears.

Moments later the forward lookouts reported breakers ahead, and almost simultaneously the *John* struck the Manacles. Her forward movement, assisted by the swell, carried her over the outer chain of rocks to crash down again inside the Manacles. The only thing to do was to try and get the ship into shallow water as quickly as possible. The land could be dimly seen against the night sky, and the helmsman steered as best he could for the shore. An anchor was dropped in an attempt to slow the ship before she struck again, but failed to hold and the *John* went broadside on to the rocks off Lowland Point.

Of the four lifeboats on board, three were in their chocks, only one slung over the side ready for use, and no sooner had the ship struck than the captain, four of the crew and one passenger climbed in, saying they were going to fetch help. Captain Rawle shouted for men to lower away, but as no one paid any attention he and one of the crew were forced to climb back on deck and lower the boat themselves. As a ship's lifeboat it was in poor shape, lacking a plug for the bung-hole, and without either rowlocks or thole pins. The hole was plugged with cloth, thole pins were improvised from three sailors' knives and the stem of the passenger's pipe and, not surprisingly, it was with some difficulty that they eventually reached Lowland Point.

Once the captain had left the *John*, some of the passengers attempted to launch a boat but it was smashed against the side and sank. The crew, apart from the steward, did nothing to help and sat in the rigging drinking pilfered spirits. The flood tide set in just after midnight, and by 2 am heavy seas were breaking over the deck. A number of passengers tried to climb above the sea into the rigging, only to be beaten back by the crew; one young couple tied their two infants into a bed sheet and hoisted the bundle into the rigging. But either a wave caught it or the cloth tore, for it went overboard and the children drowned. Wave after wave swept the deck from bow to stern, hurling men and women against the bulwarks or carrying them overboard, while the few who did manage to climb the rigging were frozen by the bitter cold and unable to retain their handholds.

No boat could be launched during the night from Coverack or Porthoustock owing to the rough seas but, soon after dawn, the weather abated and the Coverack coastguard longboat and the Porthoustock lifeboat were able to reach the ship, now only 250 yards offshore and driving closer. In three trips the two boats rescued seventy survivors, but 193 men, women and children had died during the night. Even during the rescue, when it was obvious that everyone would be taken off in turn, the crew fought the passengers for places in the boats. They were later described as 'a drink-smelling rabble' and not a single one of them lost his possessions, let alone his life.

Both at the inquest on the victims and the subsequent court of enquiry, the captain and his entire ship's company (apart from the steward) were roundly condemned for their callous behaviour. The enquiry revealed that the ship carried no distress flares or signal gun, and that none of the boats was in a seaworthy condition. A verdict of manslaughter was returned against the captain, who was arrested and placed in Bodmin jail awaiting trial. He later received a prison sentence, as did a number of St Keverne men who were found guilty of looting from the dead as they lay on the beach. A memorial tablet in St Keverne church reads, 'Sacred to the memory of 120 people here interred, who were drowned in the wreck of the *John*, 3 May 1855. Erected by one of the survivors'.

Major disasters seemed to occur on the Manacles at intervals of fifty years, since between the sinking of the *Primrose* and *Dispatch*, and the *John*, and between the *John* and the *Mohegan* (1898), a similar period elapsed. But between the tragedies, the annual toll of ships and lives continued and unless the crews managed to escape in their own boats, or were reached by local lifeboats, they had little hope of survival. Only in the case of the *Mohegan* is a survivor reported as having been able to swim ashore.

On 11 January 1872, the Shields barque *Cabinet* went down on the outer Manacles during dense fog and a north-easterly gale, her crew of eleven being rescued by the Porthoustock lifeboat. She had left Falmouth on 31 December with Black Sea wheat for Newry but had had to put back until 10 January owing to bad weather.

Three schooners were wrecked in 1879; on 13 January the three-masted *Dunloe* of Guernsey struck at 11.40 pm during fog whilst on voyage from Granville to Cardiff in ballast. The crew escaped in their boat, returning next day to find her completely submerged. On 4 July a French schooner was lost at Godrevy and on 19 July the 122-ton *Naiad* of Gerrans, carrying coal from Port Talbot to Falmouth, went down nearby. Although lookouts had been posted at bow and stern, none saw the rocks until she struck at 2.30 am. Built by Hoskins Ltd of Plymouth, the *Naiad* was owned by a Captain Medlin of Falmouth.

At 7.0 pm on the evening of 14 October 1898, the 7,000-ton passenger liner *Mohegan*, owned by the Atlantic Transport Co, should have been ten miles south of Falmouth. Instead, she was off St Keverne and only one mile from the shore, heading for destruction at thirteen knots. The Coverack coastguard, the first to see the danger, fired a warning rocket and she appeared to alter course. But it was too late; she struck the Manacles and sank outside the Varses, leaving only her masts and funnel above water. Among the 106 drowned were her captain, all the deck officers, a stowaway and most of the passengers. It was a disaster on a scale the Manacles has not equalled since.

The *Mohegan*, a new ship, was on only her second voyage to America when she sank. Originally ordered by the Wilson Furness Leyland Line as the *Cleopatra*, she had been built by Earles of Hull, but prior to launching was purchased by the Atlantic Transport Co of London on 29 July 1898, for the sum of £140,000. The *Cleopatra* was unlucky from the start. Her completion was held up by a strike and she had to be rushed through to avoid a high penalty for non-delivery not covered by the strike clause in the contract. As a result, she leaked so badly during her first Atlantic crossing that she had to be docked at New York for repairs before returning to the Tyne for a thorough overhaul.

A very modern and luxurious ship for her time, she carried about sixty first-class passengers, a crew of ninety-seven, and cattlemen to attend animals carried on deck. She was four-masted with a single funnel amidships, and her four boilers drove a triple-expansion engine which raised an indicated horse-power of 5,500, giving her maximum speed of fourteen knots. Her length was 482ft, beam 52ft and depth 35ft 7in. She was fitted with eight watertight bulkheads, and steam pumps which could pump dry every compartment in turn. An enclosed bridge extended the full width of the ship, reaching back over the engine room, above which was a music room, saloon, smoking room, and staterooms decorated in the best Victorian style.

She sailed from Tilbury on 13 October 1898 as the *Mohegan*, under the command of Captain Griffiths, commodore of the line, with fifty-three passengers, ninety-seven crew and seven cattlemen. Her general cargo included spirits, beer, lead, antimony, artificial flowers, church ornaments, glass, and seed, and with 1,050 tons of coal in her bunkers and 2,200 tons of water ballast her draught was 20ft 6in. A Trinity House pilot left her off Dover at 7.45 pm and at 2.40 pm the following day, 14 October, she passed Prawle Point and signalled a request that her progress be reported to her owners. At Rame Head she was sighted less than ten miles off shore by Joseph Burnfield, a signalman, but from there on her course and the cause of her subsequent wreck remain something of a mystery. It seems that from the moment she passed Start Point, east of Plymouth, she was on an incorrect course; but the truth died with the ship for only her officers could have given an explanation.

Four people saw the *Mohegan* during the last few minutes of her short life—boatman Snell, of the Falmouth coastguards, Mr Fooks, receiver of wrecks at Falmouth, Mr James Hill, coxswain of the Porthoustock lifeboat, and boatman Charles May of the Coverack coastguards. All saw the lights of the liner as she neared the Manacles and each, instinctively, knew that she was heading for disaster as no vessel of her size would deliberately approach so close to the Manacles. Only the Coverack coastguard could do anything to try and avert disaster, and he at once fired a rocket and lit blue flares. Coxswain Hill called his crew to the lifeboat house before the *Mohegan* had even struck the rocks, and but for his prompt action many more would have lost their lives that night.

On board, the passengers were sitting down to dinner, while in the cabins the 'nannies' were putting their charges to bed. In the quiet dark of the wheelhouse, high up on the bridge, the helmsman was steering the course given him by the man he had relieved, a

Page 89: Doomed cattle crowd the decks of the steamer *Suffolk* of London, wrecked under Old Lizard Head on 25 September 1886.

Page 90: (above) Swept by heavy seas, the Clan Line tramp *Clan Malcolm*, wrecked at the Lizard on 26 September 1935; (below) the Norddeutscher Lloyd mail steamer *Mosel*, wrecked on Bass Point, Lizard, during thick fog on 9 August 1882.

course checked both by the captain and second officer. On the wings of the bridge and on the forecastle-head, the lookouts were silent; apart from a few shore lights, there was nothing to be seen. Down in the engine-room, William Ferguson, auxiliary second engineer, was in charge of the machinery assisted by the fifth and sixth engineers. Mr Ferguson had gone on duty at 6 pm when everything was working normally, the telegraph indicator showing 'full speed ahead', engines making sixty-eight revolutions a minute, boiler pressure 197 psi. At about 6.50 pm he felt a slight shock run through the ship, almost as if she had dropped an anchor, after which the bridge signalled down to 'stop engines'. Water then began to pour in so quickly that within half a minute he had to ease the steam-pressure valves and abandon the engine-room. The ship had struck the Manacles with her starboard side, tearing a huge gash below the waterline and the sea flooded several compartments at once. Although the generators were situated well aft of the boilers, fourteen feet of water soon put them and every light in the ship out of action.

On the bridge, Captain Griffiths had ordered the crew to lower the boats and was directing passengers to their stations as each was filled. The fourth officer managed to fire four distress rockets from the bridge, but already the vessel was three parts underwater. Her list to port increased to forty degrees, rendering the starboard boats useless, and she sank within ten minutes of striking in complete darkness and with at least two boats still on their chocks. Those on deck had to swim for their lives; the luckier ones were able to reach the mizzen rigging and hang on to it.

Meanwhile the Porthoustock boat, already launched and with the coxswain burning white flares in the hope of attracting boats from the wreck, was making its way towards the outer Manacles. Soon they passed through a great deal of wreckage and then an upturned ship's boat, with two men clinging to the keel, was sighted. The men were rescued and, hearing muffled cries from beneath the capsized craft, the lifeboat crew managed to right it and found two women and a dead child floating beneath it. One of the women, a Mrs Compton-Swift, had her left leg trapped so that part of the boat had to be cut away before she could be freed. She later stated that she had been at dinner when the ship struck and had managed to board one of the port-side boats. In less than two minutes a

F

wave had capsized it, throwing its twenty-five occupants into the sea. Finding herself trapped in some wreckage, she first thought she had been drawn beneath the ship, but then realised she was inside an upturned boat and, though unable in the darkness to discern the faces of those with her, knew from their voices that they must be another woman and a child. The three were trapped for over an hour, during which the child died and the other woman, a Miss Rondebush, became very weak.

After burning three flares as a signal that more help was needed, the Porthoustock boat went on to rescue first the occupants of another boat which was half full of water, then the survivors in the mizzen rigging. During the night, all the local lifeboats—Falmouth, Coverack, Cadgwith, even the Lizard—put out to the wreck of the *Mohegan*.

Everything possible was done by the Atlantic Transport Line for victims and relatives alike, and free passages were later given to those in America who wished to visit St Keverne church where most of the dead were interred in a mass grave on the north side of the churchyard. Some bodies were embalmed and shipped to America at the company's expense. Their final gesture was the donation of a stained glass window as a memorial, which still exists. Over the mass grave a simple stone cross was erected; it carries no date or epitaph, just the single word *Mohegan*.

At the inquiry into the loss, the court were unable to reach any conclusion as to why the *Mohegan* was on a course of 'west by north', instead of the recognised 'west by south'. With her captain and every deck officer drowned, there was no one left who could know the answer. It was therefore assumed that the captain had ordered a wrong course by accident or neglect, and that no one had noticed the mistake. Many theories were put forward and for weeks the newspapers printed suggestions as to her loss; perhaps the captain bore a grudge against the company and sank the ship on purpose, or, the whole Lizard was composed of strongly magnetic material which affected the compass. Or perhaps the helmsman steered a wrong course although given a correct one by the captain. The wreck of the *Mohegan* will ever remain a mystery, but at least the tragedy brought to light many deficiencies in the life-saving equipment carried aboard ships at the time and these were later rectified.

A headless corpse was washed ashore in Caernarvon Bay some three months later, still dressed in a sea captain's uniform with buttons embossed 'A.T.L.', and there was little doubt that it was the body of Captain Griffiths. The *Mohegan* had been insured at Lloyd's and other offices for £112,000, and salvage commenced within two days of her sinking. Two vessels moored over the wreck and local divers brought up three thousand ingots of tin, followed by the antimony and lead. Her cargo was an odd assortment. Besides the church ornaments, and thousands of boxes of artificial flowers, there was china, carpets, burlap, plate glass, sloe gin, cloth, glass jars, samples, pottery, golf balls—even the intriguing item numbered 67 on the manifest, 'one empty cask'. Other items were 200 packets of lard, 10 crates of iron spindles, 55 pails of prunes, 500 casks of creosote, 163 cases of shellac, tar, rice, seed, ginger, even old rope. Shortly after the initial salvage attempt the funnel collapsed in rough seas, and within two years nothing was visible above water. No attempt was ever made to refloat her, as the huge gashes in her side could never be patched, and she lay in dangerous waters almost touching the Varses rocks on the seaward side. The ship's bell, still engraved '*Cleopatra* Hull', was salvaged by Mr Cliff of Coverack and presented to the old maritime museum at Falmouth. Intermittent salvage continued for a number of years, and the wreck was reduced by explosives. Her engine and propeller were removed and the *Falmouth Packet* reported, in October 1904, that 'after fruitless attempts for three years, Mr Sandover of the salvage ship *Mallard*, has finally landed the condenser of the *Mohegan*, weighing sixteen tons'. As the years slipped by, memories of the wreck faded, until by the late 1950s even its location had been forgotten. This roused the interest of two divers, Roy Davies and Bernard Rogers, in 1960-61, who, after considerable searching, found the *Mohegan* in seventy-five feet of water. Since then, it has been the target for hundreds of visiting divers, and a dive on the wreck can be a memorable experience. The entire hull has collapsed to seawards, leaving her huge boilers sticking up through the wreckage, the wreck lying in an almost due north-south line. Behind the boilers can be seen the huge generators that failed so quickly after she sank. As one swims the length of the ship, one has a feeling of awe, intensified by the deep gloom of the Manacles at this depth. One of her four masts has collapsed across the gaping mouth of a hatch, and now lies trapped between two winches and a pair of bollards. Fish swim lazily in and out of the gaping holes in the boilers. Broken crockery lies everywhere in the wreck, pieces of plates, saucers, cups, pots and jars, but only one intact dinner plate has yet been recovered. It carried the crest of the original owners, 'Thomas Wilsons & Co, Hull', and was presented to the Helston museum by the London diver who found it in 1966.

There were less than five witnesses to the sinking of the steamer *Cape Finisterre*, 4,610 tons gross, on 17 November 1917. It was a perfectly calm day when a German U-boat torpedoed her amidships when she was off the Manacles buoy, not long after leaving Falmouth harbour. A 300-ft column of water rose into the air and, within seconds, she lifted her bow until she stood vertical, then plunged to the bottom. Two Porthoustock brothers named Green went out in a motor-boat and picked up the sole survivor, a negro, whom they found clinging to a chicken coop still full of indignant birds. Four minesweepers in Coverack Bay at once put to sea and dropped depth charges, but saw nothing of the submarine. The *Cape Finisterre* sank in 250ft of water and remained untouched until the early 1920s, when some Italian salvage ships, after searching for the wreck for days, finally snagged it with a sweep wire. For some months the crew salvaged ingots of steel, using an observation chamber and a grab. Built in 1907 by the Russel Steamship Building Co Ltd at Glasgow, the *Cape Finisterre* was owned by the Lyle Shipping Co.

Among the many small wooden ships lost on the Manacles, and of which only copper rivets and perhaps an anchor or two now remain, have been the Newquay schooner *Idea* from Plymouth with limestone, which struck Carn Du on 1 October 1820 and floated clear, only to sink near the mouth of the Helford river, drowning her mate and two lads; the schooners *Sarah-Jane*, 9 October 1823, *Ringdove* of Gerrans, 21 February 1829; *Mary and Susan* on 7 February 1831 and the *Newmanly*, April 1837. These were followed by the Prussian ship *Helene*, 26 March 1843; the brig *Rosanna* of Sunderland, 8 March 1850, the brigantine *Mormon Maid* of Fraserburgh, 22 January 1851, and the schooners *John and Rebecca* of Fowey, 18 March 1867 and *South Down* of Dartmouth, 3 March 1876.

As sail declined, the number of ships wrecked on the Manacles fell sharply but the rocks still took their toll of the unwary or unfortunate steamship. A small Norwegian steamer, the *Juno*, struck Carn Du at 8.0 am on 3 July 1915 on voyage from Tréport to Partington in ballast. When the fog lifted, she was revealed standing on her head, her bows completely submerged and her stern high in the air. Many of her fittings were removed before she sank, including an engineer's vice which is still in daily use in a local fisherman's hut, and salvage was carried out by Leans of Falmouth, who later re-sold the wreck. A great deal of ironwork still lies to the south-east of Carn Du, but gales and salvage have scattered her remains far and wide. Some two years later, on 4 March 1919, yet another Norwegian steamer, the *Forde*, was wrecked in almost exactly the same place during dense fog, while bound from Le Havre to Wales in ballast.

The wreck of the French barquentine *Le Marne* in 1922 led indirectly to the recovery of a piece of HMS *Primrose* lost on the outer Manacles more than a century earlier. The barquentine was first sighted close by Carn Du, and appeared to stop directly over the Minstral rock. The crew were able to reach the shore in their own boat but the ship was a total wreck and was later purchased for £50 by four local men, James Cliff, Tom Rowe, Billy May and George Tripconey. For some days the men were able to work on board salvaging fittings and gear, and finally stripping the wooden hull of its copper sheathing. As the wreck broke up, parts of it floated out into the centre of the Manacles, and while recovering the last sections of sheathing from the *Le Marne* Mr Tripconey's grapnel struck into a huge piece of timber which had obviously come from another and much older wreck. It was the sternpost of a ship, thought to be at least 100 years old. Attached to the timber were a number of huge brass gudgeons that at one time had supported a rudder, and it was generally agreed that the sternpost had belonged to the *Primrose*. One of the fittings was cleaned up and presented to St Keverne Church, where it was mounted on a memorial plaque. Quite recently, a copy of the brig's plans were obtained and detailed measurements of the gudgeons left no doubt that the relic had come from the ill-fated warship.

South-west of Carn Du and the outer Manacles there is a large expanse of deep water, but close in to Lowland Point are the great Wrea and Foam rocks, the scene of numerous wrecks. The point itself is strewn with rusting plates of ships which have broken up over the years. One of the earlier sailing-ship wrecks was the 1,495-ton, iron barque *Port Chalmers* of Glasgow. She had lain at anchor in Falmouth for over two months awaiting instructions as to the disposal of her sugar cargo from Samarang and at last, on 20 March 1886, her master, Captain Hamilton, received orders for Liverpool. The barque left port at 11 am in tow of the tug *Emperor*, cast off and hoisted her own sail at 12.30 am, and headed for the Lizard.

Towards evening fog came down, and deeming it unwise to anchor owing to risk of collision the captain carried on under full sail. At 8.30 pm her lookouts sighted breakers ahead and the ship struck twice before coming to a stop. A boat was lowered and the crew, including the captain's wife, rowed clear, only to find they had left one man behind. They returned, rescued him, and remained near the wreck. At dawn, salvage lighters and tugs arrived and the crew returned aboard to rescue their belongings and the ship's papers. The *Port Chalmers* was lightened by the removal of fittings and spars, but by noon the rising tide reached the sacks of sugar and salvage was abandoned. Some time later she was sold for scrap and broken up on the beach.

A smaller wreck was the 398-ton, three-masted Norwegian barque *Ann Elizabeth*, which sailed from Cardiff on 19 November 1895 for Christiania with coal and a crew of eight. Off Start Point during the night of 21 November, an ESE gale forced Captain Simensen to put about and make for the shelter of Falmouth. But dawn on the 26th showed the Manacles close to leeward; she struck, drifted clear, and got into Contoire Bay, north of Lowland Point. Six men scrambled into a boat which capsized close inshore, two being drowned and three reaching the beach. Ordinary seaman Hensen managed to climb back aboard the wreck and was later rescued by breeches-buoy.

The cover of this book depicts the last sailing ship to be wrecked at Lowland Point, and the *Glenbervie* was long remembered by fishermen for her cargo consisted mainly of spirits. Launched in 1866 by Connells as an 800-ton, iron, full-rigged ship for the Allen Line, the *Glenbervie* was first a tea clipper along with her sister ships, *Glencarn*, *Gleniffer* and *Ravenscraig*. Later, she was engaged in the timber and codfish trade from the St Lawrence, normally completing three voyages a year before the river froze. In 1901 the Allen Line sold the ship to Branwell & Gardiner of Glasgow, who reduced her rig to a barque. She left the Thames on 10 December 1901 for Algoa Bay, West Africa, with a general cargo. She dropped her tug at Dungeness, but weather and visibility worsened as she stood down channel and neither St Anthony nor the Lizard lights were seen. Eventually, she got amongst the Manacles and went ashore near Lowland Point. Distress rockets were fired and a boat lowered, but it was far too rough for it to leave the ship. Half an hour later, the new Coverack lifeboat arrived but could approach no closer than fifty feet to the barque as she lay pounding on the rocks at Air Pool. The crew were hauled through the sea on the end of a rope, one at a time. It was the first service of the lifeboat, *Constance Melanie*, which had been placed at Coverack as a direct result of the wreck of the *Mohegan* and the stranding of the liner *Paris*.

It was high tide when the *Glenbervie* struck, and later in the day it was possible to board her dry-shod. Though her hull was badly damaged and the cabin flooded, her cargo was intact, and before long the entire district knew she was carrying 600 cases of whisky, 400 cases of brandy and barrels of rum. The Western Marine Salvage Co undertook its recovery, and several hundred tons of general cargo were removed and sent to London. But a quantity of valuable pianos and furniture in the lower holds were ruined and abandoned, as was a quantity of galvanised iron sheeting left on the beach. Several huts and fishing sheds on the Porthoustock beach were built from the iron and are still standing. Whilst working on the wreck, the salvage vessel *Greencastle* went on to the rocks alongside the wreck and would have been lost but for the timely intervention of tugs. On 26 January a ground swell parted the bows from the remainder of the ship and she went to pieces in the shallows.

The French collier *Gap*, Rouen to Barry in ballast, was wrecked at Lowland Point on 24 February 1928 and when, four years later, on 4 March 1932, the steamer *Ocklinge* was lost in the same place there was much local speculation, as there seemed no reason of weather or visibility for her to have got so far off course. She had been towed into Falmouth early the same day by the German tug *Seefalke*, having sheared the bolts of her rudder quadrant in a gale off Ushant whilst bound from Bilboa to Newport with iron ore. After hurried repairs, she sailed the same day for Wales and two hours later was aground on the point, only sixty yards offshore, flooded fore and aft. Salvage started immediately and nearly 100 labourers were employed to remove the cargo. But she was never refloated, and eventually the owners, Messrs Constants, of Cardiff, asked the Western Marine Co to break her up for scrap. At Lowland Point, there is still a huge propeller on the rocks, said to have come from her. The *Ocklinge* was the second steamer of Constants' lost off Cornwall, the *Lyminge* having been wrecked at Gurnard's Head on 19 September 1931. At the Board of Trade enquiry into the loss of the *Ocklinge*, Captain Driscoll, found guilty of making false declarations and forging documents, received a six-month prison sentence as well as having his certificate suspended for twelve months.

Half-an-hour after the *Ocklinge* had struck, the Belgian motor trawler *Omer Denise* went ashore on the opposite side of Coverack Bay, at Perprean Cove. She was found next morning, stern first on the rocks, abandoned but with her engine still running. She broke up where she lay and her crew were later picked up adrift in a small boat off the Lizard.

After the wreck of the *Ocklinge* there were no more steamship wrecks at Lowland Point until the Spanish coaster *Mina Cantiquin* was lost on 4 November 1951, although the MV *Fauvette*, carrying a cargo of empty shell cases, went aground on 3 February 1946 and was towed clear by tugs. The 662-ton *Mina Cantiquin* was homeward bound to Gijon from Newcastle with a cargo of pitch when she struck a rock off Chynhalls Point, Coverack, in a southwest gale. Badly holed forward, she fired distress signals and attempted to reach the shallows of Coverack Bay. Her crew of seventeen were rescued by the local lifeboat, leaving the coaster to drift across the bay on to Lowlands, the only life on board being the ship's dog, Pedro. Efforts were made to save him, but when the wind reached gale force the attempt had to be abandoned and the dog was lost.

From Lowland Point, the coast takes a wide sweep southwestwards before it reaches Coverack village, with its small harbour just large enough to shelter its few fishing boats. Coverack was one of the last outposts of pilchard fishing and maintained a

seine net for many years after the industry had virtually died in
Cornwall. The lifeboat station, on the end of Dolor Point, lies
beneath the windows of the 'Paris' hotel, named after the liner
Paris which stranded in May 1899.

The *Pindos*, launched in June 1890 by Williamson of Workington
as the *Eusemere*, was a steel, four-masted barque of 2,354 tons net
and 2,512 gross, built for the firm of Fisher & Sprott of London.
In 1896 she was sold to B Wencke & Co of Hamburg, and her
new owners seemed able to bring out her finer sailing qualities.

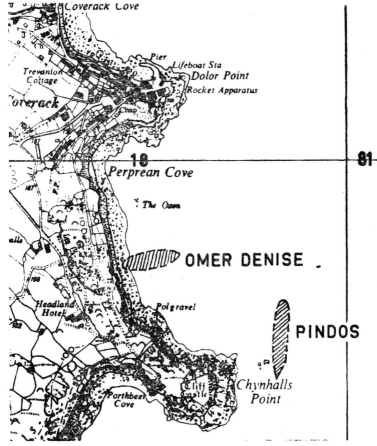

Locations of wrecks of the motor-trawler *Omer Denise* (1932) and the
2,354-ton steel barque *Pindos* (1912).

She left Hamburg for Port Talbot in late February 1911 and loaded coal brickets for Mejillones, on the west coast of South America. The weather was so bad that she took six weeks to round Cape Horn, and later was almost wrecked at Taltal. At Mejillones, she discharged and loaded nitrates and sailed for Falmouth, arriving on 1 February 1912. As an example of German discipline, the first mate ordered four men aloft to scrape and varnish the main royal yard as she entered harbour, despite the fact that it was snowing hard. She lay at Falmouth until 10 February, when she left for Hamburg to discharge in tow of the German tug *Ancona*. But they had hardly got out into Falmouth Bay than the strong south-easterly wind freshened and backed. Both ships were gradually forced backwards down the coast, and despite all the tug's efforts at 9 pm the *Pindos* was carried broadside on to Chynhalls Point, less than half a mile from Coverack village. The tug captain held her head to sea for some time to stop her broaching, but was eventually forced to slip the hawser. Meanwhile the Coverack lifeboat had put off and, aided by the glare of newly-provided acetylene searchlights, rescued the Germans by breeches-buoy from the waveswept and listing poop deck. On 20 February, the *Pindos*, together with her gear and stores, was sold for £225, but later gales soon reduced her to pieces. Over the years salvage has been carried out, but parts of her masts, rigging, plates and keel still lie on the seaward side of Chynhalls.

The *Pindos* actually settled down beside an earlier wreck, that of the 150-ton iron steamer *Rose*. She had left London for Limerick on 7 July 1866 with a crew of fifteen and thirty passengers, rounded Start Point at 5.30 pm on the 9th, then altered course and continued under sail alone. By 2 am she was in fog, and sometime during the early morning she crashed on to the rocks at Coverack. Her forward hold quickly flooded to a depth of six feet, but though her passengers were landed at Coverack pier the crew remained on board for a further week. On 16 July she broke in half and was later sold by public auction. Built by Blackwell of London in 1845, the *Rose* was a three-masted, schooner-rigged steamship with a single deck 119ft long.

On 7 March 1904, the 1,132-ton Danish steamship *G Koch* went ashore on Dolor Point, and only missed ramming the lifeboat house by yards. Bound from Hamburg to Cardiff to load coal for

Las Palmas, she was refloated two weeks later by the Western Marine Salvage Co and continued trading for another nine years before being wrecked on the Girdlestone, Orkneys, in 1913 with the loss of seven lives.

South of Chynhalls Point, the coastline rises to bleak 300-ft high cliffs where wreckers practised their trade in olden days. Black Head, an appropriately named headland which dominates the scene, took its toll of ships which missed the Lizard, claiming dozens of vessels which came too close inshore during fog. The 1,538-ton, brigantine-rigged steamer *Clan Alpine* was only one of many lost here. Owned by the River Parana Steamship Co and launched at Glasgow in 1862, she was bound from South America to Liverpool via Antwerp when she struck the headland during a blizzard on 2 February 1873. Seventeen of her crew and one passenger were saved, but thirteen others drowned, including Captain Nelson, their bodies being buried in St Keverne churchyard. The *Clan Alpine*'s cargo included timber, silver ore, copper bars, hides, potatoes, flour and rapeseed, and extensive salvage work was carried out to recover it.

Another steamer, the *Godolphin*, went on to the rocks east of Black Head on 9 January 1888, whilst bound from Bilboa with iron ore to Newport. Her wreck was bought by a group of Coverack men who salvaged her engine-room fittings, but the remainder of the vessel was abandoned. Nine years later, on 20 March 1897, another steamer, the 648-ton *Plantagenet*, joined the rusting plates lying beneath Black Head. The *Plantagenet* was making a cautious passage down Channel in fog, bound for Runcorn from St Valery with flints, when she struck the rocks, drifted clear and sank in deep water. At high tide her masts were completely underwater. Launched in 1883 by Allsop & Sons of Preston, she was owned by J Bacon of Liverpool.

The largest sailing ship ever lost on Black Head was the 1,491-ton three-masted, steel barque *Gunvor* of Fredrickstadt which, oddly enough, had sailed into Iquique as the *Pindos* sailed out on the voyage that was to end on Coverack rocks, only a short distance from Black Head. The *Gunvor* was lost at Pedn Boar on 6 April 1912, while on passage from Caleta to Falmouth with nitrates. So close inshore was she that her bowsprit overhung the rocks and the crew had only to lower a rope ladder over the bow to gain the shore. A more unusual fate for victims of Black Head befell the steamship *Veritas* of Bergen on 4 August 1907. She was on her way from Norway to South Wales with pit wood when a collision in the Channel forced her into Portland. After temporary repairs, Captain Jullesfen sailed again for Wales, but off the Lizard on 4 August a persistent leak suddenly increased to a flood which the ship's pumps could not cope with and soon the boiler fires were extinguished. The captain, his wife and a crew of fourteen abandoned ship and rowed to Coverack. Three Falmouth tugs, the *Triton, Eagle* and *Dragon*, went out to the ship, but both anchors had been dropped before the crew of the *Veritas* had abandoned her, and without steam they could not be raised. After much effort the two cables were unshackled and the tow commenced but before the ships had reached Black Head the *Veritas* had lifted her stern high in the air and sunk. Her bows struck the bottom, leaving her almost vertical, and in this position she remained for two days before finally going to the bottom. Some time later, the salvage steamer *Etna* arrived from Lundy, where she had been working on the salvage of the battleship, HMS *Montague,* and tried to move the *Veritas* closer inshore, using pontoons and barges. But the depth of water proved too great and the wreck was abandoned.

Between Black Head and Cadgwith, the coastline changes from steep cliffs to sandy beaches, then rises again as it approaches Enys Head and finally Cadgwith itself. The largest stretch of sand is at Kennack, which has seen many strandings, and at least one wreck remains in the shallows. It is a stretch of coastline that was very popular with the smuggling fraternity, Cadgwith, Carleon and Spernic coves being ideal places for the brandy boats to come ashore. History has it that the treasure of Captain Avery, the pirate, is buried in the high cliffs near Beagles Point and a number of unsuccessful attempts have been made to find it. One steamer that went ashore at Kennack was the 100-ton *Normand* of Bayonne, Nantes to Fowey in ballast, on 2 April 1914. It was very foggy at the time, but the crew managed to scramble ashore, to be found next morning by a Mr Martin, a local farmer. The *Normand* was abandoned in the shallows with a broken back and, to this day, her boiler can still be seen in the shallows. Her remains were very nearly joined by a French steamship, the 1,184-ton *Maurice Bernard*, Le Havre to Barry in ballast, on 25 May 1925, which went aground close by during a south-west gale but was refloated by tugs.

Of all the wrecks on the coast of Cornwall, only in the case of the steamers *Highland Fling* and *Suevic* has ship surgery been employed to save part of the vessel. Today, with modern cutting gear and plastic explosives, it is not difficult to cut a ship in half, but in 1907 it was an almost untried technique. The *Highland Fling*, a large iron steamer of 4,088 tons, went ashore on the Criscan rocks, a little to the west of Cadgwith on 7 January 1907. In going ashore she almost ran down the tug *Triton*, missing her by less than 200 yards in the fog.

She had left the Thames under the command of Captain Purvis on New Year's Day, bound for Buenos Aires with 3,000 tons of cement. An old vessel, launched in 1890 as the *Morayshire* for the Scottish Clan Line, she was sold to the Ducal Line in 1898, when her name was changed to *Duke of Portland*. In 1906 she was finally sold to Messrs H W Nelson, who renamed her the *Highland Fling*. Soon after leaving the Thames, a serious leak developed beneath a boiler and she put in to Falmouth where a diver found a cracked plate. It was decided that she should go into dry-dock at Cardiff, so she sailed again in thick fog on 7 January and within a very short time of leaving the harbour was hard and fast on the Criscan rocks. The crew lowered the boats and were about to abandon ship when the *Triton* appeared out of the fog and assured them they were in no danger. A towing hawser was transferred to the tug, but the steamer refused to budge; even the combined efforts of two more tugs could not refloat her. On 8 January lighters arrived from Falmouth and her cement cargo was unloaded, but still the stranded ship could not be moved. The Western Marine Salvage Co then took over the task of salvage and, after the ship's crew had been sent ashore, the remaining cargo was jettisoned, along with a number of deck fittings.

That night the *Highland Fling* began to bump and grind as the weather deteriorated. The plates in No 2 hold gave way, the forepart of the ship flooded up to the engine and boiler room bulkhead, and she began to break in two. On 12 January, a final effort to tow her off failed, despite the efforts of four tugs and assistance from the ship's own engines.

The decision was then made to separate the front portion of the ship from the as yet undamaged stern section. Dynamite charges were placed around the hull, and within a week the job was so far advanced that only a single charge of explosives was needed to sever the keel plate and divide the *Highland Fling* into two sections. But the final charge was never fired; an easterly gale blew up during the night of Sunday, 19 January, the sea parted the last iron plate and the stern portion drifted out to sea. By daylight, the tugs *Triton* and *Eagle* had managed to secure hawsers to the floating section and, after the bulkheads of the engine room had been shored up, they towed the half vessel to Falmouth. With the section becoming steadily deeper in the water and in imminent danger of sinking in Falmouth harbour, it was put on to a sand bank at high tide and lightened by unloading the coal from the bunkers. That same night, a north-westerly gale reduced the shattered bow section, still on the rocks at Cadgwith, to a pile of twisted iron. A great deal of wreckage came ashore, the complete foremast finishing up at Parnvoose. At the Board of Trade enquiry it was discovered that the deviation card for the ship's compass had been left behind in London when she sailed. It was also established that she was travelling too fast in fog, and Captain Purvis, held responsible for the loss, had his master's certificate suspended for six months.

The salvaged rear section of the *Highland Fling* was eventually manœuvred into dry-dock, but it proved too badly damaged to warrant the fitting of a new bow and was broken up for scrap metal.

CHAPTER FIVE

THE LIZARD

THE Lizard is the most southerly point of our mainland, and the 'gate post' of the English Channel. From across Mount's Bay, it appears in summer as a long sleepy blue shadow, speckled with sunshine that dances over the many faces of the cliffs. But in winter it is a menacing grey peninsula, seen only indistinctly through driving rain and spray, often completely obscured by dense fog. Low clouds scud over the cliffs and across the great moor of Goonhilly, a wild expanse which forms the backbone of the Lizard. To the emigrant of by-gone days this rocky headland represented a last forlorn glimpse of England, while to the returning sailor it meant the end of another voyage that often kept seafarers from home for three or even five years at a stretch.

Because the Lizard headland projects into the paths of a great number of ships that pass up or down Channel, it has been the scene of many more wrecks than any other point on the south coast of England. There is no record of when they began, since ships have been lost here for almost as long as man has sailed the sea, and a greek named Pytheas is known to have reached Cornwall from Marseilles as early as 300 BC. Documentary evidence of wrecks prior to the early 1500s is almost non-existent, but it takes little imagination to conjure up a picture of a lateen-rigged galley, rowed by swarthy Greeks or Phoenicians, fighting to clear the grey headland to leeward. Or, a thousand years later, a medieval carrack or caravel driven on to the Stags reef or Crenvil island, throwing its crew and armour-clad officers into the boiling surf. In later centuries, full-rigged sailing ships tore their hulls open on these same rocks. Merchant schooners, ketches, sloops and brigs, snows and brigantines, men-o'-war and packet steamers, even a battleship straight from the builder's yard, all have fetched up amongst the reefs that stretch seaward for half a mile from this famous headland.

It was not until the late sixteenth century that interest was first

105

shown in the erection of a beacon or warning light at the Lizard.
Even then, Sir John Killigrew's application of 1570 to the Lord
High Admiral to Queen Elizabeth I, for a patent to erect such a
light was rejected. It was left to the second Sir John, famous as
the founder of Falmouth, to erect the first beacon which was lit
in December 1619. The patent for the light was issued on 29 June
1619, the only stipulation being that it was to be maintained and
kept alight for fifty years at the sole expense of the Killigrews. In
return, they were empowered to collect 'dues' from passing ships
which used the light, but the patent offered no suggestions as to
how this could be achieved. This apparent concern for the safety
of shipping was not prompted solely by humanitarian motives, since
the Killigrews of early days had already established a reputation
for piracy and smuggling, in fact any enterprise that brought money
to Arwenack manor. It is very likely that their intention was to
keep an armed 'privateer' at sea to enforce payment from passing
ships—which would also have been an excellent excuse for their
other less publicised activities.

The lighting of the first beacon fire, however, aroused a storm
of local protest and, in correspondence on the subject, Sir John
Killigrew wrote the passage which serves as an introduction to this
book. Even more powerful opposition came from the Trinity
Brethren of London who were strongly opposed to private lighthouses, with the result that the Lizard light was soon extinguished
and remained unlit for the next twenty-one years, until rekindled
by another member of the Arwenack family. From 1640 onwards
the light continued to burn with nothing more efficient than a
wood or coal fire until 1812, when the first oil-burning lamps were
installed in the twin towers, eventually to be replaced by electric
light in 1878. Many stories can be told about the Lizard light,
including one of the occasion when the light was fired upon by
a British ship. A Falmouth packet was returning from America
in 1810 when, passing the headland at night, the captain noticed
that the beacon fire was very low. To warn the watchman, he
ordered a single cannon to be discharged at the cliffs, and when
there was no response from ashore a full broadside was fired
which produced an immediate brightening of the fire which lasted
all that night, and for many after.

Two of the earliest recorded shipwrecks at the Lizard are those

Page 107: The beautiful French full-rigger *Socoa* of Bayonne stranded on the Criscans near Cadgwith in August 1906.

Page 108: Timber spills out of the Norwegian ship *Hansy*, wrecked in Housel Bay, Lizard, on 13 November 1911.

of the Spaniard of 1619 and a Genoese ship in October 1667. Both were genuine 'treasure ships' of the kind beloved in fiction. The Spaniard, lost in the Polpeor Cove area, carried silver bars reputed to be worth £100,000, and one of the Killigrews, assisted by local men, set about recovering some part of the treasure, threatening death to anyone who tried to interfere. Even ten years later, when a Dutch diving engineer, Jacob Johanson, attempted to use a diving bell at the site he was prevented by force from entering the water. The Genoese wreck occurred in the vicinity of Bumble Rock, and in this case it was a consignment of silver coin that was lost. As a result of these two wrecks several applications were made to the Crown for licences to search for treasure, and impressive quantities were recovered. So much so, that the Polpeor area became a recognised testing ground for new diving apparatus. In 1704, Robert Davis, a shipbuilder from Leith, claimed to have descended several fathoms underwater in his 'diving-engine' on one of the wrecks but recovered nothing of value.

During the next hundred years most of the losses occurred amongst coastal trading ships and small merchant ships, many of which went unrecorded, the only wreck of any repute being the King's galley *Royal Anne*, bound for Barbados, which was wrecked on the Stags reef during November of 1720, with only three survivors. Two hundred and seven members of the crew drowned, in addition to her captain, all the lieutenants, twenty-four gentlemen and Lord Belhaven. Most of the bodies were buried in a clifftop grave at Pistol meadow. A few weeks later a contemporary newspaper recorded that 'the *Jolly Bachelor* and the *Henrietta*, yacht, are going down to the Lizard with a newly-invented diving engine to fish upon the wreck of the *Royal Anne* galley'. Unfortunately, their 'catch', if any, is not recorded.

Many other vessels followed in the wake of the King's galley, schooners, sloops, brigs, ketches and the occasional Indiaman. On 21 December 1754, a fine snow from the West Indies was wrecked because the light had been allowed to burn low. Occasionally local craft were lost and a Penzance-owned sloop that struck the Lizard in October 1813 instantly went to pieces with the loss of all hands. Another Penzance sloop, the *Mayflower*, loaded with a general cargo, sprang a leak and sank close inshore on 7 February 1824. The schooner *Xanthus*, London to Liverpool, went on to the Stags

G

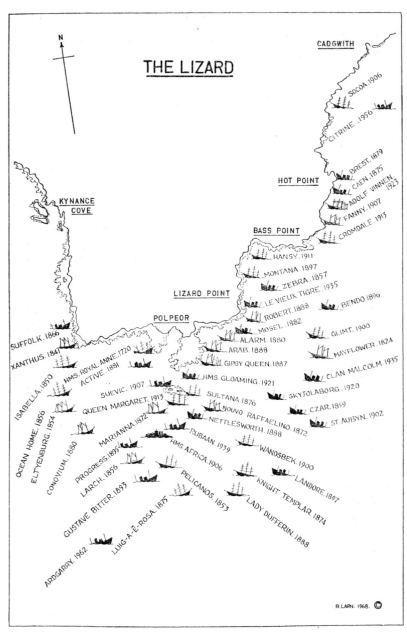

Wreck locations from Cadgwith to Kynance Cove, and off the Lizard.

in thick fog on 26 March 1841 and the brig *Isabella*, Odessa to Falmouth with wheat, was wrecked in the same place during a ssw gale on 27 March 1850. The Greek brig *Pelicanos*, Falmouth to Bridgewater with flour, was caught close inshore with a ground sea running on 1 May 1853 and was wrecked at the Lizard, although the crew were saved. The galliot *Eltyenburg* was in collision with the *Joanna Catherina* off the headland during an ENE gale in November 1854. Five of the six crew were drowned when the galliot sank, carrying to the bottom a cargo of tin ingots destined for Malta. The Padstow schooner *Larch*, Port Talbot to Plymouth with coal, was wrecked on the Stags in thick fog on 27 June 1856.

The first steamer lost at the Lizard was the *Zebra*, an iron, screw packet, Le Havre to Liverpool with passengers and general cargo, which struck in dense fog on 22 July 1856, and was beached and broke up near Hot Point. Less than two months later the American emigrant ship *Ocean Home*, Rotterdam to New York, was run down and sunk by the full-rigger *Cherubim* of London on 1 September 1856 with the loss of eighty-four lives. The frigate *Exmouth*, homeward bound from Lisbon, went aground at the Lizard on 12 May, 1857, remaining on the rocks for two hours and doing great damage to her hull. A fisherman, Sam Hitchens, went aboard and helped pilot her to safety, a service for which he received five guineas.

Two years later, the *Czar* of Hull was wrecked on the Lizard. This 1,100-ton, iron, barque-rigged screw steamer began her last voyage on 16 January 1859, when she sailed down the Thames from the arsenal at Woolwich bound for the Malta garrison. Under the command of Captain Robert Jackson, she carried 1,600 tons of government stores which included fifty-one 68-pounder muzzle-loading Lancaster cannon, shot and shell, uniform clothing, hides, spirits, oil, sugar and cinnamon. As she cleared the Downs the weather became rough and blustery, but it was not until 21 January, when some fifty miles west of the Bishop Rock, that a full wsw gale broke upon her. Rolling heavily in the deep troughs, the *Czar* developed boiler trouble and Captain Jackson put about for Falmouth. The weather worsened, and by the early afternoon of 22 January she was close inshore with the captain at the wheel, attempting to reach the shelter of the high cliffs east of the Lizard.

As she rounded the headland she struck the Vrogue Rock, less than half a mile from Bass Point, and fell broadside on to the sea, badly holed. As she rolled and pitched her lower yards dipped into the sea, until finally she broke in two abaft the funnel, the two halves sinking as they drifted apart. Two seamen and a male passenger were swept off the forecastle and, minutes later, were joined by the occupants of one of the ship's boats, which swamped whilst being lowered. A second boat managed to reach Parnvoose Cove with three survivors. Half-a-dozen craft then put out from shore led by the coastguard's cutter, which managed to get close enough to the sinking bows to rescue three of the crew who had been clinging to yardarms. Before nightfall one able seaman was recovered from the sea, after which the search was abandoned. Captain Jackson was drowned while trying to reach his wife and five-year-old son, trapped in the cabin when the ship broke in two, and when his body was recovered next day off Black Head it was laid to rest with the remainder of his crew in Landewednack churchyard. Years later, on 7 June 1900, when the salvage steamer *Mallard* was in the area working the wreck of the *Wandsbeck*, a Falmouth pilot named Bolitho, who held the rights to the wreck of the *Czar*, persuaded the *Mallard*'s master to put a diver down on her. The diver, John Rolling, found the wreck of the *Czar* collapsed but intact, lying in a bed of seaweed twelve feet deep in about twelve fathoms. A considerable number of cannon and cannon balls were sighted, but at dusk bad weather forced them to abandon the survey, though not before one of the 68-pounder guns had been raised. When landed at Falmouth docks, the gun completely filled a railway wagon. Only a month before this incident, the second officer of *Czar*, then living in retirement in Tasmania, had sent a substantial sum of money to be divided amongst any of his rescuers who were still living.

The first lifeboat at the Lizard was placed there by the Royal National Lifeboat Institute as a direct result of the wreck of the *Czar*. Its first location was most unsatisfactory since it was kept in a boathouse on the cliff-top, so that launching and recovery took place on the steep incline leading to Polpeor Cove. The task was made the more difficult by having to negotiate a sharp bend in the road with a sheer drop of at least 100ft on the seaward side. It was down this road, which still exists, that the old lifeboat crews would crawl on hands and knees for fear that gale-force winds would catch their bulky oilskins and send them over the cliff face. All that remains today of the first lifeboat or its equipment are the wooden bollards set at the bend of the road, to which blocks and tackle were attached to pull the lifeboat back uphill. Less than six years after its installation at the Lizard, this lifeboat, the *Anna Maria*, was herself wrecked with the loss of three crew. The accident occurred, not at the scene of a wreck as might have been expected, but on a normal quarterly practice.

The day chosen for the launch was 2 January 1866, a rough blustery day with a fresh sw gale that put doubts in the mind of Peter Mitchell, the coxswain, as to whether or not the practice should continue. The final decision lay with the local secretary and the Reverend Robinson electing to go ahead as planned the boat was duly launched. For an hour it was rowed and sailed back and forth amongst the rocks; then, as it turned towards Polpeor beach, disaster suddenly struck. Two great seas struck the boat in quick succession, capsizing her, but she was self-righting and most of the crew were able to scramble back on board. But the coxswain, second coxswain Richard Harris and crewman Nicholas Stephens were missing, as were all the oars in the boat, and when, shortly afterwards, the *Anna Maria* struck the rocks those aboard were thrown into the sea for a second time. Meanwhile, the first three men had been swept behind Shag Rock, kept afloat by their regulation lifejackets but at the mercy of wind and tide. One was washed out to sea and the others disappeared. The body of Richard Harris was found later in a cove near Bumble Rock, along with the lifejackets of the other two, but their bodies did not come ashore for some time. As for the lifeboat, her anchor had fallen out when she capsized and she rode, full of water, for at least an hour. Then the line parted and she went ashore to be dashed to pieces. On 7 March 1881, her successor, the *Anna Maria II*, capsized at the entrance to Church Cove in a ground sea whilst returning from a similar practice launch, but righted herself and no lives were lost.

During the early morning of 9 February 1869, a ship's lifeboat, 28 feet long, was found on the beach between Polurrian and Mullion Cove, its bows stove in and empty except for some bags of clothing and a lifebelt marked 'Calcutta. London'. The *Calcutta* was a full-rigged ship of 2,000 tons register, which had been carrying a crew of fifty-two plus twelve passengers and a cargo consisting of 250 miles of copper telegraph cable for the Persian Gulf. Two days previously she had been in collision during fog 150 miles SW of the Lizard with the barque *Emma* of Memel, which was carrying coal from Cardiff to Barcelona. Although badly damaged, the *Calcutta* stayed afloat but the barque sank within two minutes, drowning her captain and six of the eleven crew. With her steering gear completely disabled, the *Calcutta* limped towards the Lizard, but was still some distance offshore when fifteen of the crew sought the captain's permission to abandon ship in one of the boats. Led by the first mate, the boat was prepared and lowered, followed closely by a second with a further eight crew aboard, all of whom reached shore safely. As the ship approached the Lizard a third boat, containing twenty-one passengers and crew, was launched, followed by a fourth, but this one capsized, drowning the captain and all the occupants. Only eight men now remained aboard and they set to work lightening ship by throwing the telegraph cable overboard. By the time the lifeboat arrived to rescue them something like seventy-five miles of cable had been put over the side and still lies strung out across the seabed somewhere. HMS *Terrible* was despatched to locate the drifting derelict and managed to bring her into Plymouth Sound. Nothing further was ever seen of the twenty-one occupants of the third boat to leave the *Calcutta*, though their damaged lifeboat was mute evidence of their fate.

The following decade saw a vast number of wrecks at the Lizard and two deserving special mention were both Genoese barques carrying cargoes of rice, which had left the same port on the same day and were wrecked at the same place at the same time. One was the 707-ton *Marianna*, Captain Maglione; the other the 202-ton *Nouvo Raffaelino*, Captain Durante. Sailing from Bassein, Burma, in May 1872, they parted company in the Indian Ocean and for three months sailed alone. They met up again off the Isles of Scilly and continued towards Falmouth in company until fog led them to separate yet again on 20 September. At 4 pm the following day they went aground on the eastern Stags, unaware of each other's presence until both crews met on reaching the Lizard. The two ships burst open as the sea swelled their rice cargoes and they were sold by public auction, fetching about £70 each.

Two years later, the 800-ton barque *Knight Templar* of Falmouth, deep laden with wheat from Valparaiso, also went on to the Stags and became a total loss during the night of 23 April 1874. Launched at Little Falmouth in 1868, she was bound for her home port when fog was encountered and she went ashore while trying to make a landfall. The iron steamer *Caen*, of and for Cardiff in ballast from Caen, was wrecked during thick fog below Hot Point on 26 January 1875, and on 26 October that year the brig *Luiga ē Rosa* of Mecklenburg, Bremen to Cardiff in ballast, but last from Plymouth, piled up on the Stag Rock on an equally murky night. Her lights had been seen from ashore some time earlier and the lifeboat crew were already manning their boat when her distress rockets flared up into the sky. She went rapidly to pieces the next day and the lifeboat collected stores and gear sufficient to fill two carts.

Vessels wrecked at the Lizard were almost invariably auctioned off in the village hall or on the beach itself, where evidence of the wreck for sale would lie at the feet of prospective customers. One name that appears in the records of auctions shortly after that of the *Luiga ē Rosa* is that of the 140-ton brig *Sultana* of St Johns, Newfoundland. Owned by John Chapman of Liverpool, she was laden with superphosphates and bound from London for Wexford when she was wrecked in foggy weather on 31 January 1876, her master having sighted nothing since she passed the Eddystone the previous evening. The crew took to their boat but remained alongside all night in the hope of re-boarding her. But at dawn the mainmast fell through the bottom and the brig sank in heavy seas.

A lighter incident of about this time relates to a Quebec-registered vessel, bound for Hull, whose crew were able to clamber on to Crenvil Rock when she went on to the Stags. By daylight, one man could be seen clutching a cask, another a live pig, and when they had later managed to scramble ashore they were met by the ship's cat which had swum ashore ahead of them but had lost its tail in the wreck. Solemnly they walked up to the village, one man with a nine-gallon cask of rum, another with the squealing pig, a third carrying a ginger cat without a tail. Arriving at the village tavern, they drank the rum, exchanged the pig for the price of a ride to Falmouth and presented the cat to the landlord of the inn, where it remained until it died of old age.

Despite improvements to the Lizard lighthouse in 1878, including installation of a mechanical foghorn and the substitution of elec-

tricity for the oil lamps, ships still came ashore there and few were
as fortunate as the 240-ton wooden brig *Scotscraig*, owned by the
Dundee Shipping Co, which got right in amongst the rocks known
as the Inner Cledges on 15 June 1879. This thirteen-year old vessel
had left Falmouth only an hour or so before, carrying a cargo of
Cuban sugar. With the assistance of the Lizard lifeboat she managed
to clear the rocks, and survived to sail again. Less than three
months later, at 8.30 pm on 6 September, a steamship struck the
rocks almost beneath the duty coastguards' lookout windows but
the fog was so thick that the first they knew of it was when they
heard a tremendous crash, followed by screams and shouts. It
took the Cadgwith lifeboat thirty minutes to locate the wreck in
the fog, the vessel eventually being found on the rocks between
Polpeor and Church Cove. As the lifeboat pulled alongside the
wreck, it was almost overwhelmed by panic-stricken passengers
who threw themselves over the ship's rail and fought to secure a
place aboard the lifeboat. The coxswain was soon forced to stand
clear of the ship for fear of being sunk and, reinforced by fishing
craft, completed the rescue when the passengers had been calmed
down by the crew. As none of the passengers could speak English
it was only when Captain Richard Elder and his crew came ashore
that the ship was identified as the 1,472-ton iron screw steamer
Brest, of Glasgow, owned by Samuel McIver of the Cunard Steamship Co and built in 1874 by Blackwoods Ltd of Port Glasgow. A
sister ship of the *Stromboli*, wrecked only a few miles to the west
eighteen months previously, the *Brest* had sailed from Le Havre
the previous day for Liverpool with 134 passengers, mostly French,
German, Italian and Swiss emigrants bound for America, some
of whom had already suffered shipwreck in the Mediterranean.
Despite their panic behaviour, only five drowned although all lost
their personal possessions, no small disaster since most were carrying with them everything they owned. A tug was chartered to take
them to Falmouth, but the survivors refused to risk another sea
voyage and walked the twenty odd miles instead. By the time the
wreck was sold on 25 October a great deal of her cargo had been
salvaged and the bodies of those drowned recovered from a cave
near Crane Ledge, or drifting among the rocks. During early
November the *Brest* broke up completely and barely showed above
the surface at high tide.

Page 117: Her canvas still set, the Aberdeen full-rigger *Cromdale*, wrecked on Bass Point, Lizard, on 23 May 1913.

Page 118: (above) The lovely white barque *Queen Margaret* sinking on the Stags at the Lizard on 15 May 1913; (below) the German five-masted schooner *Adolf Vinnen*, decks awash, wrecked in Housel Bay on her maiden voyage on 9 February 1923.

Page 119: The 700-ton Glasgow barque *Abernyte,* wrecked below Rill
Head in fog on 8 May 1898.

Page 120: (above) One of the earliest wreck photographs; salvage work on the Glasgow steamer *John MacIntyre*, beached at Gue Graze on 17 April 1865; (below) waves pound the steamer *Brankelow*, which went ashore near Gunwalloe on 21 April 1890.

During the 1880s, the two major losses at the Lizard were the steamers *Mosel* and *Suffolk*, and though both were vessels of considerable size and carried a total of 720 persons, not a single life was lost. Prior to the wreck of these two ships there was the customary toll of smaller vessels. The schooner *Conovium*, London to Dublin with cement, was lost on the Stags in fog on 5 May 1880 and her crew barely had time to launch their boat before she rolled over and sank. Another schooner, the *Alarm* of Faversham, bound from Pembroke to London with coal, was found abandoned and sinking by the Falmouth pilot-cutter No 14 on 30 September 1880, her crew having been rescued by a passing vessel. The 337-ton iron collier *Active*, Captain Siddell, Neath to Caen with coal, holed herself on the Stags in thick, rough weather on 5 January 1881. Her crew took to the ship's boats and were picked up by the Porthleven fishing-boat *Ellen* just after the collier had capsized and sunk. The *Active* had been built in 1874 and was owned by H F Swan of Newcastle.

The *Mosel*, owned by the Norddeutsher Lloyd Line, was no newcomer to the English Channel when she struck Bass Point on 9 August 1882 for she had been plying across the North Atlantic with emigrants from Bremen to New York, via Southampton, for almost nine years. In 1875, two years after her launch, a bomb planted on board by anarchists exploded prematurely in Bremen docks killing eighty-one people, injuring a further fifty-one and extensively damaging the ship. Early in 1882, the *Mosel* was fitted with new engines and sailed for New York on 6 August. Besides his crew of one hundred, Captain Julius Hesse had the responsibility of twenty saloon-class passengers and 600 emigrants. In addition, she carried a valuable cargo, specie, mail and 400 tons of English woollen goods.

At 7.30 am on 9 August, with the first and fourth officers on the bridge, the *Mosel* neared the Lizard. Occasional fog-banks impaired visibility and the lookouts had nothing more than infrequent glimpses of the shore. But the ship had passed this way dozens of times before and, confident in their course, her officers held on at her full cruising speed of fourteen knots. Just after 8.0 am the *Mosel* ran into a heavier bank of fog and ten minutes later steamed headlong into Bass Point, directly beneath Lloyd's signal station. She was so close to the cliffs that the duty signalman climbed down, jumped on to the forecastle and spoke to the captain and officers in the saloon. In no immediate danger, the passengers were ordered to pack their baggage. The Falmouth tug *Rosetta* took off the bullion, mail and some of the saloon passengers, while a proportion of the general cargo was transferred to the tugs *Victor, Kimberly* and *Sylph.* By noon, the rising tide had flooded the engine room cutting off the steam pressure and rendering the winches useless. Soon afterwards a small fire broke out in the engine room and it was decided to abandon ship. All the passengers and crew were landed safely, the emigrants being housed in the warehouse of the Falmouth Dock Co. On 11 August, the Irish packet, *Countess of Dublin,* took the saloon passengers aboard for America, the remainder travelling on the *Herman,* a sister-ship of the *Mosel.* The wreck settled lower in the sea, and at high water lay bows-on to the cliff, with the stern completely under water. Divers sent down to examine the hull found plates torn open from the stem to about eighty feet aft, but considered that salvage was still possible. Work commenced on patching the holes but was soon stopped by ground swells, and on 24 August the *Mosel* broke in half. The wreck was only partially salvaged between winter gales and the greater part of it still lies below Bass Point.

The second big steamship wreck was the *Suffolk* which in company with her sister ships, the *Surrey* and *Sussex,* maintained a regular service between London and Baltimore in the late 1880s. Although technically owned by three separate shipping companies, the three ships were managed by the one firm of Hooper, Murrell & Williams Ltd of London. Within less than a year, the *Sussex* was wrecked at Bryher, Isles of Scilly in December 1885, and the *Suffolk* at the Lizard on 28 September 1886. Nor did the *Surrey* escape unscathed, since she was extensively damaged in a collision off Bishop Rock with the German ship *Uranus* on 4 January 1884.

Launched in 1882 by R H Green of Blackwall, the *Suffolk* was a schooner-rigged, three-masted iron steamer of 1,924 tons net. Her dimensions were an overall length of 300ft, a beam of 40.25ft and a depth of 22.25ft and she was fitted with a 275-hp twin-cylinder engine. Her hull was strengthened by six bulkheads, two of which were watertight, and a double bottom which extended for 194ft. Her last voyage began on 14 September, when she left Baltimore under the command of Captain W H Williams. On board were a crew of thirty-eight, two passengers, and a cargo of tobacco in casks, 8,000 bushels of wheat, 24,000 sacks of flour, 500 casks of flour, barrels of resin and general Christmas fare. In addition, the after deck was stacked with walnut logs to a height of ten feet and 161 prime New England steers were penned on the foredeck. The return voyage went smoothly enough, but bad weather off the Isles of Scilly on 28 September smashed some of the cattle pens and damaged a lifeboat. A course of east by south was set, calculated to take the *Suffolk* clear of the Lizard, but by 4.45 pm fog had set in and was so thick that Captain Williams himself went forward to join the lookouts in the bows. He had barely reached the forecastle when the black shape of a rock loomed up fine on the starboard bow. The engines were put full astern and the helm hard over but the *Suffolk* ran ashore at the old Lizard Head still doing a good six knots. Captain Williams ordered the carpenter to sound fore and aft, but even as he went forward the chief engineer arrived on the bridge to report that the stokehold was filling and the fires almost swamped. The carpenter came back with the news that the forepeak was flooded and Captain Williams ordered the boats lowered, at the same time pumping out oil to calm the seas.

Both the Lizard and Cadgwith lifeboats were launched and eventually found all forty passengers and crew afloat in the ship's boats. Some of the crew attempted to return aboard at 5 am next morning, but heavy seas prevented them approaching the ship and they stood by in the hope that the weather would moderate. By evening, however, a big ground sea was running and as the steamer settled down many of the cattle were swept overboard. Some reached the shore and huddled together on a small shingle beach, from which rescuers hauled twenty-six of them up the cliff face. The crew did eventually manage to re-board the wreck, but their visit was short-lived. No sooner had they gained the main deck than the *Suffolk* broke her back, sending the men scuttling down into the boats as the sea flooded into the holds. The surviving steers and the bulk of the cargo were auctioned off at the Lizard reading-room on 4 October. The walnut logs fetched 70s each and the flour 2s a sack, the wreck itself being bought by Leans of Falmouth for £111. On 20 October, during a westerly gale, the now funnel-less hulk capsized and disgorged its remaining cargo.

Logs drifted ashore from Cadgwith to Marazion, thousands of bags of flour turned the sea into a sickly grey mess, and the carcasses of cattle which had been buried deep in the sand of local beaches were washed out of their graves and floated about in the shallows.

During the remaining years of the 1880s, wreck followed wreck in quick succession. On 13 March 1887, the 95-ton Padstow schooner *Gipsy Queen*, London to Liverpool with cement, struck Maenheere Rock, came off and sank a mile offshore, her crew being saved by lifeboat. The three-masted *Lady Dufferin*, wrecked on 10 March 1888, was followed by the steamship *Nettlesworth*, Cardiff to Kronstadt with coal on 19 July; the schooner *Robert* of and from Caernarvon to London with slates, followed on 29 July and the Dublin schooner *Arab* on 28 September. The *Nettlesworth*, owned by R Gordan of Sunderland, was the sister ship of the *Sestos* which, at the time of the wreck, was in Falmouth docks, having been almost cut in half by a British ironclad off Wolf Rock on 17 July 1888. The 894-ton wooden barque *Lady Dufferin*, launched by Yeo of Prince Edward Island in 1873, had sailed from Newport with 1,200 tons of railway lines, sleepers and ties, destined for the South American railway depot at Rio Plata. She met a south-west gale off the Scillies and was forced to turn back to Falmouth. Off the Lizard, several great seas washed right over the ship and shortly before 10.30 pm, completely unmanageable, she was thrown on to Mulvin Ledges, 200 yards west of Polpeor Cove. Her crew were rescued by the lifeboat and after the storm the ship was unrecognisable, a mass of broken timbers, twisted railway lines and sleepers. Some of the lines were salvaged but the sleepers were carried out to sea to be cast up on beaches for miles around, and kept many a Cornish fire burning that winter. The figurehead of the *Lady Dufferin* was salvaged and stood in the garden of a private house at the Lizard for many years, but is now inside one of the 'serpentine' workshops.

Wrecks like that of the *Lady Dufferin* emphasised the difficulty of launching from Polpeor in southerly gales, and so in 1885 a second lifeboat was placed in the slightly more sheltered Church Cove. However, it never found favour with the Lizard crew and after little service the station was closed in 1899. The final development of the Polpeor station was the building of yet another boat-house, this time with a slipway so that the boat could be launched directly into the sea, the old house being converted into an engine-house. A turntable was built in the forecourt of the old house so that, upon recovery, the lifeboat was hauled up the beach on to the table, turned through 90 degrees and put back into its boat-house via the 'back-door'. The new engine-house and turntable were completed in 1914, just in time to meet the emergencies of the First World War, but many more ships were to be wrecked in the intervening years.

Taking some of the larger ships, and in chronological order, the 564-ton steamship *Gustave Bitter* of London was wrecked between the Enoch and Maenheere rocks on 4 March 1893, with the loss of her second officer. The rest of her crew were rescued by the Lizard and Cadgwith lifeboats and the ship, which had been bound from London to the Manchester Ship Canal with a general cargo, was sold as she lay to a Falmouth diving contractor for £22. Five months later, on 13 August, another steamship, the *Auric* of Belfast, bound from Caen to Swansea in ballast, stranded at Carleon Cove, near Cadgwith, in fog but was successfully refloated with the aid of tugs.

Home waters proved no protection for the three-masted, schooner-rigged steamship *Progress* of Penzance, which sank four miles west of the Lizard on 19 June 1895 after colliding in fog with the packet *Lady Martin*. Owned by J H Bennett of Penzance and built by E Lindsay of Newcastle in 1872, she was bound from Gloucester to London and was the first steamer to be registered at Penzance.

Fog, too, contributed to the loss of the Liverpool collier *Landore*, built by Harveys of Hayle, which stranded on the Lizard rocks on 23 November 1897, fortunately without loss of life. In 1900, the insatiable Stags reef claimed two more victims within six months of each other, first the three-masted steel ship *Wandsbek* of Hamburg on 26 May and then, on 24 November, the Norwegian barque *Glimt* of Stavanger. The *Wandsbek*, bound from Portland (Oregon) to Liverpool via Falmouth, was owned by Knohr & Burchard and had been launched at Hamburg only two years earlier. Caught out by strong tides, she went ashore in a flat calm and her wreck was sold to Captain Richards of Liverpool for £55. There was more excuse for the *Glimt*, bound from Rosario to Falmouth with wheat, as she found the Stags in thick weather with a heavy ground swell and her crew were saved only by an exceptionally daring rescue operation staged by the Lizard and Cadgwith lifeboats. The barque, built at Drammen twenty years earlier, became a total loss.

So the toll continued into the turn of the century. On 19 August 1902 the steamer *St Aubyn* of London, bound from Cardiff to London with coal, struck Maenheere Rock in squally weather and, leaking badly, was beached in Housel Bay. Later, after her cargo had been jettisoned and temporary repairs made, she was refloated with the aid of tugs.

Even battleships could fall foul of the Lizard, though one that 'got away' was HMS *Africa* which came close inshore among the Lizard rocks while undergoing builders' trials on 29 May 1906 and narrowly missed going aground. A warship of 16,350 tons, she carried a complement of 777 and had been built at Chatham at a cost of one and a half million pounds.

Two months later, on 31 July, the steel, three-masted ship *Socoa* of Bayonne stranded near Cadgwith in thick weather while on passage from Stettin to San Francisco. She was carrying cement intended for the rebuilding of that earthquake-shattered city and 50,000 barrels of it had to be jettisoned before she could be refloated. Later re-named the *Thiers,* she survived for another twenty-one years before being broken up.

The year 1907 was a particularly memorable one for the Lizard, the victims ranging from the little 52-ton Bideford ketch *Fanny,* wrecked on Bass Point in thick fog on 23 July, to the 12,500-ton White Star liner *Suevic,* wrecked on the Maenheere rocks on the night of 17 March while carrying a total complement of 456 passengers and crew. All were rescued—the greatest number of people ever to be saved from a wreck since the RNLI was founded in 1824—thanks to the magnificent efforts of the four local lifeboats. Of these the Cadgwith boat brought 227 survivors ashore, the Lizard boat 167, the Coverack boat 44 and Porthleven 18. Of the 456 survivors, 160 were women and children.

The *Suevic,* homeward bound from Australia, carried a crew of 141, plus 382 passengers and one stowaway; her cargo was general, and included frozen meats, butter and copper bars. She was on her way to Liverpool via Plymouth when an error of navigation and bad visibility combined to put her ashore on the Maenheere rocks. Two days after she went ashore, a railway company steamer arrived alongside to disembark the passengers' luggage, and was followed later by every available lighter and coaster in the West Country. On 20 March in calm conditions unloading of the cargo into the smaller vessels began and was completed exactly one hour before the weather deteriorated on 27 March.

Divers inspected the hull, but the *Suevic* was so badly damaged in the forepart that explosives were used to detach the bow section from the remainder. The after portion, containing all the valuable machinery, boilers and passenger accommodation, then floated free and, virtually undamaged, was towed to Southampton and dry-docked. A new bow section was built at Belfast, then towed to Southampton where the two ends were mated and the *Suevic* was re-born to sail again. So confident of success were the owners that they advertised her next sailing for 14 January 1908, while the bow section was still on the stocks at Belfast. During the First World War the *Suevic* served as a troopship, and in 1929 she was sold to a Norwegian whaling company. Re-named the *Skyttern*, she survived as a whale factory ship until 1 April 1942 when her crew deliberately scuttled her in the Skagerrak rather than let her fall into German hands.

In the years between the wreck of the *Suevic* and the outbreak of the First World War, three large and well-known square-rigged sailing ships were lost at the Lizard. The first of the three was the 1,597-ton steel ship *Hansy*, launched at Dumbarton by Alexander Macmillan & Sons in 1885 as the *Aberfoyle*. In the course of a somewhat chequered career, she had been picked up in Bass Strait, Tasmania, in 1896 by a steamer which had found her crippled and with her master and chief officer dead on board. Three years later she was sold to Crawford & Rowath of Glasgow and they, in turn, passed her on to her final owners, Akties Hansy of Frederickstadt in 1910. The *Hansy* left Sundsvall, Sweden, on 3 October 1911 with a cargo of timber and pig-iron for Melbourne and after a rough passage down Channel was caught by a hard ssw gale off the Lizard. While trying to claw off the coast she missed stays in coming about, became trapped in Housel Bay and was wrecked at Carn Table. The crew were rescued by breeches-buoy from the shore and the master, Captain Kiltvo, and the mate were later taken off by the lifeboat. Two days later, when the weather had moderated and a salvage party were able to board the wreck, they found a pig feasting on potatoes in what remained of the crew's quarters, while two goats eyed them amiably from the comfort of a bunk. For weeks after the stranding, great quantities of timber were washed out of the wreck and thankfully collected by the local fishing boats.

The other two full-rigger casualties of the years between 1907 and 1914 were both lost in May of 1913 but under very different circumstances. They were the four-masted steel barque *Queen Margaret* of 2,144 tons gross, launched by Macmillan of Dumbarton in 1893 and the 1,903-ton three-masted ship *Cromdale* of Aberdeen, owned by D. Rose and built at Glasgow in 1891 by Barclay Curle & Co. The *Queen Margaret* was one of the only two British ships ever to carry three skysails and her reputation for speed, grace and good treatment of crews was legendary among seafarers. When she left Barry docks in July 1912 with a cargo of coal for Montevideo, she carried a crew of twenty-five under the command of Captain Bousfield of Ripley, Yorkshire, making his first voyage as master and accompanied by his wife and son.

Montevideo was reached without special incident and after discharging her coal, the *Queen Margaret* went on to Sydney to load wheat and sailed for Falmouth on 17 January 1913. One hundred and thirty days out, at 4.0 am on 13 May, the barque was close-hauled off the Lizard waiting for daylight to communicate with Lloyd's signal station and report her arrival. As soon as visibility allowed, Captain Bousfield signalled his identity with a string of flags and was given in return a message from his owners instructing him to discharge his cargo at Limerick and then go on to Glasgow to pay off his crew. The wind being very light and variable, Captain Bousfield passed a message through Lloyd's requesting the owners' permission to engage tugs to take him clear of Land's End. While awaiting a reply to the message, which had to be relayed to London, the ship beat slowly back and forth in front of the headland and had just come about to stand westward again when she suddenly shuddered and ground to a halt. Incredulously, master and crew looked over the side to see rocks and weed only a few feet underwater. The *Queen Margaret* was firmly impaled on Maen-heere Rock at the eastern end of the Stags reef, less than half a

Page 129: The French pitwood schooner *Olympe*, wrecked in Gunwalloc Church Cove on 3 October 1910.

Page 130: (above) Tremendous seas sweep the 2,297-ton Genoa steamer *Tripolitania* aground on Loe Bar on Boxing Day 1912; (below) salvage work was kept up on the *Tripolitania* for nearly a year, but she was never refloated.

mile from Polpeor, and despite the combined efforts of tugs from Falmouth she was still hard aground after the next high tide. On the ebb, she fell over on to her port side until her yardarms touched the water, then her four tall masts broke off and the elegant tracery of her rigging and clewed-up 'gulls wings' crashed down into the sea. Later, her long, slim hull bulged and parted under pressure of the swollen wheat and when the time came to auction off all that remained of this once-lovely ship, the *Queen Margaret* changed owners for the paltry sum of £50.

Eighteen days later, the *Cromdale* came ashore less than half a mile away from the *Queen Margaret*. One hundred and twenty-four days out from Taltal, Chile, with a cargo of nitrates, she was already a week overdue at Falmouth when, nearing the Lizard, she ran into dense fog on the evening of 23 May. Her master, Captain Arthur, had earlier been able to check his position with a passing steamer and was not unduly worried until several hours had passed without sight or sound of the Lizard or St Anthony lighthouses. Then, at 9.50 pm it was the helmsman and not the look-out who first saw a blurred flash in the murk dead ahead. Seconds later breakers were seen and before course could be altered the *Cromdale* had grounded on the rocks below Bass Point. Badly holed, she settled rapidly by the stern and in less than ten minutes had to be abandoned.

The first distress rocket, fired from a boat by the first mate, exploded almost in front of the coastguards' lookout, and the Lizard and Cadgwith lifeboats were soon afloat and helping in the rescue. Next morning, when the fog lifted, the *Cromdale* was an awesome spectacle, poop deck under water and bows on the rocks below the high cliffs, every sail set but hanging limply from the yards in the still air. At low water, her crew boarded her and managed to recover some personal belongings and the ship's instruments. The wreck was later put up for auction but, with a ruined cargo, she was of little value apart from her sailing gear and Harris Brothers of Falmouth bought her for £41, later reselling her to a third party. A week after she came ashore the *Cromdale* broke up in a heavy SSW gale and very little salvage work was ever carried out on the remains.

Some six months prior to the loss of the *Cromdale*, during the Christmas of 1912, the 3,103-ton steamship *Sola* disappeared off

H

the Lizard with thirty-four passengers and crew. Owned by a British railway company, she was on her way to South America with railway equipment and staff and is believed to have been overwhelmed by the severe gales which raged all that week. One of her lifeboats and several bodies came ashore at Gunwalloe, more bodies were washed up at the Lizard, and her second boat was found jammed inside a cave, but exactly what happened to the *Sola* will never be known.

German submarine activity during the First World War was responsible for the sinking of a vast tonnage of merchant shipping within sight of the Lizard. Between 1916-18 alone, thirty-five ships, representing some 70,000 tons, were sent to the bottom by torpedoes or scuttling charges. Among these many victims were: *Pearl*, 144 tons, 30.9.1916; *Lucent*, 1,409 tons, 12.2.1917; *Polymnia*, 2,426 tons, 15.5.17; *Tyne*, 2,909 tons, 17.6.17; *Noya*, 4,286 tons, 30.8.17; *Sommenia*, 3,317 tons, 15.9.17; *Garthclyde*, 2,124 tons, 15.10.17; *Foylemore*, 3,831 tons, 16.12.17; *Lydie*, 2,559 tons, 9.2.1918; *Cheviot Grange*, 3,691 tons, 21.2.18; *Lady Cory Wright*, 2,516 tons, 26.3.18; *Henley*, 3,249 tons, 10.4.18; *Mountby*, 3,263 tons, 10.5.18; *Limbourne*, 1,219 tons, 29.9.18; and *Westwood*, 1,968 tons, 3.10.18.

The war over, the Lizard was still in business and one of the first post-war wrecks was that of the 617-ton steel steamer *Skyjolaborg* of Hangesund, Rouen to Swansea in ballast, which struck the Maenheere Rock during fog on 18 January 1920. The Cadgwith lifeboat went out but found her abandoned, Captain Macland and his crew having already rowed into Mullion.

The smallest naval vessel to be lost on the headland was probably the auxiliary drifter HMS *Gloaming*, which was wrecked there in 1921. The 94-ton *Gloaming*, which had been built for the Admiralty in 1918 by J G Forbes, left Pembroke Dock for Portland on 3 March 1921 as part of an escort to the 1st Submarine Flotilla. The flotilla consisted of five steam submarines, *K5, K8, K12, K15* and *K9*, and the escort of the cruisers *Inconstant* and *Pandora*, plus the tender *Gloaming*.

By nightfall on 4 March the flotilla was closing on the Lizard, with the *Gloaming* well out ahead. Her commanding officer, Lieutenant Whitfield, and her crew, apart from a petty officer at the helm, were asleep in their bunks. At 3.30 am she struck the Cledges reef with such violence that the crew were thrown to the deck and several injured. The *Gloaming* listed heavily to starboard and had to be abandoned. At high water next day she rolled over and disappeared, almost directly over the site of the *Suevic*'s bow section.

Forty-five years later, some holiday-makers looking for crabs at low water near Polpeor were attracted by the glint of metal and found between the rocks a ship's bell, somewhat battered but clearly marked *Gloaming*. Members of the Naval Air Command sub-aqua club from the nearby air station at Culdrose undertook to search for the wreck and found it some 500 yards offshore, lying in thirty-five feet of water. Very little remained but the engine block and propeller shafting, boiler and fittings. Positive identification was made from the 43-hp steam reciprocating engine, manufactured by Cooper & Craig of Dundee in 1918. Another interesting but dangerous find was a quantity of 3-in fixed ammunition, loose and in boxes on the seabed; obviously submarine gun ammunition carried by the tender. As the site was remote, with little chance of being disturbed, it was considered prudent to leave them alone but when, in the following year, two local youths found the ammunition whilst snorkelling and reported it to the police, the Devonport Command Bomb and Mine Disposal unit were called in to detonate it underwater.

During May 1922, two ships came ashore at the Lizard on the same night, the 168-ton auxiliary schooner *Viola*, built by Pickards of Appledore in October 1872, which had served during the first world war as a 'Q' ship, and the 1,968-ton steel tanker *St Patrice* of Swansea. The *Viola* had left Teignmouth for Glasgow on 19 May with china clay. She put in to Brixham for oil fuel, but soon after sailing encountered fog and sighted nothing until 4 am on 21 May, when she grounded on the rocks at Kennack Sands and broke her back. Less than an hour later, the *St Patrice* went on Mulvin ledges, only three miles away. The tanker had left her home port for Jarrow-on-Tyne the previous day, with a cargo of fuel oil. Launched by the Antwerp Engineering Co of Hoboken in 1919, she had been bought from the Société Navalede of Le Havre only six weeks previously by British Tankers Ltd of Swansea. After a three-month salvage operation she was re-floated and towed to Falmouth for temporary repairs, but sank in a gale off Heligoland on her way to Hamburg.

When the *Adolf Vinnen* came ashore in 1923 she was a new ship, only nine days out of her builders' hands. Owned by Vinnens of Bremen, she was one of five steel, five-masted auxiliary schooners built by Krupps of Kiel between 1922-23. Of over 2,000 tons gross tonnage, the *Adolf Vinnen* was fitted with a diesel engine originally destined for U-boats and carried the peculiar sail plan known as 'jackass rig'. She left the builders on 1 February 1923 for Bruns-büttel, via the Kiel Canal, where final fitting-out took place. On 9 February she sailed on her maiden voyage, in ballast for Barry to load coal. Her master, Captain Muller, had also commanded an earlier *Adolf Vinnen*, a 3,000-ton barque which had been requisitioned after the First World War by the United States and renamed *Mae Dollar*. As the *Adolf Vinnen* left the North Sea and entered the Channel she ran into strong headwinds. These increased and veered SSW so that when the Lizard was sighted on 23 February she was dangerously close to the land. Failing to work clear, she drove ashore at 5.30 pm only seventy yards off Bass Point and very close to the wreck of the *Mosel*, lost in 1882. A crowd of spectators had gathered long before she struck and the new motor lifeboat *Frederick H Pilley* was being launched even as the big schooner hit the rocks. Seventeen of her crew were saved by breeches-buoy but Captain Muller, his officers and the steward decided to remain on board. During the night, heavy seas swept the wreck from end to end and they were almost swept from the rigging. The sea was so rough that the Lizard lifeboat, unable to approach Polpeor station, had to make for the shelter of Falmouth. Next day, the captain and his comrades were rescued by breeches-buoy and the ship left to the mercies of the sea. By 16 March, all four topmasts had collapsed and were followed shortly after by the mainmasts. The wreck remains near Bass Point, but is often completely engulfed in sand and only uncovers at infrequent intervals.

Like most other shipping companies, the White Star Line suffered heavy losses during the war years and a welcome post-war replace-ment was the 8,000-ton *Bardic*, launched by Harland & Wolff in 1919. After employment as a general cargo and passenger ship on the Australian run, the *Bardic* was laid up throughout 1923 whilst being converted into a refrigerator ship for the carriage of bulk meat. On 6 August 1924 she left Sydney and docked in Liverpool on 26 August, where part of the cargo was discharged, after which she sailed for London on the 30th. The weather was foggy and disaster was only narrowly averted off the Longships when an Atlantic liner almost ran her down. The passengers and crew were already going to lifeboat stations as the ships passed, only yards apart. Fog closed down as the *Bardic* continued along the south coast, and the forward look-out had barely had time to report a foghorn ahead before the ship had ground to a standstill on the Vasiler Rock, one of the most dangerous of the exposed rocks in the Lizard reef.

The combined efforts of the *Bardic*'s 1,138-hp engines and two tugs failed to refloat her. By daylight, she was well down by the head, almost every double bottom tank was punctured, and the engine-room as well as Nos 1 and 3 holds were all flooded. The Liverpool Salvage Association then took over and she was eventually refloated on 29 September, after twenty-nine days aground. Listing badly, she was towed to Falmouth and beached alongside the eastern breakwater. After extensive repairs she sailed again in 1925. In 1926 the Aberdeen Line bought her and she was re-named the *Horatius*; after which the Shaw Savill Line owned her for a few years under the name *Kumara*, until finally the Greek Marathon Steamship Co Ltd of Pireas bought her in 1937 and changed her name to *Marathon*. On 9 March 1941, the *Marathon* was shelled and sunk by the German battleship *Scharnhorst* off the Cape Verde Islands.

Although there were a few minor incidents in the next ten years, there was a marked decrease in Lizard wreck incidents, and after 1925 a number of years went by without a single casualty. However, Boxing Day, 1927, saw the Lizard lifeboat again at sea in an easterly gale and a blizzard rescuing two of the crew of the Thames barge *Lady Daphne* of Rochester, bound from Weymouth to Fowey. Her master had already been lost overboard and, after being abandoned, the barge drifted all the way to Round Island, Isles of Scilly, where it was blown ashore virtually undamaged.

In 1935 a large trawler, a 12,000-ton tanker and a Glasgow tramp all came ashore within a period of six months. At 8 pm on 27 March 1935 the Boulogne steam trawler *Le Vieux Tigre* grounded below Bass Point. Twenty-nine crew and two dogs were landed, and by morning only the top of the ship's bridge, funnel and stern were above water. The trawler's tabby cat must have had a life to spare

as she was marooned on the wreck for two days until the crew
of a Cadgwith fishing-boat coaxed her off. The 'Old Tiger' later
drifted under the high cliffs and broke up in heavy ground seas.
The Danzig tanker *D L Harper*, Venezuela to Hamburg, crude oil,
went on to the Mulvin Rock in thick fog on 20 June but was saved
and refloated, unlike the 5,994-ton Clan Lines steamer *Clan Malcolm* of Glasgow, wrecked at Green Lane at 9 pm on 26 September
while bound from Port Natal via London to Glasgow. Dense fog
cloaked the headland at the time, and the coastguards were unaware
of the wreck until they saw her distress rockets. Although the
German tug *Seefalke* reached her in a matter of hours, the identity
of the ship was not known ashore until the Lizard lifeboat returned
after eighteen hours' duty. The *Clan Malcolm* was badly damaged,
and a salvage diver declared her a total loss. On 30 September the
underwriters confirmed the loss officially, a personal tragedy for
Captain Pollack, the master, for whom this was a last command
before retiring. On 3 November a south-east gale smashed deck
fittings, decks and hatch covers; she survived one night of this
pounding, but began to break up the following day. Her deck was
swept almost clean, and after a sagging deck line had showed her
keel to be broken Cadgwith Cove was soon ten feet deep in
wreckage. Some time later the *Clan Malcolm*, which was launched
in 1917 by Craig Taylor & Co of Stockton, broke in two and
vanished. On 14 February 1936, the 5,112-ton Hartlepool steamship
Lackenby, London to Cardiff in ballast, went ashore close by in
foggy weather, but refloated without assistance.

Surprisingly few ships were sunk on or near the Lizard during
the Second World War by comparison with the 1914-18 War and one
of the few lost on the headland itself was the 324-ton Glasgow
collier *Rubaan*, which struck the Dales in thick weather on the
night of 16 December 1939. She had been launched in 1921 as the
Tod Head by Cran & Somerville of Leith.

At the height of a gale on 26 November 1954 the tanker *Casino*
radioed that her crew had sighted a sinking vessel seventeen miles
south-west of the Lizard. So severe was the gale that the Lizard
lifeboat *Duke of York* could not be launched. A later message
from the tanker stated that the unknown vessel was believed to
have sunk, but that survivors had been seen in a boat, also men
in the sea. In appalling conditions, the lifeboat was launched with

coxswain George Mitchell at the helm, a name which has been connected with the Lizard lifeboat since 1859 when the first lifeboat was placed at the headland. The boat searched far and wide for survivors, only abandoning the search at dusk when there was no further hope. The day following the wreck, the Coverack boat recovered two bodies fourteen miles east of the Lizard which were identified as those of members of the crew of the Dutch coaster *Carpo*, bound from Swansea to Amsterdam with coal and a crew of twelve, none of whom survived.

Among more recent wrecks off the Lizard have been the 800-ton Glasgow motor-vessel *Citrine* which, while on passage from Llandulas to London with stone, radioed at 1 am on 2 January 1956 that a hard NW gale and heavy seas had stove in all her hatches, and that she was making for the shelter of the Lizard's eastern cliff. The Lizard and Cadgwith lifeboats found her between Black Head and the Lizard and stood by while her master tried to beach her at Kennack Sands. With less than a mile to go the coaster sank. All ten of the crew were saved by an extremely daring rescue, though the seventy-year old ship's cook later died from exposure.

During a tremendous ENE gale and blizzard on 29 December 1962, the Greenock motor-coaster *Ardgarry*, Swansea for Rouen with anthracite, vanished close to the Lizard. Two broken boats, one washed up at Scilly and the other near Land's End, were all that was ever found of her and her crew of eleven men.

CHAPTER SIX

KYNANCE COVE TO LOE BAR

AROUND the western corner of the Lizard Point lie the sands of Kynance, and then the high cliffs which form the outer horn of Mount's Bay. Exposed and precipitous, they lack even the slight shelter that the inner part of the bay sometimes gets from the high land above Penzance, and run almost unbroken from Rill Head to Gunwalloe, where they give way to Loe Bar, that great bank of sand which dams the estuary of Helston's River Cober and separates it from the sea. To sailing ships coming up Channel before a south-westerly gale, this six-mile stretch of coast offered a dead lee shore, from which there was no escape for any that failed to weather the Lizard or miscalculated a landfall in fog. Mullion Cove, half way along, was the only haven but it had grave disadvantages. There was no pier to shelter the little harbour until the 1870s, and even then it was all but inaccessible in bad weather, even to experienced local men. Half a mile offshore was a further hazard, the low rugged shape of Mullion Island, which stood in the path of any ship trying to wear off the coast or making for the cove. Other equally dangerous rocks and ledges fringed the cliffs; the Lion, Asparagus Island, Rill ledges, the Horse, and Kinsale Rock. To go south-eastwards meant facing the Lizard reefs, north-westwards the dangers of Gunwalloe and Loe Bar; for a sailing ship to be trapped under these cliffs meant certain destruction.

Loe Bar is mentioned in connection with some of the earliest Cornish wrecks known in any detail. On 20 February 1492 a wine-laden ship came ashore there, and one 'John Beull of Ambell' and a gang of heavily armed retainers seized eight butts of wine from the tenants of Winnianton Manor. The rest was saved and stored at nearby farms. John Beull must have been a daring man, as the lords of Winnianton were the powerful Arundel family, whose ruth-

138

less seizures of wrecks and wrecked goods all along the west Cornish shore were unparalleled, and usually unopposed.

Gunwalloe was the scene of an even bigger disturbance when on 19 January 1526 the great Flemish carrack *St Anthony*, owned by King John III of Portugal and laden with bullion, plate and silver to the value of £16,000, was driven ashore while bound from Flanders to Lisbon by 'an outrageous tempest of the sea'. She became a total wreck and only forty-five of the crew survived. Under the direction of Francis Person, the king's factor, the local people spent all that day and the following night salvaging specie. Two days after the wreck three local magistrates, William Godolphin, Thomas St Aubyn and John Millaton, captain of the Mount, accompanied by forty servants, attacked the crew and carried off goods valued at £10,000. When news of this outrage reached the King of Portugal he appealed to Henry VIII's Court of Star Chamber for speedy justice, and submitted the following inventory of the cargo:

'8,000 cakes of copper valued at £3,234; 18 cakes of silver at £2,250; silver vessels, ewers, pots, bowls and other plate worth £2,576; precious stones, pearls, chain, brooches and jewels worth £2,664; rich cloths of Arras and tapestry, £766; Holland cloth, linen etc, £610; satins, velvet and silk, £400; 21,000 barbers' bowls or basins, £164; candle sticks, £418; a great chest of salamanders and instruments of music, £50; complete suits of armour and harness for the king and his mount, £210; guns, both brass and iron, worth £2,740.'

In answer to the charges the three gentlemen alleged that Alvero de Mera, alias Diego de Alvero, the chief ruler of the cargo, fearing that the country people assisting the salvage would carry it off to their homes, had begged them to come to his aid. They did so at noon the morrow of the wreck, St Aubyn coming later to help, as they put it, 'the good work'. Furthermore, they declared that Diego Vaal, master of the ship, and El Jerome de Corfe, a Portuguese gentleman, entreated them to buy £20 worth of the salved goods, in order to provide them and the shipwrecked sailors with the necessities of life. This, they insisted, was all they had taken for themselves.

Winnianton Manor court rolls bear many references to treasure recovered in later years, and leave no doubt that a great deal was left unsalvaged. In 1529 John, son of James Tangy, complained that he had salvaged a silver crucifix, and Godolphin, St Aubyn and Millaton had seized it on the pretext that it belonged to some person drowned there whose goods they had bought. In 1575, Henry Williams found a silver flute weighing one pound, worth £4 13s 4d, and this was sent to Sir John Arundel as lord of the manor.

Legends of the wealth lost with the great carrack endured for generations, and unlikely though it may seem, another 'treasure ship' was lost there in the 1780s. Also Spanish, but unnamed, she struck below the cliffs midway between Gunwalloe Church Cove and the fishing cove half a mile westwards. She broached to and, according to legend, spilled her cargo of gold specie or pieces of silver, supposedly between two-and-a-half and nineteen tons, into a gully. In 1845 a limited company began work to recover the treasure; a dam was built across the mouth of the gully with the intention of pumping it dry at low water and digging into the exposed sands. The night before everything was ready, a south-west gale blew up, and by dawn the result of two months' labour had vanished. In 1847 another company hired a gang of tin miners to cut a passage and steps down the cliff and sink a shaft three feet in diameter and twenty-five feet deep in the rocks, in spite of operations being limited to low tide. The miners then drove forty feet under the gully, the idea being that embedded coins would simply drop into the tunnel. No coins appeared but the sea did, and the tinners escaped drowning by a hair's breadth, abandoning their tools in the rush for the surface. The breach could not be sealed, and for the second time a bid for the treasure of 'Dollar Cove', as the gully had become known, came to nothing.

Thirty years elapsed before a Mr Boyd, with two engineers, two divers, a diver's mate, four seamen, a cook and a large watchdog, set up their tents on the familiar camping ground above the cove. His idea was to pump out and sieve the contents of the 1847 shaft. A large suction pump, driven by a belt from a threshing machine on the clifftop, rapidly cleared the shaft and tunnel which had sealed itself against the sea, and the tools left by the miners were found, but no coins came to light. Sand was sucked and sieved by the ton, and when finances began to run low it was decided to blow up the tunnel in the hope of bringing the treasure

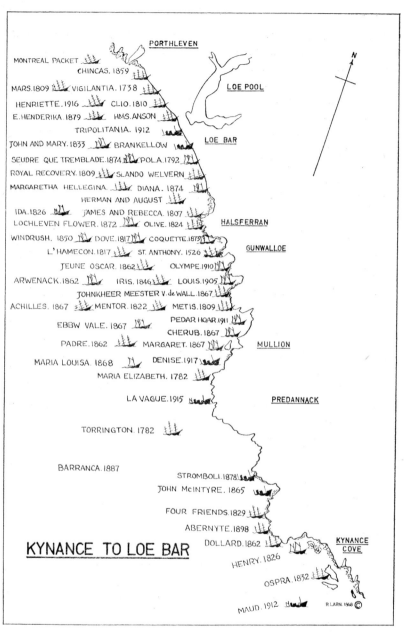

PORTHLEVEN

MONTREAL PACKET
CHINCAS. 1859

MARS.1809   VIGILANTIA. 1738

HENRIETTE.1916   CLIO. 1810

E.HENDERIKA. 1879   HMS.ANSON

TRIPOLITANIA. 1912

JOHN AND MARY. 1833   BRANKELLOW

SEUDRE QUE TREMBLADE.1874   POLA.1792

ROYAL RECOVERY. 1809   SLANDO WELVERN

MARGARETHA HELLEGINA.   DIANA. 1874

HERMAN AND AUGUST

IDA.1826   JAMES AND REBECCA. 1807

LOCHLEVEN FLOWER. 1872   OLIVE. 1824

WINDRUSH. 1850   DOVE.1817   COQUETTE.1873

L'HAMECON.1817   ST. ANTHONY. 1526

JEUNE OSCAR. 1862   OLYMPE.1910

ARWENACK.1862   IRIS.1846   LOUIS.1905

JOHNKHEER MEESTER V. de WALL.1867

ACHILLES. 1867   MENTOR. 1822   METIS.1809

PEDAR HOAR.1911

EBBW VALE. 1867   CHERUB. 1867

PADRE.1862   MARGARET.1867

MARIA LOUISA. 1868   DENISE.1917

MARIA ELIZABETH. 1782

LA VAGUE.1915

TORRINGTON. 1782

BARRANCA.1887

STROMBOLI.1878

JOHN McINTYRE. 1865

FOUR FRIENDS.1829

ABERNYTE.1898

DOLLARD.1862

HENRY. 1826

OSPRA. 1832

MAUD. 1912   R.LARN. 1968 ©

LOE POOL

LOE BAR

HALSFERRAN

GUNWALLOE

MULLION

PREDANNACK

KYNANCE COVE

KYNANCE TO LOE BAR

Wreck locations between Kynance Cove and Porthleven, with Loe Bar.

down with the roof. More sand passed through the sieves but without result, and the work was abandoned. Next day a man from Winnianton, exploring the vacated works, found two silver dollars within minutes.

Despite the succession of dismal failures, the buried wealth at Dollar Cove continued to attract treasure seekers. In 1877 Vivian, Grylls and Kendall, bankers of Helston, sold 200 shares at £3 each to finance another attempt. Their circular emphasised that not one but several ships carrying specie had been wrecked between 1784 and 1794. John Toy, promoter and manager of the scheme, had apparently spent years around the cove, occasionally picking up dollars, and was so convinced of success that he had taken out a licence to search for buried treasure, certain that divers working inside an iron caisson would succeed where other methods had failed. Nothing was found during the first season, and though an unspecified quantity of coin was recovered the following year, it was insufficient to repay the shareholders and the company went into voluntary liquidation.

There was yet another attempt in June 1890, involving the Liverpool salvage steamer *Zephyr*, which achieved little except the near drowning of her owner, captain and two men, when their boat was driven ashore while investigating the cove. The last man to fall for the lure of the treasure was a London businessman, who was so certain he could see the outline of the ship that he hired a sand suction dredger; thousands of tons of sand were shifted but no coins were found. Since then Dollar Cove has been quiet, though coins are still occasionally found, the last one in the summer of 1966, and several sub-aqua clubs have spent a diving holiday there but left empty-handed. There is vast movement of the seabed in Mount's Bay from time to time, and thousands of tons of sand can be scoured away or dumped overnight, and parts of Gunwalloe cove can alter in depth by as much as twenty feet at a time. Probably the treasure will never be found, if it is there at all, but there will always be legend, and men ready to try for hidden gold.

Besides treasure ships, there were many ordinary wrecks; the records of Winnianton's neighbouring manor, Predannack Wartha, reveal that at a Lady Day court in 1723 a case involved the salvage of a cable and anchor supposed to have been 'dropt by the

men of the shippe that was sank before Mullion Island'. In 1730
the salvors of two large anchors recovered from a wreck had to
pay the lord of Predannack 6s, a fifteenth of their value, the usual
charge for landing salvage on any of the beaches to which he
held wreck rights. This toll must have been more profitable when,
in 1744, William Johns of Penzance landed timber, anchors, guns,
barrels of pewter, bundles of iron hoops and copper, at Meres, the

Location of Spanish treasure ship wrecked in Gunwalloe Cove in the 1780s.

western side of Polurrian Cove near Mullion. The complete bottom
of a ship was landed at Mullion in 1755, and a large yard and
part of a sail at Porthpeor. Even more welcome debris of the ocean
were barrels of butter and wine, casks of pitch, hides and baulks
of timber, which was usually sold to the benefit of the manor.

Though details of salvaged goods and ships by name alone are
plentiful, it is not until the late eighteenth century that more
detailed stories come to light. In December 1779, the wine-laden
Dutch ship *Slando Welvern* was wrecked in Gunwalloe. In 1782
the brig *Maria Elizabeth*, Malaga for Hamburg with wine and

fruit, was lost below Predannack Head, and the ship *Torrington*, Oporto to Southampton with wines, on Loe Bar, during a winter's gale. The brig *Pola*, laden with hemp and cider, came ashore at Gunwalloe in January 1792. On 11 November 1799 the *Sherbourne Mercury* reported that 'on Monday night last a foreign vessel (brig) was wrecked at Mullion near the Lizard . . . her crew all perished.' There was an unusual wreck on Loe Bar on 18 May 1802, when a large French mackerel boat drove ashore during a heavy south-westerly gale. Eight of her crew were lost, but the six survivors, first fed and clothed by Mr John Rogers of Penrose, were lodged at the 'Fishmongers Arms', an old thatched inn that once stood close to the waterfront at Porthleven, until a subscription could be raised to send them home.

In the short space of seven weeks, in the winter of 1807, there were two disastrous wrecks within two miles of each other. The government transport *James and Rebecca* was returning home with a squadron of the 9th Light Dragoons, veterans of General White-lock's ill-fated Buenos Aires expedition, when shortly before mid-night on 6 November she struck below Halsferran cliffs just east of Gunwalloe. Of about 200 people on board, more than half were taken off in a rope chair along a hawser from the mizzen top, a line having been floated ashore with a lifebuoy, but about eighty people, including troopers, some of their wives and children, some of the crew, and Captain Rochester, were still aboard when she broke up at eleven o'clock next morning. Many were dragged from the sea alive, but ten sailors, twenty-eight troopers and three child-ren were lost. They were buried in a common grave on the clifftop at Halsferran, without Christian ceremony except for the simple recitation of the Lord's Prayer by a local man, among the last shipwreck victims to be buried in this way.

The frigate *Anson*, a 44-gun fifth-rater commanded by Captain Charles Lydiard, was towed out of Falmouth Roads by her boats on Christmas Eve 1807, watered and provisioned, to take up her station with the Brest blockade fleet. It was blowing hard from the WSW as she made down Channel, and when, forty-eight hours later, Ile de Bas off Ushant was sighted the storm was so bad that Captain Lydiard put back for Falmouth. The weather also drew in hazy and thick, and at 3 pm on 28 December he and the officers discovered that the *Anson* was well to leeward of the Lizard. Being a cut-down third-rater, she was no dainty sailer and efforts to clear the land failed. At dusk, off Loe Bar, the best bower anchor was let go and the topgallants were struck. The *Anson* rode safely until 5 am on the 29th, when her cables parted; the small bower was dropped and held her for another two hours, then it also parted and Captain Lydiard ordered the helmsman to run her ashore. She broached to and her mainmast fell, making a bridge of escape for many of her crew, while others were pulled ashore. Nevertheless, over 120 lives were lost, including Captain Lydiard who was

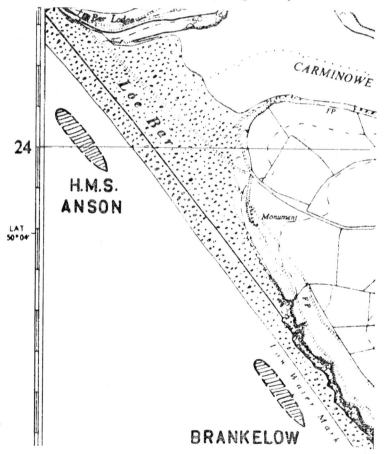

Locations of HMS *Anson*, wrecked on Loe Bar in 1807, and the *Brankelow* in 1890.

swept away while trying to save a young boy. He was interred with military honours at Falmouth, but at the request of his widow his body was removed to the family vault at Haslemere, Surrey. The wreck of the *Anson* inspired Henry Trengrouse, son of a Helston cabinet maker, to start experiments with a line-throwing apparatus which was later to contribute to the saving of life at sea.

The *Anson* must be one of the best-salvaged wrecks on the Cornish coast; she was dived on frequently during the late nineteenth century, and in April 1905 a Penzance company raised a large cannon. Several others were raised over the years, and a ship's bell which was found is reputed to be that of the *Anson*. In 1964, divers of the Naval Air Command sub-aqua club found and salvaged one of her huge brass pintle and rudder supports, and two iron cannon, a thirty-two pounder and a twenty-eight pounder. The larger one weighs three and a half tons and now stands outside Helston museum. There are still nine or ten cannon on the wreck site, but they are often buried beneath the shifting sand.

On 6 April 1808, the Hamburg ship *Herman and August*, Oporto to London with wine, was lost on Loe Bar in a south-west gale. Joseph Dale, a young Gunwalloe man who had distinguished himself during the wreck of the *James and Rebecca*, perished while trying to save a sailor who was eventually dragged from the sea by a man on horseback. On 6 January 1809, the 110-ton brig *Royal Recovery*, Corbett master, Liverpool for London with salt, was wrecked on Loe Bar; just over a month later the big sloop *Mars*, Captain May, outward bound from Dartmouth for Teneriffe, came ashore close by, and in November that year the barque *Metis*, Cunningham master, drove ashore at Polurrian. The Scots sloop *Clio* of Kincardine, bound from the Azores with barilla, and a wine-laden Spanish polacca brig, bound for Plymouth, were lost on Loe Bar in the same gale on 16 November. The Spaniards who had been twenty-four hours in the rigging were saved; Captain Marshall and the *Clio*'s owner were lost, leaving only three survivors from the sloop.

More fortunate were the crew of a French sloop, bound from Bordeaux to Rouen with wine, which was lost on Loe Bar on 24 October 1815, but Captain Guillème and eleven sailors perished when the brig *L'Hameçon*, Marseilles for Havre de Grace with wine, struck nearby at the height of a south-westerly gale on 24

Page 147: A clifftop grave of un-named sailors near Porthleven; circa 1740.

Page 148: (above) Relics recovered from Cornish wrecks for museum purposes. The intact dinner plate is from the liner *Mohegan*; (below) a muzzle-loading Lancaster gun recovered in May 1900 from the steamer *Czar*, wrecked at the Lizard in 1859.

January 1817. Two more lives were lost on 1 July that year, when the Dartmouth sloop *Dove*, Neath for Plymouth with culm, was wrecked in Gunwalloe fishing cove, just east of the church, where the victims were later buried. The brig *Montreal Packet* was embayed and driven on to Loe Bar on 11 December 1819, while bound from Tarragona to London with nuts; she lay deep in the surf and her crew of six were swept from the rigging before the helpless gaze of the people on the beach. On 5 March 1822 the brig *Mentor*, bound from the Azores to London with fruit, struck below the cliff just east of Gunwalloe. Captain Thomas Osborne, who had gone below after twelve hours of duty, and the crew, except for one man who was drowned, were marooned on a rock for two hours, the captain shivering in only his shirt. At low tide they got ashore and walked over the desolate moors to a farm. The preventive and customs men soon arrived but only a few boxes of oranges were salvaged before the *Mentor* broke up.

Though this melancholy catalogue continues well into the nine-teenth century, it is relieved by the daring rescues performed by local men. The first silver medals awarded by the R.N.L.I. went to William Rowe of Porthleven, for swimming out with a rope which saved the crew of the collier brig *Olive*, wrecked beneath Halsferran cliffs on 27 April 1824, and John Freeman of Gunwalloe for assisting him. Frederick Rogers of Penrose led a daring bid to save the captain and mate of the ketch *Ida* of Stockholm, wrecked on the western end of Loe Bar in a ssw gale on 5 February 1826, while bound from Messina with oranges. The rest of the crew, including the mate's two sons, had been swept overboard, but this was not the only loss of life; a young woman from Cury was carried into Loe Pool by breakers surging right over the bar, and a young Helston man was swept off the rocks. Another man, helping to unload the *Ida*'s cargo, received a fractured skull from a falling box of oranges, and a fisherman who tried to steal some fruit lost his fingers when a dragoon brought his sabre down across his hand.

There were many other gallant rescues; the crew of the 47-ton Scilly Isles schooner *John and Mary*, Captain Mumford, Cork to Plymouth with provisions, were dragged ashore when she struck Loe Bar on 7 February 1833. John Kitto of Porthleven waded out and flung a lifeline on board the Norwegian ketch *Elizabeth*, of and for Bergen from Ivica with salt, wrecked at Gunwalloe on 20

I

November 1846. Aided by Henry Cuttance of the 'Ship Inn', Halsferran, John Freeman, Solomon Rowe, John Sheppard and coastguards Bell and Cotton of Mullion, Kitto pulled Captain Niels
Ellertsen and three other men ashore, a brave act which brought
them an award from the King of Norway. Henry Cuttance, who
had himself avoided probable death on Loe Bar when he escaped
from the *Anson*'s press gang after they captured him in Falmouth
before her last voyage, figured prominently the following year when
the Russian barque *Iris* of Bjorneborg, 100 days out from Volo, in
Turkish Salonica, drove under the cliffs between Poldhu Cove and
Mullion on 10 October 1846. Her carpenter, bosun and an able
seaman reached a nearby farmhouse, and at dawn her captain
and a sailor were seen huddled in a cleft in an outlying rock.
Cuttance organised the rescue; a light line was flung across and
food and hot coffee sent over, which kept them alive until a hawser
and rope chair were rigged, and they were brought ashore after
being marooned for ten hours. But there was no such rescue for
Captain Samuel Brewer and the crew of the Falmouth schooner
Windrush, lost during a ssw gale on 24 November 1850 while
homeward bound from Malaga with oranges. A box of documents
identifying her was washed up as the sale of her cargo began on
Gunwalloe beach.

The largest sailing vessel wrecked on Loe Bar was the 1,894-ton
wooden full-rigger *Chincas*, Thomas Dawson master, which left
Liverpool in October 1859, bound for Rio de Janiero with 3,000
tons of cannel coal. Bad weather forced her into Cork for repairs
and she sailed again only to encounter the *Royal Charter* gale; Captain Dawson, his ship battered and leaking, put about for Falmouth,
but the gale veered and drove the *Chincas* into Mount's Bay. She
scraped past Mullion and anchored off Loe Bar, but the cables
soon parted and at 5 am on 7 November 1859 she was in the surf.
A Gunwalloe man alerted Porthleven coastguards, who found the
ship's great hulk broadside to the seas, dismasted and slowly driving
in over the sands. Captain Dawson and his crew waited until a
wave receded, then, running and wading, rushed up the beach into
the arms of their rescuers, but nine men were swept away and
drowned.

The tide ebbed and the bar was crowded with labourers, horses
and carts and hundreds of spectators, as gear and stores were

salvaged. At dusk, the flooding tide surged over the ship and within an hour the *Chincas*, which had been launched only the year before at Richibucto, New Brunswick, was shattered. Her cargo of cannel coal was eagerly scooped up by the villagers, but they did not realise its high burning qualities and many a cottage grate was cracked or stove burnt out that winter. Pieces of the coal can still be found, and they burn as brightly as they did over a hundred years ago.

One of the greatest hazards encountered in Mount's Bay was the sudden shift of the wind from eastwards to south-west; ships coming up Channel would be blown into the bay, those entering or leaving it would be pinned against the eastern cliffs, and chaos would result off Mullion, where scores of ketches, brigs and schooners usually anchored in the shelter of the tall cliffs. In 1862 alone, this veering of a storm caused four wrecks. The brig *Dollard* of Finsterwalde, Jan Koster master, Trieste to Falmouth with 1,100 quarters of wheat, failed to clear the Lizard in a gale which shifted to south-west by west. Her foreyard broke and at 6.30 am on 11 January she drove under Rill Head. Only an able seaman reached the rocks; Captain Koster, his son Jan who acted as mate, and four other men perished. Eleven days later a squally SSE breeze veered south-west and rose to a hard gale, and at dawn the survivors of the 460-ton Austrian barque *Pardre*, also bound from Trieste to Falmouth, were discovered marooned on Kinsale Rock at Poldhu. By the time help arrived only four Italian sailors were left to be rescued, Captain Bojdanovich, his wife and baby son, and ten men having been swept off the rock.

The brigantine *Jeune Oscar*, Algeria for Dunkirk with iron ore, was wrecked in the same way at Gunwalloe on 17 October, though all were saved by the Manby rocket apparatus, but there were no survivors from the 92-ton Truro schooner *Arwenack*, lost close by on 13 December while bound from Devoran to Swansea with copper. She had been dismasted off the Lizard and drifted into the bay unseen, and not until the southerly gale began to ease at dawn was her broken wreckage discovered under the Gunwalloe cliffs.

It was in Mullion Roads that the sudden veering of the wind had its worst effect, as the wrecks in January 1867 show. For two days a furious SE to ESE gale had raged and vessel after vessel had stood in beneath the shelter of Mullion cliffs. Suddenly, on the night of

5 January, the wind veered ssw and a frantic scramble ensued as nineteen schooners raised anchor and headed seaward. The *Cherub*, of Swansea, Cardiff to Caen with coals, and the *Margaret* of Teignmouth collided. George Mudge of the *Margaret* leapt on to the *Cherub*, only to find that she was crippled and uncontrollable, and he came ashore with her crew in their punt at Polurrian. At dawn the *Margaret*, her bows slightly damaged, lay anchored with three other schooners; the weather was sunny and clear, the gale dropped away to a light breeze, but the glass was falling, a heavy ground sea broke on the beach, and the tide was ebbing away from beneath them. As the *Margaret* was beyond rocket range, a mounted messenger was dispatched to Porthleven for the lifeboat, and when it was realised she would not arrive in time another messenger set off for the Lizard.

Attempts were made to get the *Margaret*'s crew to float a line ashore, but they remained seemingly ignorant of their peril, calmly leaning on the bulwarks waiting for rescue. At almost dead low water the schooner parted her cable, broached-to, broke in half amidships and disintegrated. Captain Bowden clung to the wreckage but though rocket lines were fired across him he failed to grasp them and was swept away among the wreckage. The other schooners lay further out in greater safety, and one, the *Hearty* of Jersey, took off the crew of the iron schooner *Ebbw Vale* of Swansea, Ardrossan to Plymouth with bar iron, and eventually landed them at Plymouth. The *Ebbw Vale* broke her cable in the rising south-west gale that evening and drove in close to the other two wrecks.

The crew of the *Margaret* perished in broad daylight; those on board the Dutch East Indiaman *Jonkheer Meester Van Der Wall Putteshock* died unseen in pitch darkness. Commanded by Captain Klass Lammerts, and 140 days out from Batavia for Amsterdam with passengers and a cargo of coffee, arrowroot and tin worth £50,000, she was sighted by a Mousehole pilot on the afternoon of 24 March 1867, tacking back and forth between the Lizard and Gunwalloe. The Mousehole pilots had recently had poor treatment from foreign captains, so when she appeared to be in no particular danger they decided not to go out. At 4 pm she missed stays off Mullion Island, but came around again and stood seaward. The strong ssw gale worsened, and darkness hid the *Jonkheer Meester*.

Nothing more was seen until 2 am, when distress rockets rose from the Mullion cliffs, and an hour later a coastguard found wreckage around Poldhu Cove and called out the rocket brigade and lifeboat.

Dawn came and more debris, including the entire poop of the barque, were found south of Poldhu, and the bodies of two women, one about forty and the other twenty-five, a three-day-old baby, and several sailors were picked up. Then a bedraggled sailor was discovered stumbling about the rocks. He was hurried to the vicarage, where the Rev Harvey interrogated him, but as he neither spoke nor understood English nothing could be learned except that he was Greek, and had joined the ship in Batavia. He knew neither her name nor that of her captain, nor could he give any reason for the lady's watch and chain in his possession. The mystery deepened at an inquest held at the old inn at Mullion the following week when, through an interpreter, he identified himself as Georgio Buffani, sailor on board he knew not what vessel. From a list of Dutch Indiamen he pointed out the *Kosmopoliet*, but shortly after the verdict was returned of death by drowning in the wreck of the *Kosmopoliet*, two Dutch sea captains arrived in Falmouth and expressed the opinion that, in all probability, the ship was really the *Jonkheer Meester*. This was finally proved when Captain Lammerts's masonic diploma was washed ashore. Most of the 850 tons of coffee also came ashore, together with the bamboo baskets holding the sugar, and a box containing gold coins, banknotes and jewellery. Later, a will, identifying one of the women as a governess retiring after years in India, was found in the broken poop section. Local fishermen using a waterglass and long tongs recovered the tin blocks from six fathoms, receiving £15 per ton salvaged.

Other ships followed the *Jonkheer Meester* to a violent end on these cliffs. On 21 October 1867 the Glasgow barque *Achilles*, Miramichi to London with log wood, was wrecked at Polurrian in fog and a strong south-west wind, without loss of life. The 80-ton Padstow smack *Maria Louisa*, John Massey master, Plymouth to Penzance with slates, was lost on the Treguin Rock at the tip of Mullion Island, during a WNW gale on 22 January 1868. Mullion's new lifeboat, the result of the wrecks of the *Margaret* and the *Jonkheer Meester*, could not launch through the tremendous surf and all on board died. It was particularly tragic as the smack had been bought by public subscription for Captain Casey of Padstow after he had been crippled in a wreck off the north coast in 1859. Halsferran cliffs saw yet another serious wreck on 23 November 1872, when the Sunderland barque *Lochleven Flower*, Berdyansk to Falmouth with wheat, drove ashore during a severe SSW gale, her master, Captain Hallywell, and his crew being drowned while trying to row through the surf on Loe Bar.

Mullion lifeboat made a bid to save life on 2 March 1873, when the 617-ton iron barque *Boyne* of Scarborough, Wheelan master, 120 days out from Samarang to Falmouth with sugar, struck Meres ledges on the western side of Polurrian Cove. She broached-to in heavy seas, and as her crew struggled to secure a rocket line from the cliffs she broke in half. Even as the lifeboat, the *Daniel J Draper*, approached, Captain Wheelan was drowned trying to swim ashore, and the two men by then left aboard were swept off as the lifeboat was almost within reach. The only survivors were three able seamen and an apprentice who got away in a boat just before the barque struck, and managed to pull into Mullion.

On 26 November 1873 the French pitwood schooner *Coquette* of Douarnenez was wrecked under Halsferran cliffs, her cabin boy being drowned. Another French schooner laden with pitwood, the *Seudre que Tremblade* of Marennes, Honnebont to Cardiff, was wrecked on Loe Bar during a SSW gale on 22 September 1874; even as late as this the reputation of the Mount's Bay wreckers caused Captain Perrot and his crew to shun their rescuers until the customs men arrived. One of the last sailing ships lost at Gunwalloe was the 350-ton Austrian barque *Diana*, Bonafaccio Catarnich master, crippled off the Wolf Rock by a gale which backed from north-west to south-west, while on voyage from Falmouth to Dublin with wheat from Trieste, on 8 December 1874. The captain and the pilot decided to put back for Falmouth, but the ship was embayed and driven ashore at Creeg-an-Pella, a small cove east of Gunwalloe. Her crew were saved by rocket line, but hopes of refloating the eight-year old barque were dashed when she broke up a month later in a south-westerly gale.

The effect of the new Wolf Rock lighthouse, and improvements to those at the Lizard and Longships, coupled with the decline of certain types of sailing ship, resulted in a decrease in wrecks in this area from the late 1870s onwards. Less than a dozen are recorded between 1877 and 1916. The Dutch galliot *Margaretha*

Hellegina, bound from Larahie to Gloucester with beans, was beached and broke up on Loe Bar after striking a submerged rock on 22 April 1877. Another Dutch galliot, the *Elizabeth Henderika,* was lost at Poldhu Cove on 31 December 1879, on voyage from Le Havre to Bilboa with empty casks. The Glasgow iron ship *Barranca,* nine days out from the Thames with general cargo for East London, foundered between Kynance and Loe Bar on 22 January 1887. Distress guns were heard in the foggy darkness and at dawn her wreckage strewed the rocks, no survivors being left to tell how it happened.

Fog also caused the wreck of the 700-ton Glasgow iron barque *Abernyte,* Cardwell master, Caleta Buena for Falmouth with nitrates, under Rill Head on 8 May 1898. Her crew rowed sea-wards, leaving the barque slowly settling below the cliffs, and were picked up at dawn by Falmouth pilot cutter No 6. The *Abernyte,* launched at Dumbarton in 1875 by Mackellar & Co, broke up in heavy ground seas during the evening. She was not the first wreck about the Rill; the Rochester schooner *Henry,* from Sicily with lemons, was lost in a nearby gully on 8 February 1826; the brig *Four Friends,* Liverpool for Plymouth with salt, ran into the 'Pound' on 17 October 1829, and the Danish brig *Ospra,* Havana for Hamburg with coffee and sugar, was preserved in local legend as the 'coffee wreck' when she struck Asparagus Island in fog on 6 May 1832.

Some of the last wrecks between Mullion and Loe Bar were French ships. The 145-ton ketch *Louis* of Boulogne was wrecked on Cricabello Point, near Poldhu Cove, on 26 March 1905, while bound from Guernsey to Llanelly with stone. Captain Gonyean was drowned in his cabin while trying to secure his papers and money, and able seaman Pierre Pettiton drowned while swimming ashore, but the mate and two seamen reached the rocks safely. A south-westerly gale blew the 180-ton schooner *Olympe,* of and from Lannion for Swansea with pitwood, into Gunwalloe Church Cove on 3 October 1910. Captain Jean Francois Bonami and his crew were hauled through the surf by a human chain formed by workers from the nearby Poldhu Hotel. A year later the 69-ton ketch *Pedar Hoar* of Bordeaux, also laden with pitwood, from Granville to Wales, caught fire and sank off Mullion in an ESE gale on 11 October 1911, and the last sailing ship actually wrecked on

Loe Bar was the brigantine *Henriette*, lost during dense fog on 13 October 1916.

In comparison with the vast number of sailing ships, less than a dozen steamers have been wrecked in this part of Mount's Bay. Two of the earliest were in the gorge-like cove of Gue Graze, between Mullion and Kynance. On 17 April 1865 the 630-ton iron steamer *John MacIntyre* of Glasgow, London for Cardiff in ballast, clipped a rock off the Lizard. She ran for Penzance but, filling fast, had to be beached below Gue Graze. Tugs and salvage lighters from Falmouth began work, the holes were plugged with bags of Kynance clay, and the steamer, which had been launched only two years before by Palmers of Newcastle, was eventually refloated. Thirteen years later the 734-ton iron steamer *Stromboli*, bound from Le Havre to Liverpool with general cargo and passengers, steamed too close to the Lizard while signalling Lloyd's station and struck the Maenheere Rock. With two of the five watertight compartments holed, Captain Jones steered into Mount's Bay, but flooding in the engine room forced him to beach her on the north-west tip of Gew Graze. The weather was fine and calm, and the sixteen passengers and most of the crew, including the second officer who had been wrecked at the Lizard in 1856 in the steamer *Zebra*, were helped ashore by the coastguards, and luggage, deck fittings, stores and some cargo were salvaged. Tugs arrived from Falmouth at noon, but the *Stromboli*, which had been launched in 1856 by J L Thompson of Glasgow for the Mediterranean service of Burns & MacIver (later Cunard Steamship Co), was doomed. By 5 pm she was submerged and during the night a heavy swell broke her in two. Most of her cargo of sugar, silk, cambrics and velveteens was ruined by the sea. The wreck was salvaged in later years and all that now remains is a boiler and some iron plating.

Three other steamers were lost around Kynance and Mullion; the steam trawler *Maud* of Fleetwood broke tow off the Lizard on 11 February 1912 while bound from the Isle of Man, where she had stranded, to Hull for repairs. Her crew reached the tug safely, but the *Maud* was swept ashore at Kynance. Another steam trawler, the *La Vague* of Boulogne, homeward bound from the fishing grounds, was lost in fog under Vellan Head on 9 June, 1915, and in the same month in 1917 the *Denise* of Caen, built by Grahams of Sunderland in 1912, was wrecked half a mile south of

Page 157: Eighteenth-century soldiers meet resistance from wreckers on the shores of Mount's Bay.

Page 158: (above) An early photograph; the Sunderland barque *William* wrecked in Porthleven harbour on 24 November 1865; (below) the last sailing ship wrecked near Porthleven, the French schooner *St Anne*, lost during a sw gale on 3 November 1931.

Page 159: (above) The Penzance schooner *Mary Hannah* wrecked outside Newlyn harbour on 3 February 1899; (below) the Newcastle steamer *Cragoswald* firmly impaled on Low Lee ledge on 30 April 1911. She survived to be torpedoed in the 1914-18 war.

Page 160: The Boulogne trawler *Marguerite*, wrecked in Talland Bay in fog on 2 May 1922.

Location of the 734-ton steamer *Stromboli*, wrecked on the tip of Gew-Graze in 1878.

Mullion near Men-te-heul. She lies in forty feet of water under high cliffs and although very broken up some fittings, including anchor cable, bollards and two boilers, are still there.

The two largest steamers were wrecked further west, and though separated by over twenty years each provoked a similar surge of salvage activity. The 1,661-ton brigantine-rigged *Brankelow* of Liverpool was under charter to the Russian government, laden with coal from Cardiff to Kronstadt, when she grounded near Gunwalloe in a light south-westerly breeze and slight haze at 12.30 am on 21 April 1890. Porthleven LSA soon fired a rocket line aboard but it was mysteriously severed, a boat trying to pull ashore capsized and confusion reigned for some time. Finally her crew of twenty-nine did come ashore, except for Captain Stewart who remained

on board until late afternoon, by which time the *Brankelow* was
settling deep into the sands. Tugs and salvage gear were rushed
to Gunwalloe, but a strong south-west gale on 26 April put an
end to operations, and on 9 May the underwriters, via Edward
Mitchell, auctioneer of Lelant, offered her for sale. Prices were
ridiculous even for those days; the coal cargo, valued at £825,
brought a top bid of £1 before it was withdrawn, and the
Brankelow, worth £25,000 afloat, was sold to a London firm for
£405. They re-sold her that evening for £840, but further storms
caused her new owners to abandon hopes of refloating her, and
the engines and all fittings were removed. On 11 June, again under
new ownership, the now empty hulk broke in three during a gale,
but salvage work continued until she broke up completely that
autumn. The *Brankelow*, which was owned by the Brankelow
Steamship Co, was built by M Pearse of Stockton in 1882.

Location of the steamer *Denise* of Caen, wrecked half a mile south of
Mullion in 1917.

The 2,297-ton steamer *Tripolitania* of Genoa sailed from her home port on 18 December 1912, in water ballast for Barry docks, under the command of Captain Elia Reppito, and when deep in the Bay of Biscay encountered the worst storm to sweep the Channel for fifty years. Gusting to over 100 mph, the wsw gale caught her high-riding hull as it would a sail, and by 6 am on Boxing Day, when the Wolf Rock was sighted, she was in grave difficulties. She scraped past the Land's End cliffs, and though water was pumped into her holds to force her deeper into the sea, she drove on. By noon the *Tripolitania* was inside the Lizard and, knowing she was doomed, Captain Reppito called the crew on to the bridge and told them that he was going to beach on Loe Bar. At full speed she surged up the coast, then the wheel was put hard over and she was run ashore in heavy surf. Without waiting for rescue to arrive, the Italians flung a rope over the bows and though the first man who slid down was swept away, twenty-seven others got safely ashore. During the next few days the *Tripolitania* was driven farther up the bar sands, but she was little damaged and the work of refloating her began. Scores of labourers dug away the sand which continually built up around her, coffer dams were erected and channels cut back to the sea. Months passed, and she still remained on the bar. In August 1913 hopes of salvage were still good, but on 4 November a south-west gale and high spring tide destroyed a year's work in a night. By dawn she had wallowed her way 300 yards further inshore and settled down even deeper; over the next two years she was broken up where she lay. The *Tripolitania* was launched on the Mersey in 1905 as the *Drumgarth*, for John Heron & Co of Liverpool. She later became the *Lord Cromer*, and in December 1911 passed to Luigi Pillagura of Genoa. By a coincidence, her last captain before she was sold to the Italians was Captain J J Beckerleg of Marazion, whose home was only half a dozen miles from Loe Bar.

CHAPTER SEVEN

MOUNT'S BAY

'From Wicked Rocks and Shelving Sands,
From Breague and Germoe men's hands,
Dear Lord Deliver Us.'

SO ran the old mariner's prayer, and well might he pray for deliverance from the inhabitants of the eastern shores of Mount's Bay, for even at a period when it was the local custom to loot stranded ships and maltreat their crews, they earned themselves the worst reputation for wrecking in the whole of Cornwall. A letter written in 1710 described the tinners of Germoe as 'a mad people, without fear of God or of the world', and a hundred years later they would still 'cut a large trading vessel to pieces on one tide . . . strip half-dead men of their clothing, and cut down all who resist them'. Even when ships were driven ashore relatively undamaged, they would in a matter of hours become a looted shambles as the tinners from the great mines of Wheal Vor and Wheal Reath, which lay in the wild moors between the coast and the Godolphin Hills, descended in a ravening horde. Everything that could be was battered loose, wrenched free or just lifted off the decks, and often the very hull timbers themselves would be stolen. The wreckers would not only fell anyone who tried to stop them; they often fought savagely among themselves, and if the cargo happened to be wines or spirits, the results could be appalling. Casks and barrels would be broached, and a drunken mob of men, women and children would run riot on the beach. Few people, even representatives of authority, dared to interfere, and one Helston man who helped the authorities in an abortive attempt to save a Dutch ship lost near Porthleven in the 1750s was caught on the way home through the woods near the town and given a beating which left him half dead by the roadside.

Occasionally, when the collector of customs and the magistrates had military support, a wreck might be protected from the ravages of the local people. When the *Naboth's Vineyard* of Rotterdam, homeward bound from Bayonne with a cargo of wine, was wrecked near Porthleven on 29 December 1738, the authorities, backed by soldiers, were able to get there in time, and to the jeers and threats of a large gathering of tinners, whisk the barrels away to the customs store at Penzance. It was a very different story in December 1748, when another Dutch merchantman, the *Yonge Alcida*, bound from Bordeaux to Amsterdam with wines, struck and went to pieces on Porthleven beach. The customs officer, one Sampson who had been stationed in the village for only six months, was forced to stand by, powerless, as the wines disappeared down the throats of the tinners and fishermen. What was not drunk on the beach was trundled away into the countryside, meanwhile the wives and sons of the wreckers dragged up timbers, cordage and anything else of value, and plundered the Dutchmen's sea-chests.

Not surprisingly, the following month the frustrated Mr Sampson is found writing a bitter letter of complaint to the commissioners of customs, stating that unless troops could be called upon to reinforce him it would be quite impossible to keep order and prevent wrecking. But because of the interminable wars against the French, few soldiers could be spared for home garrison duty, especially in out of the way corners like Cornwall. At the time the *Yonge Alcida* was wrecked there were only sixty redcoats stationed between Penzance and the Tamar, and they had just been sent to Scotland to help police the clans, still smarting under the repression of the Stuart Rebellion.

It was not only the poor who indulged in such 'wrecking'; during a search for the looted cargo of the *Lady Lucy* of Rotterdam, wrecked off Porthleven in 1739, the customs officers discovered four hogsheads of best cognac in the cellar of the vicar of Cury, a few miles from the scene of the wreck. Similar stories were commonplace along the eastern shores of Mount's Bay two hundred years ago, and they were not confined solely to Porthleven; Prussia Cove, Praa Sands, and the long sweep of the Eastern Green, from Marazion to Penzance, all witnessed scenes of pillage, drunkenness and wholesale rioting.

The London *General Evening Post* for 7 March 1751 reported that when a large ship laden with brandy and fruit drove ashore near Porthleven on 2 March and her crew were drowned, the 'cliffs as usual were covered with hundreds of greedy cormorants, waiting for their prey, which no sooner came within their reach, but was swallowed up by them, more barbarous in their nature than cannibals'.

Other early wrecks include the *Adriana*, Nicholas Hans master, of and for Amsterdam from Bordeaux with 800 hogsheads of wine, east of St Michael's Mount on 3 January 1756; the *Charming Molly*, Captain Power, of and from Cork for Portsmouth with butter, brandy and tallow, somewhere on the eastern shore on 20 December 1759, with one man lost; and the *Favourite* of New York, also wrecked somewhere on the eastern land, on 31 March 1790. Four of the five drowned on her were recovered and buried at Germoe, one of the bodies having a quilted girdle containing forty-two golden guineas.

A hard equinoctial gale blew the East Indiaman *Delhi*, deep laden for London with spices, coffee, and indigo, into Mount's Bay shortly before dawn on 20 October 1815. She dropped anchor close to St Michael's Mount, but it dragged and Captain Gowing ordered the second to be let go. In their near panic the crew cut the stopper and the anchor got caught up on the gunwale, leaving the *Delhi* helpless on the edge of the surf. A pilot cutter tried to reach her, and was almost alongside when the crew again panicked and cut away the masts, leaving the ship to drive on to the beach near Marazion. Although the seas were high, all on board got ashore safely, but as the tide ebbed from around the *Delhi* several hundred pairs of eyes were riveted on the rich bales and casks that were being stacked on the beach. A large crowd began to mill around threateningly, and the Lloyd's agent from Penzance and several trustworthy local men were slowly hemmed in. The situation looked ugly until Mr Oxnam, a merchant of the town who was also a colonel in the yeomanry, called out his men and put a cordon across the beach to keep the crowd at bay.

Meanwhile the gale had sent another vessel, the Russian galliot *Flora*, bound from Bordeaux to Riga in the Baltic with wines, on to the shore at Praa Sands. She struck at high water, so was all too easily accessible from the beach on the ebb. The tinners, joined by many others who had been baulked of their loot at Marazion, swarmed all over the galliot. They stole everything, even the clothes off the backs of the crew. Colonel Oxnam and his men already had their hands full protecting the *Delhi*, and by the time they had ridden over the downs above Praa Sands it was too late. The *Flora* was in pieces, and even then they had difficulty in driving the drunken mob away from the wreck and rescuing the naked and exhausted Russian crew.

On 4 January 1817 the London brig *Resolution*, homeward bound with a big cargo of wines and oranges from Oporto, was driven on to the beach at Porthleven, a little to the east of the 'Fishmonger's Arms'. As usual, the tinners and fishermen, accompanied by most of the population from Porthleven to Prussia Cove, pounced on the cargo of wines and within an hour a regular orgy was in full swing around the stranded brig. A customs man galloped off to Falmouth with the news and returned with a sergeant, three corporals and twelve privates of the Inniskilling Dragoons, then garrisoning the fort at Pendennis Castle. But not even the presence of armed troopers could stop the looting, and the dragoons were soon driven from the beach by the jeering mob who continued their rioting throughout that night and all the next day. One drunken man fell off the rocks and was drowned, another collapsed and died on the way home, and many others nearly died of alcoholic poisoning. On the night of the 5th twenty more Inniskillings arrived, and the riot was at an end. Of the *Resolution*'s cargo of 363 pipes and 12 hogsheads of port wine, only fifty-nine were recovered intact and lodged safely in the newly-built custom house on the western side of the harbour. After a dispute concerning the wine between the collector and a Falmouth gentleman, it was sold for nearly a thousand pounds. It found its way into the cellars of most of the local gentry, and for many years special occasions, births and marriages were toasted in 'old Resolution'.

In April of the following year the Swedish brig *Victoria*, bound from Cette, in Southern France, to Amsterdam, missed stays while running for shelter and drove ashore just outside Penzance harbour. Almost within minutes, the local people had scrambled aboard and were still busy stealing her stores and deck gear when a detachment of the Penzance Yeomanry, under the command of a Lieutenant Johns, galloped up with the customs men and magistrates. The wreckers hurriedly made off across the beach, pursued by the cavalry, and the brig's cargo was unloaded and escorted into Penzance. Hardly had the last wagon-load been stacked in the custom house cellars than Lieutenant Johns and his troopers had to set off for Hayle, where they were urgently needed to protect three more wrecks from the depredations of the wreckers who lived along the desolate shores of St Ives Bay.

But there was another side to the coin, and many local men lost their lives in trying to rescue the crews of wrecked ships. In January 1796 a large transport, bound from Cork to Portsmouth with the 26th Dragoons on board, parted from her convoy, became embayed and ran ashore less than a cable's length from the rocks at Porthleven. Despite huge seas, 'nine men of Breague' joined themselves by rope and waded out towards her, but they were engulfed by a great breaker and never seen again. Soon afterwards the transport went to pieces and not one of the 400 officers, troopers and sailors on board survived. Sixteen years later the entire crew of a Swedish ship, wrecked not far away, were saved by the exertions of a local man named Tobias Roberts, who had already distinguished himself during the loss of the *Anson* in 1807.

In 1828 there was again heroism instead of brutality, when the South Sea whaler *Phoenix* was lost at Praa Sands. She was only a fortnight out of the Thames, bound for the Pacific on a three-year voyage, when she ran into a heavy gale west of the Scillies and, crippled aloft, had to turn and fly before the storm for the shelter of Falmouth. The weather was very thick, and although he was not sure of his position her master, Captain John Phillips, let her run free. It was a fatal mistake; the *Phoenix* was blown deep into Mount's Bay and at 4 am on 7 December 1828 she was on the Stones reef off Praa Sands. Two seamen and four apprentices got clear to seaward in a boat, but the mate and seven men who tried to get ashore through the surf were capsized. This time it was 'eight seamen of Helston' who plunged in with a rope about their waists and dragged the struggling sailors to safety. The *Phoenix* meanwhile washed off the reef and drove on to the sands where she was battered to pieces, and Captain Phillips, his chief mate and thirteen men died with her. Those still drifting offshore were rescued by a gig manned by an assortment of coastguards, pilots and fishermen, who had pulled through mountainous seas to reach them.

In 1841 a similar rescue bid by three coastguards and two volunteers ended in disaster, when a schooner was seen rolling in heavy

Page 169: The Penlee lifeboat approaching the 30,000-ton battleship *Warspite*, wrecked at Prussia Cove on 23 April 1947 while on her way to the breaker's yard.

Page 170: (above) German-built, British-owned, and destined for Japan, the 4,068-ton steamer *Ansgir* was wrecked near Mousehole on 1 December 1920; (below) the steamers *South America* and *Abertay* wrecked side by side in St Loy Bay in 1912.

seas off Praa Sands, without masts or rigging, and they put off to her in the coastguard galley. This was a stout, seaworthy craft, but the surf at Praa that morning was appalling, and they had not gone far before a wave turned the galley over and all were drowned. Only half an hour later the revenue cutter *Sylvia* and a Dartmouth trawler, the *Four Brothers*, reached the schooner, the Cardiff-owned *Mary Stewart* bound for Constantinople with iron, and took off her crew of eleven. Next day the schooner herself was towed in, leaving only the rescuers as the victims of an unnecessary accident.

The winds which brought the wreckers their prey were the westerly gales, which come howling up out of the Atlantic during the autumn and winter months. Once a brig, barque or schooner was blown deep into Mount's Bay, she was trapped in the surf-swept northern corner, around the little monastery island of St Michael's Mount, with little chance of ever getting back into the open channel. To escape by sailing along under the eastern cliffs in the hope of eventually rounding the Lizard was to court almost certain disaster in the breakers of Praa Sands or Loe Bar, or on the rocks beneath the big headlands of Cudden, Trewavas or Rinsey. There was the added danger of outlying reefs; the Willow, a short distance south-west of Trewavas Head, and the Stones, a mile off Praa Sands, barely awash at low water, and a deadly menace to ships beating to east or west close to the shore.

Penzance, the only real port of refuge in bad weather, lay on the opposite side of the bay, a dead beat to windward along the fringes of the Eastern Green, a mile and a half of wave-pounded sands, with the Long Rock, the Hogus and the Cressars standing out of the shallow water. Even when a distressed ship did arrive off the harbour mouth at Penzance, she could still meet destruction by colliding with the pier wall, or with another ship similarly running for shelter. Action by the pilot gigs or lifeboat was usually prompt and often daring, but even so, many sailing vessels were lost while trying to enter the harbour.

In February 1855 a fleet of sixty sail had been sheltering in Mount's Bay for several days when, on the morning of the 9th, the strong south-easterly breeze veered south-west and freshened to a hard gale. Most of the vessels made Penzance or ran seawards, but the Welsh brig *Diana*, Samuel Hollow master, Swansea for Southampton with coal, was wrecked when only yards from safety. As

K

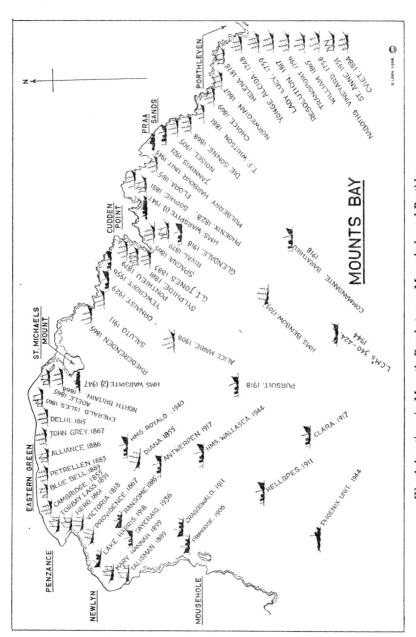

Wreck locations in Mount's Bay between Mousehole and Porthleven.

she rounded the lighthouse pier her starboard tiller chain parted and she was driven stern first on to the rocks behind. Ropes were flung down to the brig from the harbour wall and eight men were hauled up safely. Captain Hollow collected three broken ribs on the way up, but even so he was lucky. The ninth man, a young St Ives sailor called William Trevorrow, got entangled in some wreckage and was killed when he fell between the side of the brig and the quay wall. A little later the barque *Cambridge* of Littlehampton, homeward bound from Swansea with culm, went ashore off the railway-station breakwater. She had been in a collision during the scramble for the safety of the harbour and her stern was smashed. She limped in, but when almost inside the pier an iron bar used as a temporary tiller snapped and she drifted away to leeward. The crew of the *Cambridge* were unharmed, and the sails, yards and stores were removed from her damaged hull.

It was not often that a sailing ship was embayed and yet managed to reach Penzance; even if she did, she was not always any safer. During one of the worst storms in history to sweep West Cornwall, in March 1867, the Plymouth barque *Gambia* was embayed, and shortly before noon, with her cargo of beer and spirits washing about in five feet of water, put down her helm and ran for Penzance. She 'came on bravely', to quote a contemporary newspaper, but just as she turned to come in a big sea smashed her rudder and she sheered off and hit the pierhead. With bowsprit gone and bows stove in, she wallowed clear, straight into the path of the Jersey collier brig *Providence*, which had come storming up from westwards under bare poles. The noise of the *Gambia* striking the granite wall had hardly echoed through the dockside streets when there came another rending crash as the brig tore into her amidships. Battered and out of control, the barque had the good fortune to be washed into the harbour mouth; it was the *Providence* which was carried away to leeward by the heavy seas. She crashed into the opposite pier wall and hung there just long enough for her crew to leap to safety. Then she drifted on to the beach in front of the long stone breakwater which protected the railway station from the worst of the seas, and by dusk she was a wreck.

Such collisions were not uncommon, and before the harbour works were extended and the basin and lock gates erected Penzance could at times be a highly dangerous place in which to ride out a gale. A heavy run of sea swirling around and between the piers could play havoc among the ranks of moored ships, and many were the smashed yards, bulwarks and figureheads when the forest of masts below the tower of St Mary's Church got entangled in a hard blow. If the storm was really bad, the backwash of the seas might pluck a vessel from her moorings and out into the surf off the station breakwater or Chyandour, a few hundred yards farther on. The 123-ton polacca brig *Hero* of Bideford broke loose in one such gale, on 18 February 1861. She had put in with a damaged foremast while on voyage from Newport to Plymouth with coal. The harbour was crowded with windbound ships, so she tied up to a buoy in the middle of the harbour with the *John*, also of Bideford, and the *George* of St Ives.

By evening the wind had freshened to a SSW gale and Captain Fowler was warned that the *Hero* was in a dangerous place, so he went aboard to check the moorings. At 10.30 pm all three broke adrift. The *George* and the *John* hoisted sail and beached in the harbour, but the *Hero* swung out into the harbour mouth. The captain at first refused help from a pilot gig; two of the *John*'s crew went aboard to lend a hand, but soon the *Hero* was in serious trouble and Captain Fowler recalled the gig to take a hawser back to the buoy. It parted, a second was too short, and then the gig was disabled. Two local men who had also gone aboard the *Hero* returned to their boat, advising Captain Fowler and his crew to abandon ship as well, as it was now too late to save her. They agreed but dallied, the crew to collect their belongings and the captain going below to fetch his watch, and by the time they put off in their boat they had lost the shelter of the pier and were capsized. Only young William Jupp, of Southsea, survived, rescued by a rope from the pierhead; Captain Fowler, three of the *Hero*'s crew and two of the *John*'s crew were drowned. The *Hero* drifted on to the rocks below the railway station and by daylight was gutted and broken.

When a gale blew hard from the south-west, Porthleven was the worst place for a sailing ship to run to for shelter; hardly safer was the harbour at St Michael's Mount, where Norwegian timber used to be unloaded for pitwood in the tin mines. One of the most spectacular shipwrecks in the whole of Mount's Bay happened at Porthleven on 24 November 1865. A southerly gale had been blowing for three days, and already the *Adele*, the *Emerald Isles*, the *Spragna*, the *Tobacco*, the *Rhederenden* and an unknown schooner had been lost or stranded between Eastern Green and Cudden Point. At the height of the storm the 300-ton Sunderland barque *William*, Wright master, from Odessa, in the Black Sea, to Falmouth for orders with a cargo of linseed, ran for Porthleven's narrow, rock-strewn harbour entrance. A flag was hoisted to guide her in and as she scraped past the outer pier one of her crew, over-anxious to save himself, leapt on to the jetty. His feet had barely touched the smooth granite flagstones when a wave knocked him over the edge. Anthony Pascoe, a local man who rushed out to his assistance, was also swept into the sea, but his brother managed to drag him out. The unfortunate sailor failed to get hold of any of the lifebuoys thrown to him and soon vanished. The *William* careered on into the harbour, missed the inner entrance and smashed her bows against the jetty. The force of the sea jammed her into the angle of the wall, with her stern resting on the roadway twenty feet above. Captain Wright and his exhausted crew climbed ashore over the broken wreckage of the poop. Before the *William* broke up, an early photographer braved the wind and flying spray to set up his apparatus and take what must be one of the earliest Cornish wreck photographs. (See page 158)

When lifeboat stations were established at Penzance and Porth-leven in the 1860s, the people of Mount's Bay showed that they could be as courageous in saving ships and lives as they had been callous in destroying them in the past. In the great storm of 5-7 January 1867 four big schooners and the 500-ton Glasgow barque *John Grey* were lost within half a mile of the Mount, and a Nor-wegian ship went to pieces under Rinsey Head without a single survivor. The *John Grey*, forty days out from Demerara, for the Thames, with a cargo of rum, sugar and coconuts, had lost half her original crew through fever in the West Indies, and Captain Blackney had had to sign on anybody he could get hold of for the voyage home. She arrived off Scilly just after Christmas 1866, but the weather turned bad and for another ten days she thrashed to and fro in the mouth of the Channel. High winds and heavy seas ripped her sails and smashed yards and bulwarks, and on 4 January a full gale from the south swept down on her. At dawn on the 6th the wind fell away and Captain Blackney took advantage of the favourable breeze, but the lull only lasted a few hours and by nightfall the *John Grey* was again rolling through a rising sea and a south-westerly gale.

By daylight on 7 January the barque had been carried deep into Mount's Bay. The gale veered SSW and she was pinned close in to the cliffs between the Mount and Porthleven. Nothing would make her go against the storm, and the day passed with the *John Grey* beating up and down, slowly drifting closer to the rocks. As dusk fell a Penzance pilot cutter offered help but the captain, for reasons of his own, curtly refused; it was his undoing, for half an hour later when the barque floundered in the shoals off Cudden Point and he recalled the pilots, they were unable to get near him. The *John Grey* drifted to leeward and ran into the breakers between the Long Rock and the Hogus rocks, a short way west of the Mount. The morale of the scratch crew was not up to the strain of their ordeal, and they had sought to restore it from the cargo of rum. To quell his drunken sailors, Captain Blackney got his revolver from the cabin and for the next five hours he and his crew faced each other while the barque rolled and shuddered in the surf.

At Penzance, the lifeboat crew were having their own troubles. One wheel of the lifeboat carriage had broken on the way home from Longrock two nights previously, after rescuing the crews of the stranded schooners, and the call to go out to the *John Grey* found them immobile. The town was searched for suitable wheels; even a pair off a heavy granite wagon from a local quarry had crumpled under the four-ton weight of the lifeboat. A mason's drag was found at Alverton, at the other end of the town, which would support the carriage and at last the lifeboat left Penzance. The seven-horse team soon covered the short distance to Longrock, but even so it was nearly eleven o'clock at night before they lumbered on to the sands. Two or three hundred men risked life and limb to launch the lifeboat into the surf. The coxswain, Thomas Carbis, an experienced Trinity pilot and boatman with several rescues to his credit, edged her alongside the *John Grey* and shouted to the crew to jump. But the crew seemed oddly reluctant to leave the doomed ship and the surprised lifeboatmen then saw Captain Blackney, revolver still in hand, facing his crew and defying them to abandon ship.

Coxswain Carbis kept the lifeboat ranging alongside until eventually fifteen men summoned up courage, made a dash for the side and leapt aboard. Captain Blackney, both mates, steward, carpenter, an able seaman and a Frenchman travelling as a passenger, still refused to come off, and the lifeboat crew reluctantly turned shorewards. It was close on half-past one in the morning when the lifeboat was pulled up into the shelter of Marazion railway station. The Hayle lifeboat, the *Isis*, which had been sent for when the Penzance boat was without wheels for her carriage, arrived on the beach, but her coxswain, Edwin Trevaskis, another veteran boatman, dared not launch. The flood tide was already bringing in a mass of wreckage, the waves hurling great spars and jagged timbers with a force which would have smashed the *Isis* and her crew. Shouts from those who had stayed aboard the *John Grey* could now be plainly heard above the noise of the storm, but nothing could be done for them. Around three o'clock the black silhouette of the *John Grey's* masts vanished, and it was all over.

When dawn broke the whole corner of the beach from Longrock to Marazion village was choked with wreckage. The bodies of Captain Blackney and the others lay sprawled among the casks of rum and the hundreds of coconuts which littered the sands. The captain's persistence in refusing to abandon his ship was never explained, but may have been the action of a man at the end of his tether after an impossibly trying voyage.

A year had passed since the loss of the *John Grey* when the German barque *Die Sonne* of Pillau, bound from Cardiff to Barcelona with coal, was wrecked at Praa Sands. A heavy WNW gale off the Longships had forced her master, Captain Bruno Burier, to run for Falmouth, but the *Die Sonne* became embayed, struck the Stones and drove on to the beach. Before the lifeboat could arrive from Penzance, and though several rocket lines were fired on board by the coastguards, the barque was battered to pieces. Captain Burier, twelve Prussian sailors and two Scilly pilots who had tried to get her into safety were drowned within sight and sound of the shore.

The wreck of the timber barque *North Britain* at Longrock in December 1868 showed the fatal similarity of the eastern shores—particularly when obscured by misty rain—to the Devon side of

Plymouth Sound. The *North Britain* sailed from Quebec on 5 November 1868, bound for Southampton with 950 tons of provincial timber. Captain John Rogers usually made the Channel thirty miles south of the Scillies, but on this voyage, due to easterly gales, he was well behind his reckoning. At daylight on 6 December when land was sighted, it was taken to be Bolt Tail, on the Devonshire coast. Captain Rogers accordingly steered along the shore looking for the eastern entrance of Plymouth breakwater, but at eleven o'clock the lookouts raised the cry of 'Breakers on the lee bow!' All hands were called, and minutes later broken water was also sighted off the weather bow. The *North Britain* had sailed into the northern corner of Mount's Bay and was hopelessly embayed. An attempt to get into Penzance was defeated by heavy seas and the low tide, though a pilot cutter got close enough to read the barque's name under her counter. Captain Rogers dropped anchor off the Mount, but three cables parted in rapid succession and by noon she was in the surf. Six of the crew perished, but the rest were saved after an incredibly difficult rescue by the Penzance lifeboat. A month later another five sailors were drowned when the Shields barque *Choice*, bound to Falmouth for orders with maize from Sulina, followed in the wake of the *Die Sonne* and ended on Praa Sands.

From 1869 to 1898, four large sailing ships, about a dozen schooners and a score of ketches, cutters and trawlers were wrecked on the four miles of coast between Porthleven and Penzance. Most of the small vessels were local and only a few were refloated. The dandy ketch *Alliance* and the schooner *Golden Light*, driven ashore at Chyandour on 7 December 1886, were both from Penzance. So were the schooners *Jane and Mary*, *Helena*, *Alpha*, *Fenna and Wilhelmina*, *Mary James* and *Mary Hannah*, stranded between 1870 and 1899. Many were from other West Country ports, and a few were foreign. The schooners *Rose* of Plymouth, and *Treaty* of Goole, were stranded outside Penzance harbour in a SSE gale on 1 February 1873. The *Ponthieu*, a 'natty French brig' as she was described in a local paper, was wrecked at Perranuthnoe on 17 May 1879 while on voyage from the Pomeron River, in Spain, to Liverpool with iron ore. Five months later the Jersey cutter *Rival*, homeward bound with coals from Newport, struck and foundered on the Stones off Praa Sands. The sailing trawlers *Bluebell* of

Plymouth, and *Talisman* of Dartmouth, were lost near Penzance on 29 January 1889 in thick fog and a strong south-west gale. The large Brixham schooner *Torbay Lass* was wrecked on the Cressars, off Penzance pier, two years later on 8 December 1891. She was in tow from the Mount, where she had just unloaded coal from Runcorn, to Penzance, but the tug *Merlin,* skippered by a local shipwright called Bernardo Speshott, failed to raise sufficient steam and allowed the schooner to drift on to the rocks. The packet *Lady of the Isles* towed the *Torbay Lass* clear, only to have her sink a few hundred yards off the reef.

There were two wrecks on 14 February 1881, when a SSW gale was blowing, with fog and heavy seas, just the weather for getting blown into Mount's Bay. Sure enough, the schooner *Sylphide* of Vannes, on voyage from Audierne to Cardiff with potatoes, was wrecked at Perranuthnoe in the early hours; her crew were saved by rocket line but she soon broke up as the weather was rough all day. At 7 pm the 574-ton American barque *T F Whitson* of Bearspaw, Maine, drifted ashore at Praa Sands after being embayed, on voyage from Victoria, Vancouver Island, to London, Nickel master, with wool and tinned salmon. The crew were saved by rocket line, after the terrified Chinese cook had been thrust forcibly into the breeches-buoy and sent ashore first. Shortly before midnight the coastguards left on watch over the barque saw she was on fire and the fire brigade was called from Penzance. Meanwhile a bucket chain was organised, but despite all efforts she burned for another forty-eight hours. It was thought that the lamp over the binnacle had been left lit when the crew abandoned ship and that the rolling of the barque had overturned it.

Meanwhile the cargo had been unloaded by horse and cart and by boat, and a lot of it had been stolen. A week later three local men and one of the crew of the *T F Whitson* found to have been selling salmon for three shillings for a dozen tins, were brought before the magistrates. In defence of one man it was urged that charges should not be pressed as it would be found that half of Helston was implicated, and not only in humble quarters, either.

After the slight comedy of the *T F Whitson* came the tragedies. In the following October the French schooner *Sophie* of Regneville was lost with all hands outside Prussia Cove in a heavy south-east gale. Nothing was seen of her until dawn, when wreckage was washed in and the body of the ship's boy was found. Two years later, on 1 September 1883, Captain Norton and eleven men died when the Newport barque *G I Jones* was lost near Cudden Point in a furious ssw gale, while bound from Charlestown to Falmouth for orders with phosphates. Only four months later, on 26 January 1884, the Austrian brigantine *Cviet*, San Domingo to Falmouth with logwood, was wrecked outside Porthleven harbour with the loss of three lives. But fortunately, when the 335-ton barque *Petrellen*, homeward bound to Porsgrund in ballast, was driven on to the sand flats at Longrock, none of the crew was drowned. She had put into Mount's Bay for her chief mate to get treatment for an injured foot, and had been anchored there for a fortnight when the weather turned rough. It was while she was trying to get clear on the evening of 1 February 1885 that she was wrecked.

Some vessels stranded on these beaches and were salvaged. The Norwegian brig *Otto*, which had the distinction of being wrecked in a pool of treacle in a submerged forest (her cargo of sugar having dissolved from her damaged holds as she sat on the beach among the trunks of a prehistoric wood uncovered by the storm), was repaired and refloated, and sold on 17 February 1873 to a Penzance general merchant named Denley. She had further extensive repairs, and on 17 June she sailed for Wales under her new name of *Providence*. Thirty years later, re-rigged as a schooner, she was still in the coasting trade. With her were the *Nulli Secundus*, originally the German brigantine *Tobacco*, which stranded on the Eastern Green during the November gales of 1865, and the brigantine *Jeune Hortense*, which stranded at Longrock in May 1888. Not only the coaster fleet of Penzance, but those of other Cornish ports could boast ships that had been salvaged after stranding.

Coast dwellers in Cornwall are accustomed to strange sights but an old lady who lived in a cottage above Praa Sands was somewhat alarmed when, on an August night in 1905, she saw the dark face of a negro pressed against the rain-spattered panes of her parlour window. He was the cook of the 441-tons register iron barque *Noisel*, the last big sailing ship to fall victim to the old wreckers' haunt of Praa Sands. The *Noisel* was a distinctly polyglot vessel. She was commanded by a Cornish sea captain named Symons, then living in Plymouth, who had recently bought her in a French port. On 31 July 1905 the *Noisel* sailed from Cherbourg under charter to a German firm, loaded with 600 tons of broken armour plate from the turrets of an obsolete French battleship, bound for Savona, where the cargo would be sent on to a foundry near Genoa. As crew she carried Wilhelm Bartels, mate, a German who had married and settled in Le Havre, a French bosun and four able seamen, a Pole from Danzig, and David David Allen, the negro cook from New York; a rare mixture even for the latter days of sail.

The *Noisel* had hardly cleared Ushant when the long summer heatwave ended in a severe storm. The wind rose to a hard southwest gale and the little barque was carried a long way off course; worse, her rolling and tossing caused the great slabs of armour plate to shift. Her list increased and Captain Symons put about and ran for the shelter of Plymouth. The flash of the Lizard light appeared over the barque's weather bow at 8 pm on 7 August, but she refused to clear the land and was driven into Mount's Bay. She scraped past the Rinsey cliffs and would not come about, so Captain Symons dropped one anchor. It held, but the cable parted, and when the second anchor was let go it failed to grip the sandy bottom. The helpless barque wallowed for a few minutes, then crashed into the breakers at Praa Sands, swung broadside on and broke her back. The masts began to whip and shudder and, afraid of being killed by falling yards, six of the crew jumped overboard and swam for the beach. Three were pulled ashore by local men, and two more by Francis Andrews of nearby Pengersick, who was trying to rescue the sixth man, an able seaman called Lucien Vogel, when a big wave flattened them. Andrews was dragged to safety but Vogel was sucked back under the bilges, struck his head on the plating and disappeared.

Meanwhile the coastguards were alerted by a mounted messenger, but as it was summertime the horses which pulled the rocket cart were loose in the fields, and it was some time before they were caught and harnessed up. The coastguards arrived to find only Captain Symons and the mate still on board, and as the barque was so close in it was decided to throw a line to them rather than fire a rocket. One of the coastguards, a rope about his waist, waited until a breaker receded, then rushed out as close to the *Noisel* as he dared and hurled a leaded cane line aboard. The next second he was tossed head over heels up the beach by the returning sea, hauled out, and promptly fainted. However, the line was secured, the breeches-buoy sent across and Bartels and the captain were brought ashore, though not before the mainmast had fallen, taking the mizzen top with it. The survivors, including the cook who had wandered off in search of help—which was when he peered into the cottage window—were taken to a nearby farmhouse where the roll was called and it was discovered that Nicholas Borvon, able seaman of Brest, was missing, although no one had seen him go overboard. The bodies of Borvon and Vogel were recovered a fortnight after the wreck, near Porthleven. The *Noisel*, which was only partially insured, became a total wreck and it is still possible, when heavy seas scoop the sand off Praa beach, to see, embedded in the clay beneath, the great slabs of armour plate which were her cargo.

The winter of 1911 saw the last large sailing vessel wrecked on the eastern shore. The iron barque *Saluto*, an elderly product of a Nantes shipyard, launched in 1867 as the *National*, which had passed to Norwegian owners, sailed from the Thames on 22 November in sand ballast for Barbados. Gale followed gale, and when she was far out beyond the Scillies she sprang a leak. The pumps were manned until they were choked by the ballast turning into mud, and her master, Captain Johann Olsshen, had to run for Falmouth. At dawn on 8 December the *Saluto*, blown far off course and embayed, dropped anchor less than a mile from Cudden Point. The Penzance lifeboat came out, took off the crew, and landed them at Newlyn amidst a cheering throng, augmented by the strains of the Salvation Army band playing 'Oh God Our Help in Ages Past'. A Lowestoft drifter had put out in the wake of the lifeboat to take the barque in tow, but half an hour after the rescue the *Saluto* dragged ashore at Perranuthnoe. She did not break up at once and next morning Captain Olsshen, two men and a coastguard returned aboard. While they were busy salvaging effects and papers, the wind suddenly freshened and they had to abandon ship. The dinghy capsized as the captain jumped into it and he and the coastguard struggled in the water until they were rescued from the shore. The two sailors had to spend a dangerously uncomfortable night on board the derelict *Saluto* before they were taken off by breeches-buoy next morning.

The little French schooner *St Anne* was the last to be embayed and wrecked in Mount's Bay, tossed ashore on Porthleven beach by a south-west gale on 3 November 1931. She had sailed from Cardiff the previous morning, homeward bound to Vannes with coal, but the fine weather soon changed. Her rudder was smashed by heavy seas and several sails were blown away before she crawled past the Wolf Rock in darkness and was carried to leeward towards Mount's Bay. Throughout the morning of the 3rd she ran before the storm and the sight of the battered schooner brought to readiness every lifeboat and LSA company between Penzance and the Lizard. The master of the *St Anne*, Captain le Bitter, headed for Porthleven harbour but was foiled by tremendous seas. The *St Anne* hauled off a little to the east but, unable to stand up to the gale, she was flung ashore just outside the harbour mouth. The crew climbed into the rigging and clung there as the schooner rolled in the surf. A man swam out with a line but was driven back when almost on the point of securing it to the bowsprit guys. The Porthleven rocket brigade's first rocket was swept away over the stern into the sea, but the second fell straight and true, just forward of the mainmast, where it was easily secured. One by one the five men and a boy were brought ashore, the last crew to be wrecked in a fashion which for two centuries had brought tragedy and heroism to the eastern shores of Mount's Bay.

Though the northern corner of Mount's Bay was such a deadly trap for sailing ships, steamers were less at the mercy of the wind and fewer than a dozen have been wrecked or stranded between Penzance and Porthleven. In March 1912 the Cardiff steamer *Northlands* did what no sailing ship could have done; she escaped going ashore by steaming along the entire length of the coast from Cudden to the Lizard only a few hundred yards from the shore, somehow dodging the reefs, against a hard south-west gale. The Greek steamer *Jannikis* and the French collier *Ornaist* both survived stranding at Perranuthnoe in the 1920s. On 27 January 1936, the *Taycraig*, Cornish-owned despite her London registration, dragged her anchors in a south-west gale and wrapped herself around the tall post-and-cage beacon which marks the Gear rocks, just off Penzance promenade. Her crew were rescued by the lifeboat, but the *Taycraig*, which was in ballast for Newlyn to load roadstone, sank until her funnel and masts stood out of the water and defied all efforts to salvage her. More recently, in July 1956, the

827-ton steam coaster *Yewcroft*, bound from the Thames to Bristol with cement, wandered off course in dense fog and grounded near Cudden Point. A few hours later, as the tide ebbed from beneath her, she broke her back.

A large Spanish cannon was raised near Low Lee Ledge, half a mile off Penlee Point, in October 1916, and another in 1967, which may have come from a West Indiaman wrecked on the Low Lee on 2 December 1771. They prove that sailing ships were wrecked there in past centuries; certainly several steamers have struck the reef. One was the collier *Ransome* on 17 April 1885, as she entered the bay with coal for Newlyn. It was only a glancing blow and with pumps going at full bore she ran for Penzance, only to sink a hundred yards off the pierhead and break up within forty-eight hours. On 3 August 1906, the Liverpool coaster *Primrose* rammed her bows on the reef in thick fog, and by morning her stern had risen twenty feet in the air, poised for her final plunge into deep water. The largest steamer was the 2,085-ton *Cragoswald* of Newcastle. She had sailed from Barry in the early hours of 28 April 1911, bound for Venice with 4,800 tons of coal, but when twelve hours out her chief engineer was taken seriously ill and Captain Albert Crowthers altered course for Mount's Bay to land him. As the weather was foggy, the captain steered a careful course past the Runnelstone and was almost in the bay when he made a bad mistake. A large black and white check can buoy was seen bobbing in the heavy seas, and was taken to be that marking Mount Mopus ledge, between St Michael's Mount and Porthleven. But they had been confused by the mist and rain, and a few minutes later, as the *Cragoswald* passed carefully to port of the buoy, there came a tremendous crash and she shuddered to a stop. Though she was going very slowly, her bows were firmly impaled and for the next four days she hung precariously on the Low Lee while salvage craft, tugs and divers fussed about her. Twice the salvors were driven off by rough seas, but on the morning of 2 May the *Cragoswald* floated free and was towed to Penzance. Five days later, escorted by tugs, she left Mount's Bay under her own steam for the repair docks at Falmouth. After only seven months she was ashore again, this time in Jury's Gap, near Dungeness, during the south-west gale which wrecked the barque *Saluto* in Mount's Bay. The *Cragoswald* spent a week on the beach before being refloated, and she lasted until 18 April 1917, when a German U-boat torpedoed her 60 miles west by south of the Bishop Rock.

It was a case of so near and yet so far when the 2,774-ton steel screw steamer *Hellopes* sank off Penzance on 29 December 1911. She had been launched in 1889 by J Reid & Co of Port Glasgow for the British & South African Steamship Co and had traded under their flag until a grounding at the Cape damaged her so badly that they decided to sell her for scrap. She was on her last voyage, from the Mersey to a breaker's yard at Falmouth, and had accomplished about four hundred miles with a heavy list due to her coal cargo shifting, and in a howling NNW gale. She rounded Land's End on the point of sinking and reached Mount's Bay almost on her beam ends, only to go down within a quarter of a mile of safety.

Enemy action in both world wars left sunken ships on the bottom of Mount's Bay, and during the 1914-18 war it was common to see the crew of a torpedoed or mined steamer rowing into Penzance, or stepping ashore at Newlyn or Porthleven from a fishing-boat. On 20 November 1917 the 1,637-ton Belgian steamer *Antwerpen* sank a short way off Penzance after being torpedoed two miles SSW of the Runnelstone. In the following year the steamers *Pursuit* and *Commandante Barathieu* were sunk in the bay and the big American steamer *Lake Harris*, resplendent in her dazzle-paint camouflage, was beached in front of Penzance railway station after an encounter with a U-boat. The Stones off Praa Sands claimed one of those mysterious vessels, the 'Q'-ships, when in August 1918 the steamer *Glendale*, laden with a cargo of Portuguese wine, was wrecked in thick fog. Her crew escaped unharmed and a lot of the cargo drifted ashore, but the *Glendale* still lies deep among the Stones.

The minesweeper *Royalo*, far removed from her peacetime occupation as a Grimsby trawler, was blown up near St Michael's Mount on 1 September 1940. She was engaged in the dangerous task of sweeping a string of magnetic mines laid by a German aircraft. Around noon there was a shattering explosion and the *Royalo* was enveloped in a great column of water. The Penlee lifeboat put off, but by the time she and other boats arrived the *Royalo* had gone. Launched in June 1916 by Cook, Wellington & Gemmel of Beverly, Goole, as a steel, ketch-rigged trawler of 248 tons gross, the *Royalo* had been requisitioned by the Admiralty at the outbreak of war. In January 1944 the 547-ton naval trawler *Wallasea,* less than a year old, suffered a similar fate when an E-boat torpedoed her as she was escorting a convoy past Mount's Bay. Later the same year her wreck was joined by two landing craft (mechanised), *LCMs 340* and *424* which were swept off the Liberty ship *John L Manson* as she ploughed past the bay in a gale. Perhaps the oddest of the wartime casualties was a large pontoon, part of the Mulberry Harbour used in the Normandy landings, which broke adrift while being towed home late in August 1945. The south-west gale swept this gigantic piece of steel and reinforced concrete, which measured 160ft by 40ft, into a gulley near Praa Sands, and for fear of it becoming a navigational hazard it had to be destroyed.

Few coasts have wrecked a battleship, but the Cornish coast, having allowed HMS *Africa* to escape unscathed when she got among the Lizard rocks in 1906, claimed one on 23 April 1947 when the old *Warspite* cheated the breaker's yard by stranding at Prussia Cove. One of the great battleships resulting from the 'Dreadnought Race' between Britain and Imperial Germany in the years before the First World War, the *Warspite* was launched in March 1915, the second of five great sisters of a class which took its name from the first, the *Queen Elizabeth.* Though weighed down by a vast amount of armour-plating, the then modern innovation of oil fuel gave them a speed of twenty-five knots, so that they were as fast as the battle cruisers of the Grand Fleet but without the cruiser's serious disadvantage of having to sacrifice armour for the sake of speed.

The early career of the *Warspite* was not auspicious. In the winter of 1915 she collided with the *Barham* and was considerably damaged. She was repaired in time to take part in the Battle of Jutland but at a critical moment in the engagement her helm jammed, she was hit thirteen times by big shells and was ordered back to Rosyth. Even then she almost met disaster as *U-51* narrowly missed torpedoeing her as she entered the Firth of Forth. Six weeks later she was damaged in another collision and by the time she was back in service the war was nearly ended, and soon the two great battlefleets which clashed at Jutland had vanished, the British to the breakers' yards and the German to the bottom of Scapa Flow. But the 'Queen Elizabeths' remained in service,

Page 187: The Dieppe trawler *Vert Prairial*, capsized below the Porthcurno cliffs on 13 March 1956. Her crew of seventeen were lost.

Page 188: (above) The Belgian trawler *Vierge Marie* near Tater Du on 13 January 1937, the first of a tragic series of similar wrecks; (below) all that could be seen of the Spanish coaster *Juan Ferrer* on the morning of 23 October 1963, below Carn Boscawen.

and during the late 1920s were refitted and altered, particularly amidships. Ten years later they underwent another major rebuild and modernisation in time for the outbreak of the Second World War. The part played by the *Warspite* is well known. She saw action in every theatre of the war, from Norway to the Mediterranean, and survived the attentions of the Luftwaffe, U-boats and the Italian Navy, once giving the latter an unwelcome surprise by scoring a direct hit on the cruiser *Giulio Cesare* at a range of fourteen miles.

At the end of the war the 'Queen Elizabeth' class (except for the *Barham*, torpedoed in the Mediterranean), nearly thirty years old, was consigned to the breaker's yard. The *Warspite* was the first to go, and after her guns had been removed she left Portsmouth on 19 April 1947, in tow of the tugs *Bustler* and *Melinda III* for Clydeside. It was a voyage she was never to finish. Shortly before midnight on 21 April, while the tugs fought to hold her in a southwest gale, the *Bustler*'s hawser parted southwards of the Wolf Rock light. Though the *Warspite* was a long way off the land, the Portsmouth duty staff officer asked Penlee and Lizard lifeboats to stand by, but at eight o'clock on the 22nd the gale appeared to moderate and the crews stood down.

For the next twenty hours the battleship and the tugs rode out the storm, but drifted closer to Mount's Bay. At midday on 23 April the *Melinda III* was forced to slip her hawser and the warship's towing crew dropped anchor. It failed to hold and in less than an hour the *Warspite* was ashore on Mount Mopus Ledge, an isolated reef a mile south-west of Cudden Point. The Penlee lifeboat crossed the bay and her coxswain hailed Captain Baxter of the towing party to say that, as it was now low water, the flood tide would carry the battleship off the reef and on to the eastern shore. The captain declined to abandon ship and the lifeboat put into Newlyn, as it was too rough to return to the lifeboat house. As the tide rose the *Warspite* did indeed float clear of Mount Mopus and drifted on to the rocks at Prussia Cove.

Swept by huge waves, the great battleship, still in her wartime camouflage, lay a little to the east of the old smugglers' cove, with her bows to the storm. There was hardly any shelter for the lifeboat to lie alongside and the seas broke with tremendous force over the great side bulges and around 'B' turret. A narrow channel

L

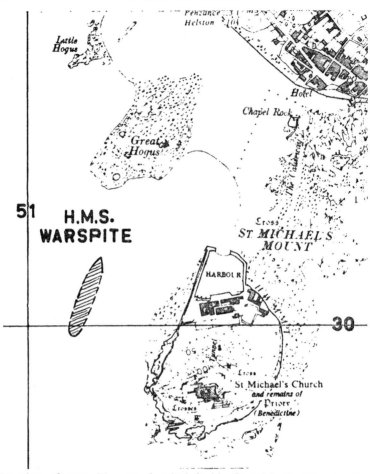

Location of HMS *Warspite*, beached beside St Michael's Mount after grounding in Prussia Cove.

between the *Warspite* and the shore offered the only opportunity for the lifeboat to get near, and the coxswain managed to bring her to the end of the quarter deck. Two lines were flung aboard and in spite of the lifeboat rising and falling twenty feet at a time as the breakers roared in around the *Warspite*, the incredibly difficult and dangerous rescue began. Thirty-five hair-raising minutes later, Captain Baxter and his crew were safely on board and at eight o'clock that evening they stepped ashore at Newlyn.

The south-westerly gale did more damage to the *Warspite* than her service in either of the two wars; she could not be towed to the breaker's yard, and within a few days it was decided to demolish her where she lay. But the old warship was eventually moved to Marazion and beached beside St Michael's Mount for ease of access. There she remained for more than five years, a battered, rusting hulk, surmounted by a couple of tall ungainly derricks which were used to load scrap metal into a variety of vessels, including an ancient tank landing craft, for transportation to Penzance pier. In those years she became a familiar sight and name; the old *Warspite* would have been forgotten sooner if the Cornish coast and weather had not accomplished in a few days what thirty years and two wars had failed to do, as well as saving her from a more ignominious end.

CHAPTER EIGHT

MOUSEHOLE TO TOL-PEDN-PENWITH

A SHORT distance beyond the once-thriving fishing village of
Mousehole rises the first of the tall granite cliffs of the Land's
End peninsula. From Mousehole (which in 1595 was sacked
by a squadron of Spanish galleons, leaving only one house, the
famous Keigwin Arms, standing amid the smoking ruins) to the
bleak heights of Tol-Pedn-Penwith, ten miles to the west, the land
stretches in an unbroken succession of steep-sided coves and high
out-thrust headlands. In all but a few places the vast, monolithic
blocks of granite which form the coastline tumble tier upon tier
down into the sea, like the stairway of some legendary Cornish
giant. Here and there the moors and tiny stone-hedged fields, with
their sprinkling of squat, grey-roofed cottages, squeeze their way
to the sea's edge through narrow gorse-filled valleys, and tucked
beneath these sheltering slopes lie some of the ancient 'ports' of the
Hundred of Penwith; Porthcurno, Porthgwarra and Penberth, with
their brightly painted crabbers drawn up on the beach, or slip-
ways paved by flat-topped boulders laid across the head of the
cove.

Though deep water lies close to the shore, there are many
isolated rocks fringing the coastline, some of them submerged, some
standing out of the water at the tip of a headland. Only a few
hundred yards from Mousehole harbour lies the low, craggy mass
of St Clement's Island, which gave the village its ancient name of
Porthenys, the island port. Like St George's Island at Looe, it was
something of a mixed blessing; although it formed a natural breakwater for the little harbour, the island was at times a serious hazard
to the fishing fleet returning home in bad weather, or to any vessel
that passed too close to the shore. A gale from south or east blowing into Mousehole made St Clement's a greater danger than usual,
and several ships were wrecked upon it after being carried to leeward while entering or leaving Mount's Bay. In June 1817, two

large mackerel drivers sank a short way off the island during a SSE gale with the loss of all fourteen fishermen. Wrecked on the island itself was the Genoese brig *Concezione*, on 17 November 1852, while bound from London to Newport in ballast. There were no lives lost on this occasion and the following morning her dismasted and broken hulk was towed off by a tug which happened to be lying wind-bound in the bay. On 13 January 1888 the Bristol fishing smack *Bonito* failed to gain sufficient sea-room after leaving Newlyn in a south-east gale and was blown on to the island's seaward tip. Her crew pulled ashore near Penlee Point and the *Bonito*, after several hours on the rocks, washed clear on the flooding tide and was towed in by three Mousehole luggers, little the worse for her experience.

The most notable wreck on St Clement's Island occurred on 1 November 1907, when the Thames sailing barge *Baltic*, bound for Newlyn from the Medway with a cargo of cement for the harbour extension works, got off course after rounding the Lizard. The night was so dark and thick that her plight was hidden from the shore, and nearly an hour went by before the flickering light of a paraffin-soaked mattress burning on the foredeck was seen from the village. The coastguards sent word to the lifeboat station at Newlyn, while six Mousehole fishermen decided to make a rescue bid of their own. They manned the crabber *White Lady*, but as the harbour mouth was closed by the large timber baulks which keep out the rough seas in winter, they had to manhandle her over the pier and down into the sea outside. Big waves were dashing against the exposed harbour wall, making it a hard struggle to row the crabber clear of the rocks and shallow water. At last it was accomplished and the fishermen pulled towards the glimmer of foam which distinguished the dark mass of the island from the darkness around. The tide was ebbing fast and jagged ledges and rocks were coming awash; it took five attempts to find a landing place for the *White Lady*. Then fisherman Stanley Drew leaped on to the rocks with the Mousehole pierhead light in one hand and managed to scramble across to where the shipwrecked people were huddled. Headed by a young Irish sailor, Adam Torrie, who had risked his life to get on to the island over the *Baltic*'s bowsprit, Captain Langford, his wife and daughter, and mate George Baines, had abandoned the barge for the slightly better safety of the rocks.

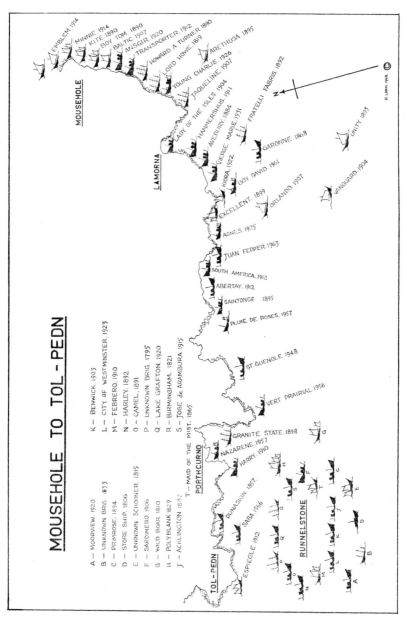

MOUSEHOLE TO TOL-PEDN

A — MOORVIEW. 1920
B — UNKNOWN BRIG. 1833
C — PRIMROSE. 1894
D — STORE SHIP. 1806
E — UNKNOWN SCHOONER. 1815
F — SARDINERO. 1906
G — WILD BOAR. 1810
H — POLYBLANK. 1829
J — ACKLINGTON. 1887

K — BENWICK. 1905
L — CITY OF WESTMINSTER. 1923
M — FEBRERO. 1910
N — HARLEY. 1892
O — CAMEL. 1891
P — UNKNOWN BRIG. 1795
Q — LAKE GRAFTON. 1920
R — BIRMINGHAM. 1821
S — JOSE de ARAMBURA. 1915
T — MAID OF THE MIST. 1865

MOUSEHOLE

EMBLEM. 1914
MINNIE. 1914
KITE. 1890
BOY TOM. 1890
BALTIC. 1907
ANSGIR. 1920
TRANSPORTER. 1912
HOWARD A TURNER. 1890
LORD HOWE. 1819
YOUNG CHARLIE. 1926
JAQUELINE. 1907
ARETHUSA. 1895

LAMORNA

LADY OF THE ISLES. 1904
HAMMERSHUS. 1911
AVEBURY. 1884
VERGE MARIE. 1922
KIORA. 1922
BOY DAVID. 1961
FRATELLI FABRIS. 1892
GARONNE. 1868
ORLANDO. 1907

UNITY. 1833
VANGUARD. 1904

EXCELLENT. 1899
AGNES. 1925
JUAN FERRER. 1963
SOUTH AMERICA. 1912
ABERTAY. 1912
SAINTONGE 1895
PLUIE DE ROSES. 1957
ST. GUENOLE. 1948
VERT PRAIRIAL. 1956

PORTHCURNO

GRANITE STATE. 1898
NAZARENE. 1957
HARRY. 1910
DUNASKIN. 1857
SABA. 1966
ESPIEGLE. 1912

TOL-PEDN

RUNNELSTONE

R. LARN. 1968.

Wreck locations between Mousehole and Tol-Pedn.

Drew carried Mrs Langford, who was nearly hysterical, back to the crabber and William Harvey followed with her daughter in his arms. The others made their way after him and when all were safely aboard the *White Lady* the fishermen headed back for Mousehole. But by this time the tide was low and the task of getting back into the harbour was even more difficult, and the women had to be hauled to the top of the wall by ropes tied under their arms.

The *Baltic* soon became a total wreck, but the bravery of the six fishermen did not go unrewarded; Stanley Drew, William H Harvey, Luther Harvey, Charles Harry, Richard Harry and Richard Thomas each received a cash award from the RNLI, as well as a silver medal which a Birmingham businessman had especially struck to commemorate their action. Adam Torrie, the Irish sailor, settled in Mousehole and married the harbourmaster's daughter, and today his descendants still live in the village, while mention of the wreck of the *Baltic* will prompt many an old fisherman to retell a story that has lost none of its flavour over the years.

Close to Mousehole, where the small fields and daffodil patches on the cliffs to the west of the village merge with the bracken-covered slopes of Penzer Point, lie the remains of the *Ansgir*, one of the largest ships ever wrecked on the Cornish coast. She was one of the many vessels of the German Merchant Marine, ranging from Atlantic liners to auxiliary schooners, surrendered to the Allies at the end of the First World War as compensation for the millions of tons of shipping sent to the bottom by the mines and torpedoes of the Imperial Navy. Almost new, completed a few weeks after the Armistice by A K Ges Neptune of Rostock, on the Baltic, she was a large, single-funnelled, two-masted steamer of 6,483 tons gross, 4,068 tons net, with a deadweight capacity of around 9,500 tons. She measured 438.5ft in length, 57.1ft in beam and 28.1ft in depth, and her single screw was driven by a four-cylinder diesel engine of 476 nhp.

At the end of the war she was taken over by the Ministry of Shipping, who placed her under the management of Gow, Harrison & Co of Glasgow. Her German crew brought her over to Leith Roads where, on 12 August 1920, the *Ansgir* hoisted the 'red duster'. Captain James S Gemmel took command of her and she went out to Hampton Roads, Virginia, where she loaded coal for

Rotterdam. This safely delivered, her next port of call was Dart-mouth and here on 29 September 1920 her crew were paid off. As customary, they all signed on afresh next day, and the *Ansgir* crossed the Atlantic again and at Baltimore took on coal for La Pallice. On arrival at the French port, Captain Gemmel was informed that the *Ansgir* had been awarded to the Japanese as part of their war reparations, and he was ordered to proceed to Barry and take on bunkers for the voyage to the Far East.

On the morning of 1 December 1920 the *Ansgir* sailed from La Pallice in water ballast for Barry. The weather was hazy, with a blustery south-west wind which promised to freshen strongly before nightfall. Ushant was sighted at two o'clock in the afternoon and an hour later Captain Gemmel set course for the Wolf Rock light. The wind increased to a hard quartering gale towards dusk and visibility was seriously impaired by heavy rain and patches of foggy drizzle. At 8 pm the third mate joined Captain Gemmel on the bridge for the eight to twelve watch and both men and the lookouts kept constant watch for the Wolf or the Longships light. The steamer rolled on through the heavy seas, gradually getting closer to the Cornish coast, but by eleven o'clock no lights had been sighted. Half an hour later the captain decided to put about, but hardly had the order been given to turn to port than the watch below were hurled from their bunks as the *Ansgir* struck the rocks a few hundred yards west of the coastguard lookout on Penzer Point, near Mousehole.

Captain Gemmel rang down for hard astern, but the steamer was driven broadside to the cliffs within minutes, the waves break-ing over her as high as her funnel. She rolled so violently that it seemed as if she would turn right over, and the boats could not be launched. A long wooden hold ladder was put over the side and down it went 19-year-old Geoffrey Davis, an apprentice from Birmingham, clad in a lifejacket and with a rope about his waist. Two more volunteers followed him and hung on to the line while he jumped clear of the side and struck out for the rocks. Waiting for him were three Mousehole fishermen who had been tending their boats in the harbour when, seeing the steamer's lights heading towards Penzer Point, they had raised the alarm in the village and then run all the way up the steep Raginnis Hill and along the clifftop lane to the scene of the wreck. The Mousehole men had a hard struggle to haul him out and once were nearly swept into the sea, but they managed to regain the rocks and pull Geoffrey Davis in with them.

More men arrived from the village and the line the apprentice had brought ashore was used to haul in a stouter rope, one end of which was secured to the *Ansgir*'s poop and the other looped around a pinnacle of granite. Then the crew started to come ashore one by one, handing themselves along the line. Meanwhile the Mousehole LSA company had left their rocket-cart by the coastguard lookout and were manhandling their apparatus down the cliffs. They reached the rocks to find that twenty of the crew had already come ashore along the line and soon rescued the remaining twenty-five by means of a quickly-rigged line for their breeches-buoy.

Dawn found the *Ansgir* still broadside on to the cliffs, listing heavily to port, with her bows facing Lamorna. She was badly damaged and in spite of being almost new had to be sold for scrap, and was broken up by the Western Marine Salvage Co of Penzance. In April 1921 she took a severe pounding from a westerly gale, but it was not until the late winter of that year that the *Ansgir* finally vanished from below the Penzer cliffs. It is still possible to find her plates and steel work jammed in the rocks below the point, and diligent search at low water can produce the occasional memento of one of the largest steamers ever wrecked between Penzance and Land's End.

A mile or so westwards of the *Ansgir*'s remains stands Carn-du, the 'Black Carn', the eastern arm of beautiful Lamorna Cove, where a hundred years ago small sailing ships loaded great blocks of granite hewn from the quarries high above the tiny pier, which was built especially for the trade. A plinth twenty feet high and weighing twenty tons was sent to the Great Exhibition of 1851 by sea from the Lamorna quarries, but the hazardous method of loading the granite from a spidery staging on the cliff face into the ships below eventually led to the stone being taken to Penzance by wagon. By the turn of the century the quarries were fast becoming derelict. A few of the stone-loaded ships were lost, but outside the cove several much larger vessels were wrecked or stranded, usually in foggy weather.

On 4 November 1884, the Cardiff collier *Avebury*, homeward bound in ballast from Lisbon, got off course towards the Wolf

Rock, missed Land's End completely in the fog and steamed on to the rocks less than a quarter of a mile west of Lamorna, near where the 1,235-ton Glasgow full-rigger *Macduff* had almost broken her iron keel nearly four years earlier. On 27 January 1890 the New Brunswicker *Howard A Turner* drifted ashore near Carn-du, derelict after being abandoned north of the Scillies while bound from Hillsboro' NB to Dublin with timber. She was refloated, but two winters later the Austrian barque *Fratelli Fabris* was less fortunate. While bound from Antwerp to Buenos Aires, she vanished off the Lamorna cliffs during a heavy southerly gale without trace or survivors, although a lone sailor in a lifeboat came within hail of Penzer Point before he disappeared in a sudden squall and was never seen again.

A big French nitrate clipper, the *Jacqueline*, was almost wrecked on Carn-du on an August night in 1907. She and one of the two tugs which had her in tow from Dunkirk to Port Talbot were caught by thick summer fog as they crossed Mount's Bay from the Lizard and ran straight into the headland. The *Jacqueline*'s bowsprit was bent up vertically by the impact, but both she and the tug slewed off the rocks as the tide rose and eventually reached Falmouth with nothing worse than a few dented plates. Among other vessels which stranded around Lamorna were the Danish steamer *Hammershus,* whose master was under the impression that he was rounding Land's End and put her ashore on the eastern side of the cove, and the famous old Scilly Islands mail steamer *Lady of the Isles.* In summertime she mixed her regular duties as packet steamer with those of a pleasure craft and it was while taking sightseers to view the scenery at Lamorna, on 1 September 1904, that she grazed the sunken ledge of the Little Heaver, which lies just off the tip of Carn-du. Her passengers were taken off and she was run ashore in the cove, close to the pierhead, where she lay submerged from bows to bridge with three big holes below her engine-room. Fortunately the weather stayed fine and a local salvage company refloated her with the aid of a tug from Falmouth and towed her into Penzance.

Though her injuries were not too serious she was an old vessel and her owners sold her to the salvage company, who had her reboilered and fitted out as a salvage steamer. In this capacity, and under her old name, she was present at every major wreck on the Cornish coast for the next thirty years, though on occasion she went back on her old run to the Scillies as a relief steamer when the regular packet, the *Scillonian*, went for her annual refit. The 'Lady', as she was always known locally, was lost on 3 October 1940. Her long career, which had begun in 1875 on the building slips of Harvey's of Hayle, was ended by a well-placed German mine, a mile off the Manacles buoy in Falmouth Bay. When the *Lady of the Isles* was stranded there may have been men still living who could just remember the last time a Scilly Packet was wrecked near Lamorna, which was in 1819. The *Lord Howe* left Penzance quay for St Mary's on the morning of 16 July, laden with merchandise and carrying several passengers. Not far beyond Mousehole she ran on to a rock off Kemyel Point and filled fast, but fishing-boats saved all on board and most of the cargo before she sank. The wreck was alleged to have been caused by the entire crew going below for dinner and leaving the ship's boy at the helm.

A small error in dead reckoning, resulting from the rotor of the patent log, trailing on its line over the stern, becoming clogged with weed and failing to register the distance run, contributed to one of the worst disasters ever to occur along the western cliffs of Cornwall. This was the wreck of the schooner-rigged, two-masted, iron steamer *Garonne*, built by C & W Earle of Hull in 1866 for William Miles Moss of Liverpool, the principal owner of a line of steamships operating out of the Mersey to Continental ports. A comparatively small ship of only 638 tons gross and 449 net, the *Garonne*'s 215-ft length was divided by four watertight bulkheads and two partial ones, and her double-direct-acting inverted cylinder compound engine of 90 hp gave her a maximum speed of about twelve knots.

On 21 May 1868, some ten weeks after having successfully passed a Board of Trade survey and being valued at £15,000, the *Garonne* sailed from Bordeaux for the Mersey with 600 tons of general cargo under the command of Captain Benjamin Drew, a middle-aged Cornishman from Mevagissey with long experience of the Liverpool-Bordeaux run. Apart from a Guernsey man and a German, the crew were all English and the sixteen passengers included four women, two of them French nurses, and eight young children.

By 1.30 pm on 22 May with Ushant nearly abeam, one-third

of the voyage to Liverpool had been completed and Captain Drew set a course to bring him close to the Longships light. As the day drew on a thick, misty drizzle settled in, the visibility rapidly deteriorated and shortly before dark a seaman, sent aft to read the patent log, discovered it out of action. Relying now on dead reckoning, uncertain of the distance run by the ship since the last log reading, Captain Drew again altered course at 10.0 pm and ordered the fore-topsail, fore-trysail and fore-staysail to be hoisted to take advantage of a favourable wind. No soundings were taken as a check on the ship's position, though the young second officer, Wilson, had ordered the deep-sea lead line to be made ready when coming on watch at 8.0 pm.

At 11.0 pm a sight of the Wolf Rock or the Longships light was well overdue and the captain went forward to alert the lookout. Twenty-five minutes later there came a shout from the second officer, 'Sir, it's the land ahead!' and back came Captain Drew's terse reply, 'Land it is. Hard a-starboard and full astern!'

Able seaman Thomas Tulloch spun the wheel hard over and down in the engine-room chief engineer Alexander Ruxton, who had been with the *Garonne* since she was built, prepared to stop and reverse the engine. But it was too late, and even as she turned the *Garonne* drove heavily on to the Bucks Rocks, a mile west of Lamorna Cove and, holed beneath her bridge, settled down amidst the breaking seas.

Captain Drew raced back to the bridge, rang for 'Stop engines' on the engine-room telegraph and ordered the fore-topsail halliards to be let go as they were in the way of launching the boats. Down in the engine-room Ruxton eased the safety valves and was opening the firebox doors when sea water welled up through the plates beneath his feet. He damped the fires, and with the rising flood at his heels scrambled up the ladders on to the deck. There he met his second in command, William Arrowsmith, who had been lying on his bunk when he heard the order to reverse engines. Arrowsmith went towards the bridge to help with the boats, but ashes and scalding water blasting up through the engine-room skylight drove him back.

Meanwhile the chief officer was burning blue distress flares and firing rockets but they were seen only by two local schooners, the *Julia* and the *Mary Boynes*, neither of which recognised their significance. Captain Drew, second officer Wilson, bosun Crichton, Fox the carpenter, able seaman Tulloch and others then set about lowering the big port-side lifeboat and the cutter. The bosun and donkeyman MacCormack jumped into the lifeboat and the cutter was soon in the water as well, manned by fireman Corcoran and the cabin boy, Frederick Walker. The third lifeboat was left in her slings and the second officer ordered the men in the port boat to pull to leeward of the poop and take off the passengers. He then returned to the bridge, but finding Captain Drew and the chief officer had left it, and with the *Garonne* listing far over with her deck almost touching the water, he struck out for the poop along the almost submerged lee rails. He arrived in time to see a wave carry three women passengers overboard, and promptly jumped in after them. He would have drowned if the cutter, which had disappeared to leeward after being launched, had not suddenly reappeared less than thirty yards away and its occupants hauled him aboard.

In the continuing confusion on board the *Garonne* attempts were now being made to launch the ship's dinghy slung over the counter, a task that was not made any easier by the several sacks of green peas for which the dinghy had served as a convenient store. Launched at last, the dinghy proved to have no bung in it and almost sank before the drainhole was plugged. Several members of the crew scrambled into it, and while the chief engineer improvised thole pins from the ropes on a lifebuoy which floated past, the others bailed furiously with a bucket and a large soup plate.

Meanwhile the port lifeboat had been pulled under the *Garonne*'s stern in obedience to the second officer's orders but the heavy seas prevented it from getting close up and the passengers still there were too frightened to jump. Only twenty minutes from the time the *Garonne* had struck, she suddenly listed right over on to her beam ends, rolled off the Bucks reef and sank.

After a fruitless search for survivors, bosun Crichton, in charge of the port lifeboat, ordered it to be rowed along the coast and at first light Thomas Carbis, coxswain of the Penzance lifeboat, saw them from the pierhead and guided them in. They were helped to the Ship Hotel on the dockside, where they learned that the dinghy had safely reached Mousehole. The cutter had also failed to get near the poop deck, where Captain Drew was last seen a few minutes before the end came, and several hours later it was taken in tow by a lugger off Lamorna and brought into Mousehole.

At dawn the *Garonne* lay only two hundred yards from the cliffs at Tater Du, in the sound between the Bucks and the shore. The sea was already washing the cargo out and barrels and cases by the score were littering the coast between St Loy and Lamorna. Before dusk she had started to break up and next morning the pitiful debris of the wreck was being gathered up. At nine o'clock an eight-year-old girl and her younger sister were found floating in the sea off Lamorna pier. A Mousehole lugger recovered the bodies of two small boys off the island during the afternoon and one of the French nurses was found by the fishing-boat *Four Sisters* near the Penlee buoy. An uncle and his nephew were washed in at Lamorna and Captain Drew was found below Carn-du, his face disfigured by a large bruise over his left eye.

As more bodies were recovered and preparations were made for the inquest it became apparent that of the *Garonne*'s sixteen passengers only two had been saved, while only three of the crew had been lost. At the subsequent enquiry, second officer Wilson, the only surviving deck officer, was heavily pressed as to his and the crew's conduct during the wreck, and also as to why he had not ordered soundings to be taken as the *Garonne* approached Land's End. Wilson, who had only been an officer for a few months, denied that there had been any indiscipline among the crew and said that soundings had not been taken as the captain and the chief officer both thought they were only approaching their reckoning, not over-running it. He also maintained that he had jumped overboard only to help passengers who had been swept into the sea, not to save his own life. Nevertheless, the court severely censured him, which perhaps was a little unjust to a young and inexperienced officer who could hardly have been expected alone to create order out of the extraordinary confusion which seems to have prevailed on the deck of the *Garonne*.

The Bucks reef is overlooked by the bulk of Carn Boscawen, the eastern flank of St Loy Bay, where in the autumn of 1912, there occurred a quite extraordinary wreck. The story really begins in the early hours of 13 March the same year, when John Richards, who lived in a small cottage above the bay, was awoken by the crack of distress rockets. Hurriedly dressing, he seized a lantern and strode down across the fields to the beach. A short way off-shore, hardly visible through the rain and fog, the tall sides of a big steamer rose like a wall from the sea. Her decks were alive with men and on Richards' shout to launch their boats and he would guide them in, there came the creak of davits and splash of oars. Two large lifeboats soon bumped on to the rocks; fifteen men and one highly agitated woman were helped ashore from one, while twenty more seamen waded in from the other.

Meanwhile another cottager had set off on his bicycle for Mouse-hole and soon the rocket wagon, drawn by its four-horse team, was pounding along the road towards Lamorna. By the time it rattled down to St Loy, the steamer had been identified as the *South America* of London. A rocket line was fired over her, but as no one was left aboard to secure it, Captain Alfred Bowling, chief officer Thom, and second officer Harold Read, a Penzance man, swam out, climbed a rope over the ship's side and set up the lines to work the breeches-buoy. As dawn lightened the sky above Carn Boscawen, the ship's instruments and the crew's baggage were landed and the *South America* was seen to be lying broadside-on near Merthen Point, at the western end of St Loy. She looked intact, but when the tide ebbed her bottom plates were seen to be badly damaged. The salvage steamer *Lady of the Isles* arrived, but even then it was obvious that refloating the stranded steamer would be a very difficult operation.

The *South America*, a steel screw steamer of 4,197 tons gross, was owned by the Nitrate Producers Co of London and had been launched in 1900 by Short Bros of Sunderland. She had sailed from Hamburg four days before the wreck, bound for Cardiff in water ballast, under charter to the Hamburg Amerika Line. The weather was poor until the evening of 12 March, when it cleared and Captain Bowling was able to morse 'All's well' to the signal station on the Lizard, but less than half an hour later the *South America* was steaming through thick banks of drizzle and frequent squalls of torrential rain, and having to steer a zigzag course across Mount's Bay to avoid the Newlyn pilchard fleet, strung out hap-hazardly from Mousehole island to the Runnelstone. At midnight Captain Bowling altered course northward to take the *South America* round Land's End. She ploughed on through the murk with the lookouts still keeping a wary eye open for the fishing boats and had just avoided a lugger lying at her nets when second officer Read saw the dark shape of the land right ahead. The helm was swung hard over, but even as the steamer's 389-hp engine was put violently into reverse there was a rumbling screech and she shuddered over the big round boulders of St Loy Bay.

In the days after the wreck, prospects of salvage grew dimmer with every tide, and a gale which blew up a week later caused more serious damage. Finally the underwriters disposed of her to the Western Marine Salvage Co of Penzance, who began to break her up. At a Board of Trade inquiry in May 1912, Captain Bowling and his officers levelled charges of looting at the people of St Loy, as a number of things, including chief officer Thom's Boer War medals and a large manilla hawser, had mysteriously disappeared. The medals were returned, but the hawser was not, and there was talk that someone had been wrecking. These accusations were bitterly resented by the local people, many of whom had given every help and opened their homes to the shipwrecked crew. After two days the findings of the court were announced. Captain Bowling was found guilty of not having navigated the *South America* with due care and in a proper and seamanlike manner; he had failed to take soundings after the shore lights were obscured and should not have altered course until he was certain of the steamer's position. In view of his previously unblemished record, he did not lose his certificate but received a severe warning. After the proceedings he withdrew his allegations about the looting of the *South America*.

During the spring and summer of 1912 the local people became familiar with the great hulk of the *South America* and the breaking gangs who swarmed over her, and many could remember similar scenes from twenty years before, when the French pitwood steamer *Saintonge* was wrecked in the bay. A few storms disturbed the work and one night in July the salvage men were called to Mousehole where another large steamer, the *Transporter* of North Shields, in ballast from St Nazaire to the Tyne, had run ashore in thick fog. Most of her crew came ashore by breeches-buoy, but found the Penzer cliffs so uninviting that they returned aboard and stayed there until the *Lady of the Isles* refloated the *Transporter* later in the day.

Page 205: (above) The Lowestoft sailing trawler *Girl Annie*, wrecked at Pardenack on 4 May 1908 in thick fog; (below) the shattered wreckage of the Liverpool barque *Khyber* covers the beach at Portloe a few hours after she struck on 15 March 1905.

City of Cardiff

Page 206: (above) One of the crew of the *City of Cardiff*, wrecked at Nanjizel on 21 March 1912, comes ashore in the breeches buoy; (below) the ship that knocked the top off the Runnelstone, the Ellerman steamer *City of Westminster*, slowly breaking up on 8 October 1923.

Autumn came and the *South America* was still slowly diminishing as the salvage men cut deeper into her big steel hull. October was an even foggier month than usual that year, and it was during the dark hours of the 14th that the extraordinary wreck occurred in St Loy, exactly seven months after the first one. At half-past three in the morning, John Richards was roused from his bed for the second time that year by unusual noises in the bay. He thought at first that the salvage men must have raised steam on the *South America*, or were engaged on some particularly noisy job, but as it seemed unlikely at that hour he took the lantern he had used to guide in the *South America*'s crew and made his way down to the shore. Thick fog swirled over the sea and it was several minutes before he saw a small steamer right against the big hulk's weather side. For a moment he thought that it must be a salvage craft, but foam churning below her counter showed that the newcomer was desperately trying to back clear. Richards called out and received a reply in a tongue he did not understand. After a while the crew appeared to give up their attempt to get clear and Richards set off to send news of the wreck.

Within an hour the *Lady of the Isles* had arrived, towing the Newlyn lifeboat, while the rocket cart from Mousehole had joined the inhabitants of St Loy on the same rocks from which they had fired the line over the *South America*. The lifeboatmen and coastguards soon discovered that the stranded steamer was the 599-ton steel screw, schooner-rigged *Abertay*, owned by Bois et Chabois of Lorient and bound for Barry with a cargo of pitwood. She had sailed from France thirty-six hours previously and encountered foggy weather right from the start. It got worse, and shortly before midnight on the 13th the wind had fallen away and the fog become so thick that the lookouts could scarcely see beyond the bows. Around three o'clock there was a tremendous crash, and her crew, confronted by the tall shape of the *South America*, thought that they were in a collision. Then the *Abertay* began to pound and roll on the rocks and they knew she was ashore.

Dawn revealed an amazing sight. The *Abertay* lay so neatly placed alongside the *South America* that it looked as though they had been deliberately moored together. But beneath the swell it was a different story; the French steamer's forefoot and bilges were a crumpled mass of metal, the plates buckled and twisted apart.

M

Her master, a tall, handsome and moustached Biscayan of about forty, suffered further misfortune on the day after the wreck, when he slipped and fell over a ledge on the cliff and was rushed to Penzance with serious injuries. The *Abertay*, which was launched by W Simon & Co of Renfrew in 1888 as a well-decked steamer, was beyond salvage and was broken up for scrap along with the *South America*.

On the same night the *Abertay* was wrecked, another French crew met disaster only a few miles westwards, when the 88-ton wooden schooner *Espiegle* of Treguier, also laden with pitwood and a week out from Brest, struck the Guthenbras Rock, below Tol-Pedn. Her headgear, bowsprit and fore-canvas were telescoped and she rebounded into deep water with her bows stove in. The 13-year-old cabin boy, Amède Kergudalan, was swept away while the punt was being launched, but the rest of the crew and their dog pulled clear safely. They climbed on to the great Guthenbras Rock shortly before 3 am (at almost the same instant the *Abertay* ran ashore at St Loy) and were marooned there until dawn, when the Tol-Pedn coastguards rescued them with breeches-buoy and cliff ladders. The nine-year-old *Espiegle* (which means 'Mischievous') vanished for nearly two weeks, until a hard gale battered her to pieces and her cargo strewed the beaches from Mousehole to Loe Bar.

No vessel was more in danger from the coast between Mousehole and Tol-Pedn than a fishing-boat running for Newlyn in bad weather. Experienced local men, tough 'East Coasties' whose spindly-funnelled drifter had ridden out countless North Sea gales, or stocky Bretons in their brightly-painted, seaworthy crabbers, each was as vulnerable as the other when the Porthcurno cliffs were hidden by thick fog or drizzly rain. Once the twinkle of the light on the Runnelstone buoy had vanished astern, assuming it was visible at all, there was no other beacon or seamark until the lights of Mount's Bay came into view. A fisherman had only his skill and instinct to guide him on such a night. As fishing craft tend to sail close to the shore, any slight miscalculation is enough to send them on to the rocks. Of the score which have stranded along this unlit and dangerous ten-mile stretch of the west Cornish coast, only three have survived; a powerful steam drifter, a stoutly-built French trawler and a modern, well-equipped motor fishing-vessel.

All three owed their salvation to the Penlee lifeboat and a good deal of luck.

At Mousehole, some sixty years ago, they had a primitive but effective method of warning the fishing fleet as it approached the harbour in fog. The youths of the village stood on the parapet of the pier and dropped heavy pieces of iron on to the jetty below with an ear-splitting clang which carried a long way seawards and saved many a lugger from running ashore. Even so, several of the Mousehole fleet were lost while homeward bound. The lugger *Boy Tom*, returning from the wreck of the *Howard A Turner* at Lamorna on 28 January 1890, missed stays as she ran for the harbour. A fresh ENE gale was blowing and her crew had to abandon her before she went ashore below the Gurnick, beyond the old harbour wall. They had just landed when the lugger *Kite*, homeward bound from the Plymouth fishery, appeared round the island, also missed stays and was similarly blown ashore. The crew of the *Boy Tom*, Captain William Thomas Polgreen, Robert Thurban, John Pender and John Richards, at once refloated their punt, put off and rescued the crew of the *Kite*. They later received £4 each for their courageous action.

The fishing boat *Unity* sank off Lamorna in December 1893, fortunately without loss of life, but when the long-liner *Arethusa* vanished off the island on 22 January 1895, her crew of three were drowned. The *Emmeline* and the *Jonadab* drove from their anchors on to the island during a NNE gale in April 1899. The *Vanguard* was cut down off the Bucks in April 1904 by the Lowestoft drifter *Berry Castle*, only one of the considerable number of Cornish fishing boats lost by collision. Another was the lugger *Orlando*, which was towing the dismasted *Emblem* home in a northerly gale in October 1907 when she changed tack, got across the tow and was rammed amidships. The *Emblem* was herself lost on 27 April 1914, when a heavy ground swell swept her out of Mousehole harbour and on to what is locally known as Hotel Rock. She was so badly damaged that as a danger to navigation she had to be burned. The second lugger *Emblem*, built to replace her, caught fire and sank off the Wolf Rock twenty years later. The fishing grounds themselves could be dangerous, too; the *Rising Sun* was almost wrecked on the Runnelstone on 17 May 1908, and the *Percy* had a narrow escape when she went tumbling through the shoal water of Carn Base. Three others lost while homeward bound were the sailing drifter *Minnie*, wrecked outside the harbour on 8 August 1914, the *Kiora* at Lamorna in the early 1920s, and the motor lugger *Agnes* below Carn Boscawen on 25 July 1925.

Not all the lost fishing boats were local. On a misty morning in May 1899 the Lowestoft steam drifter *Excellent*, one of the many East Coast boats which, until the Second World War, spent each mackerel season fishing from Newlyn, struck the Bucks and went down. The Brixham sailing trawler *Harry* dragged her anchors nearly two miles in a southerly gale before she was wrecked below what was later to find fame as the Minack Theatre at Porthcurno. On 1 June 1926 the Yarmouth drifter *Young Charlie*, outward bound from Newlyn, struck the Bucks and backed clear with water pouring into her fish hold. The Lowestoft drifters *Primevere* and *Empire Heroes* ran alongside and took her in tow for Newlyn. It seemed as if they might succeed until they drew level with Penzer Point. Then the *Young Charlie* gave a heavy lurch, broke the hawser, and with barely time for the other boats to take off her crew, she sank in eighteen fathoms off the Dominee Rock. It was small consolation to her skipper that some of her nets and gear were recovered next morning. The *Young Charlie* lay far too deep to be salvaged.

In the early hours of 13 January 1937, the Belgian motor trawler *Vierge Marie* of Ostend set the tragic pattern for many wrecks to come. A farm labourer who lived near Carn Boscawen stepped from his cottage door shortly before dawn and was greeted by the thick, pungent reek of fuel oil wafting in from the sea. Buttoning his heavy weatherproofs against the driving wind and rain, he picked his way across the fields and soon made out the lights of the *Vierge Marie*, ashore in a narrow cove just beyond Tater Du point. When he heard the shouts of her crew he wasted no time in getting to the farm where he worked, so that the news could be telephoned to Penzance. He then returned to the wreck with more men and ropes, only to see a small boat, manned by three men, capsize as the Penlee lifeboat closed in to rescue them. They were buoyed up by their lifejackets, but even so were in a bad way when they were hauled out. Artificial respiration was kept up on all three as the lifeboat sped back to Newlyn, but they died before they reached hospital.

As the light grew, the men on the cliffs could see no sign of life as the trawler rolled and slewed with every wave that broke into the small cove. Unknown to them, the farm labourer's wife had been roused by a loud knocking an hour after her husband had left and, thinking he had returned, she opened the door to be confronted by a drenched and battered stranger. In fluent English he told her that he was Captain Josef Lus and that his ship had been wrecked nearby. While the woman heated kettles and fetched blankets, he staggered off into the fog again, to return ten minutes later supporting his chief mate, Gustave Vanlee, whose legs were so badly cut that he could hardly stand.

The 200-ton *Vierge Marie* had been on her way into Newlyn after developing engine trouble off Pendeen the previous afternoon, and there had been no warning of how close the weather had brought her to the Lamorna cliffs until she struck. Captain Lus radioed an 'SOS', but the ground swell was so bad that he had to give the order to abandon ship without waiting for rescue. As the dinghy was launched a wave overturned it; the captain and mate jumped into the sea, but engineer Hessene and deckhands Yaston and Miel righted the dinghy and pulled clear, only to capsize on the point of being rescued by Penlee lifeboat. The trawler's young cabin boy, Valentine Maartens, was missing, presumed swept overboard and drowned. The *Vierge Marie* rolled over to starboard a few hours after going ashore and within a day or two was a jumbled mass of broken plating and fittings jammed beneath the cliffs at Tater Du.

Eleven years passed, and the tragedy of the *Vierge Marie* was repeated. Again, it was the usual 'wreck weather' for the western cliffs; hazy with heavy ground seas, the aftermath of a hard southwest gale. Shortly after one o'clock on the morning of 1 November 1948, the coastguard on watch at Treen saw the lights of a motor vessel emerge from a fierce squall of rain and head straight for the surf beating upon Pedn-e-Vounder sands. In response to the rapid blink of his Aldis lamp, she turned eastwards and vanished round Logan Rock headland. Though she made no signal, either to acknowledge the warning or to ask for help, he called out Treen LSA company and another coastguard and went down into Penberth Cove. There was no sign of the mysterious ship, but the wind was thick with the stench of fuel oil. Suddenly he saw a young man washing about in the surf and despite almost being swept away, dragged him out and carried him to a nearby cottage.

Search parties began to scour the cliffs. A lifejacket marked 'ST GUENOLE-ROUEN' was picked up on the rocks near the cove, and at dawn a vessel of about 500 tons was found bottom up beneath Gribba Point, less than half a mile away. The *St Guenole*, a steel tar tanker owned by Cie Mar de Transport de Goudron of Rouen, bound in ballast from Nantes to Irvine on Clydeside with a crew of twelve, was a total wreck. Twenty-three-year-old André Fourcin, the sailor saved by the coastguard, was the sole survivor.

The *St Guenole* rusted away beneath the Penberth cliffs and the memory of the wreck slowly faded, until there came a devastating reminder of that night's tragedy when the *Vert Prairial* was wrecked less than a mile away at Porthcurno on 13 March 1956. The first intimation of disaster came at 5 am when the Scilly steamer *Peninnis* picked up an almost inaudible 'SOS' prefixed by the call sign 'Dieppe 1517'. This confirmed a report just received by Land's End radio, via Stonehouse radio, Aberdeen, that the British steamer *Tiana* had also intercepted a weak 'SOS' from an unidentified vessel. 'Dieppe 1517' was definitely a French trawler and calls went out at once to the western fishing ports to discover who and where she was. It was soon learned that the call-sign belonged to the 250-ton Dieppe motor trawler *Vert Prairial* which, under command of Jean Baptiste Coppin, had sailed from Brixham shortly before six o'clock the previous evening, bound for the fishing-grounds off Trevose Head. That she was in distress was certain, but no one knew where she was until, at 5.45 am, Tol-Pedn coastguards received a telephone call from Porthcurno. Half an hour earlier a local man had been searching for driftwood on Porth Chapel beach, below Wireless Point, and had been confronted by the bows of a large trawler standing darkly out of the surf. The mystery of 'Dieppe 1517' was solved and the rescue services began at once to converge on Porthcurno. There was no sign of life aboard, although the *Vert Prairial* was known to carry a crew of seventeen. As the morning light grew, the worst fears were realised. There were no survivors. The bodies of Captain Coppin and most of the crew were recovered, and another big deep-sea trawler, the *Gai Floreal* (which was herself to strand near St Ives in 1962, and escape by little short of a miracle), took them back to Dieppe.

The *Vert Prairial*, which had fallen on her side soon after she stranded, lay exposed to the seas and soon broke up, though not before coastguards and naval frogmen had vainly searched her hull for some of the missing crew. Within a few months she had gone to pieces, although the massive cylinder block of her diesel engine still lies among the rocks below Wireless Point. How she came to run ashore could never be established with any certainty. She was an extremely well-built deep-sea trawler, launched at Sorel on the St Lawrence in 1948 and equipped with every modern aid to safe navigation. The weather was by no means rough; a fresh east-by-north breeze was blowing, with a very slight haze. Offshore the seas were choppy, but she had been built to withstand far worse conditions, and the surf breaking on the cliffs should have warned her lookouts long before she got so close that she could not escape running ashore. 'Dieppe 1517' still remains something of a mystery.

Within eighteen months, on 21 September 1957, there was another wreck at Porthcurno, with an echo of the wreck of the St Ives fishing boat *Iverna* in exactly the same place, twenty-six years before. As usual it was the early hours of a foggy morning when the pilchard driver *Nazarene* of St Ives, inward bound for Newlyn with 120 stone of fish, ran ashore on Pedn-e-Vounder beach. It was only twenty minutes to high water and Skipper Edward Toman and his crew gathered in the shelter of the wheelhouse rather than risk rowing through the surf. When the *Nazarene* ebbed dry they jumped down on to the sands but, like the *Iverna*'s crew in September 1931, the thick fog hid their plight and they faced the tall cliffs unaided. Fisherman Francis Stevens began to climb but fell, and Skipper Toman decided they should wait for daylight. At seven o'clock they reached the clifftop, and within half an hour they had knocked up the postmaster of Treen.

The fog was lifting slightly when they returned to the beach where the badly damaged *Nazarene* lay high and dry. The rest of the day was spent salvaging her nets and gear, which were brought up the cliffs in a breeches-buoy, but the weather was breaking and by nightfall there was an ugly swell. At dawn, tremendous seas were thundering down on Pedn-e-Vounder beach; by four o'clock that afternoon all that remained of the little *Nazarene* was a pile of shattered timber and her engine block half buried in the sand.

She was one of the few St Ives boats still plying her trade. Skipper Toman had sailed in her since he was a boy, as she had been built for his father at Porthleven in the 1920s.

In the following year the reputation of the 'fishing-boat grave-yard' grew. Two more local boats escaped by a hair's breadth the fate of the *Nazarene*. In July, the open gig *Swiftsure* was fishing close to Lamorna when the two Mousehole fishermen found her engine would not restart. The fresh southerly wind carried the gig so near the rocks that they had to fend her off with oars, until a motor launch came out from the cove and towed them clear. A month later the fishing-boat *Hesperian*, moving at half speed after hauling her nets, ran on to an underwater ledge between Carn Du and Penzer Point. She canted over but her skipper dared not back off for fear she would capsize and drown them all. Providentially, the *Hesperian* was a strongly-built Scotch type of motor fishing-boat, less than two years old and equipped with radio, and her signals of distress brought out the Penlee lifeboat. A line was fired across, a stout hawser sent back and inch by inch as the tide flowed the lifeboat towed her free. They were all back at Newlyn by dawn and the *Hesperian* was moored safely alongside the pier with the rest of the fishing fleet.

The fatal attraction the Lamorna and Porthcurno cliffs seemed to possess for fishing craft continued with a vengeance. Shortly after five o'clock in the morning on 1 April 1959, Skipper Albert Kernion of the crabber *Pluie de Roses*, of Audierne, was roused from his bunk when she hit the boulders not fifty feet from where the *South America* and the *Abertay* once lay together. The crew were saved, but the *Pluie de Roses*, which was only eighteen months old and represented all Skipper Kernion's savings, was beyond salvage. The motor trawler *Boy David*, a 70-tonner painted in the pale grey with the black, silver-banded funnel of the Newlyn trawling firm of Stevenson & Sons, was returning from a four-day trip off the Longships in company with the *W & S* and the *Trewarvaneth* when, at 2.15 am on 16 January 1961, she struck the Bucks. She backed clear but was sinking, and by the time the crew abandoned her the foredeck was awash. Fifteen minutes after she struck, the *Boy David* sank quietly by the head. The *W & S* picked up the crew and at three o'clock landed them at Newlyn. Weather conditions at the time of the wreck were similar to those when the

Vert Prairial was lost; a fresh easterly wind and a slight haze over the sea, which at times affected visibility.

Not only the number of fishing boats actually wrecked, but also the many that would have been lost but for a last minute warning by coastguards, prompted renewed agitation for a light or fog signal to be built on the cliffs between Lamorna and Porthcurno. Fishing vessels would then no longer have to pass ten miles of dangerous unlit coast to reach Newlyn, while any coaster which lost her bearings might have a vital last-minute warning. But even as the proposed beacon was being discussed, there came the last and one of the most tragic wrecks of all.

The early hours of 23 October 1963 found the *Juan Ferrer* of Valencia, a handsome, well-equipped motor coaster of nearly 700 tons, thrashing her way up towards Land's End on her usual run from her home port to Liverpool. The weather was bad; a strong, damp south-west wind had brought thick drizzle and occasional fierce rainstorms in from the Atlantic, and a heavy ground swell broke beneath the Lamorna cliffs. Steadily the *Juan Ferrer* rolled on through the wind and rain; at 2.30 am the lights of another vessel astern suddenly vanished as she ran into a thick bank of fog. Her young captain, 32-year-old Luis Ruiz, made for the radio room to contact Land's End and establish his position. Minutes ticked by with only the crackle of static coming through, then came a cry from the deck, 'Rocks ahead!' which sent him racing topsides. Right in front of the *Juan Ferrer*'s bows towered 'great looming shapes' as the captain later described them, and his shout for 'Full Astern' was drowned as the coaster's elegantly flared bow smashed into a wall of granite below Carn Boscawen. Deck cargo broke loose under the impact and, calling for all hands, the captain ran back to the radio room. At 3 am, Land's End radio picked up 'Juan Ferrer. Am ashore vicinity of Mount's Bay'. It was the only signal Captain Ruiz could send out before the sea put the generators out of action.

José Sevillano, a 21-year-old sailor who had been hurled from his bunk by the sudden shock, reached the deck to find the ship already heeling over into the surf. Benito Nuncy, another young seaman, joined in trying to launch the lifeboats which were carried on each side of the funnel, abaft the bridge. One boat was against the rocks, so the Spaniards turned to the other. After a struggle in the wind and darkness they lowered it, but a heavy sea smashed it against the coaster's side and it was swept away. There was one other boat, a small dinghy carried in the bows, but there was no hope of reaching it over the jumbled chaos of what had once been a neatly-stacked deck cargo.

The *Juan Ferrer* listed until her decks were almost vertical, but the rocks were only twelve feet away and Benito Nuncy jumped overboard. He was dashed on to the rocks but managed to crawl

JUAN FERRER

Location of the 700-ton motor coaster *Juan Ferrer*, wrecked at the foot of Boscawen Cliff in 1963.

up beyond reach of the waves; soon, José Sevillano, Baldomero Garcia, the 19-year-old bosun, and José Ojinaga, the 20-year-old chief engineer, also leapt overboard. Garcia vanished at once, even though he wore a lifejacket like the others, and Ojinaga was swept away as he tried to get a hold on the slippery granite. José Sevillano alone scrambled up to join Benito Nuncy on Carn Boscawen. Fifteen minutes later the galley boy, José Alonso, got ashore half-naked, and the three huddled among the boulders to shelter from the wind and driving rain. They stayed there in the hope that more of their shipmates had survived, although the *Juan Ferrer* was barely visible in the surf below.

Captain Ruiz stayed with his ship until the last possible moment, when, although a non-swimmer, he leapt off the stern as the coaster rolled over beneath him. The suction dragged him down and when he surfaced it was to hear the cries of his crew around him, but they soon faded and he was left alone in the rough seas. Supported by a bundle of wooden staves from the cargo, he trod water and drifted back and forth with the current. The first streaks of dawn gave him hope, and as he rose on a wavecrest he could just make out the distant shape of the Penlee lifeboat. He tried to shout and strike out towards her but his limbs were numb. Fortunately, his feeble cries were heard by two brothers, members of the Treen LSA company who, along with every other rescue service, had been searching for the *Juan Ferrer* since her distress call at three o'clock. The brothers signalled to the lifeboat and it closed in, hands reached down and Captain Ruiz was pulled from the sea in the last stages of exhaustion. He had been in the water for nearly four hours.

The three survivors on shore had stayed near the wreck for several hours before they struck off inland across the fields, and they were met by a rescue party at seven o'clock as they wandered up a farm lane. They were hurried to the warm hospitality of a nearby farm, while coastguards, LSA companies, an armada of rescue ships and a naval helicopter converged on Carn Boscawen. The *Juan Ferrer* lay submerged, nothing visible except the tip of her bows, rocking gently up and down with the waves swirling back and forth across the white letters of her name. Eleven of the crew had been drowned; nearly all of them young men in their early twenties. Only two of the crew were over thirty-two, and some, like the bosun, were hardly out of their teens.

Owned by Frederico Ferrer of Valencia, the *Juan Ferrer* was only three years old and had been built in her home port by AST Neptuno. She soon broke up beneath the cliffs and her stern, with its big German diesels, settled back into deep water. Nothing was salvaged, though both her engine-room telegraphs were later recovered by divers. Her cargo, several thousand bundles of staves, large sheets of thick plywood, and sporting shotguns strewed the shore from Land's End to Marazion for months after the wreck and proved extremely useful to the local people, who used it in a variety of ingenious ways. It was a coincidence of a kind which has happened a good many times that the *Juan Ferrer* had been involved in an incident off the Cornish coast only two months earlier when, on 29 August, she had towed the burnt-out and derelict motor yacht *Sheila* from Trevose Head into Hayle. Her sister ship, the *Ignacio Ferrer*, came to Penzance to take home Valencia's dead and a simple service was conducted on the end of the pier before she cast off and steamed slowly out of Mount's Bay. Four bodies recovered later were buried at Penzance.

The death of the eleven seamen at last focused attention urgently on the dangers of the coast between Lamorna and Porthcurno. Within weeks, the campaign for a light and fog signal had reached the floor of the House of Commons and the Board of Trade. It was widely discussed, films and interviews were shown on television, and finally, in January 1964, Trinity House announced that they would erect a beacon on Tater Du headland, just east of Carn Boscawen. Eighteen months later it was officially opened by the Duke of Gloucester, and since then the 30,000-candlepower light, and the resonant boom of the fog siren, seem to have put an end to the 'fishing-boat graveyard' and the tragedy of the western cliffs.

CHAPTER NINE

THE RUNNELSTONE AND LAND'S END

WHETHER the cliffs were shrouded in a thick sea fog, or whether the day was clear, there was no greater danger to shipping coming around Land's End than the Runnelstone, an underwater granite pinnacle a mile southwards of Tol-Pedn-Penwith. Marked at sea by a large Trinity House bell buoy, the Runnelstone, or Rundlestone as it was once called, stood directly in the path of any vessel which, by accident or design, steamed or sailed too close to this part of the Cornish coast. Many captains took the deliberate risk, or made the very often fatal mistake of cutting the corner too sharply at Tol-Pedn, and either forgot or badly miscalculated the position of the reef which lurked beneath the swell. There is a saying that the shallow water around the Runnelstone is due to wreck having piled upon wreck over the years, and records show that this might not be such an exaggeration as it seems. From 1880 to 1923, when a 6,000-ton Ellerman 'City' liner smashed the top off the 'Stone', as it is known locally, over thirty steamers were wrecked, stranded or badly damaged, while before the eclipse of the great fleets of sailing coasters hardly a year passed without some small schooner, smack or brigantine being lost.

One of the earliest accounts concerns the wreck of a brig. The story was written years later by the sole survivor, when he was more than ninety years old, and was published in a now long-defunct Cornish journal. Early in March 1795, the brig (which unfortunately the mariner does not name) sailed from the Thames in ballast for Barry, to load a cargo of iron for Gibraltar. She met heavy weather in the Downs and a foremast hand was lost overboard. Off the Cornish coast the gale veered north-east and, unable to weather Land's End, the captain kept the brig beating up and down between Mousehole and Tol-Pedn in the shelter of the cliffs.

The wind increased and blew the brig gradually to the west until, at 2 am on 17 March, she struck the Runnelstone.

Masts and yards crashed down as she heeled over, decks awash, and the crew of six took to their longboat. They tried to row towards the land, only a short way off, but were numb with cold and the gale blew so strongly offshore that they were soon carried out to sea, eventually capsizing in breakers off the Scillies, where all but two were drowned. It took the two survivors nearly four hours to fight their way, scrambling over rocks and swimming the intervening channels, the short distance to land and the elder of the two, the ship's mate, died from exhaustion within a week of landing on the island.

Ships of the Royal Navy were no safer than any others from the danger off Tol-Pedn; on 7 March 1806, a large stores hulk under convoy of the *Caroline* of fourteen guns, from Portsmouth, struck the Runnelstone. Lieutenant Derby of the *Caroline* succeeded in saving his charge's crew before she sank, but with her went a prodigious amount of copper bolts, brass and gunmetal fittings, and spars and yards, all of which had been destined to refit the man-o'-war hulks then lying at Milford and in the Mersey. Four years later there was a more serious affair, when the sloop *Wild Boar*, of ten guns, outward bound from Falmouth and commanded by Captain Thomas Burton, struck and foundered on the Runnelstone at dusk on 15 February 1810. Captain Burton and twelve men were rescued by a Welsh brig, but sixty-four men were lost. She was only the first of three warships to be lost on the Cornish coast that winter, and the sixth or seventh since the *Anson* disaster in 1807.

A quite unnecessary tragedy occurred on 3 July 1815 when, early in the morning, a crippled schooner floundered past Tol-Pedn, having been damaged in a fight with a privateer a few weeks previously. Off Porthgwarra, her crew suddenly abandoned ship and pulled away to a nearby brig. Three fishermen put off in a gig to try to salvage the derelict, but as they approached her they were hailed from the brig and warned that she was about to sink. Paying no heed, they scrambled aboard and went below, and only minutes later, under the horrified gaze of fisherfolk on the cliffs, the schooner suddenly heeled and sank, drowning the three men. There was further loss of life on 30 April 1821 when the Swansea brig *Birmingham*, Wales to Havre-de-Grace with iron, left the shelter of

Mount's Bay only to strike the Runnelstone. Two lads clung to wreckage and were picked up by a fishing-boat, but no trace of Captain Rotherhaugh, his wife, their young daughter and the rest of the crew was ever found.

Late in June 1825 it was reported from Penzance that a large red wooden buoy, marked 'Runnelstone' in large white letters and specially sent down by Trinity House, was lying neglected on the pier. At length, on 29 June, it was laid on the reef by Lieutenant Goldsmith of the revenue cutter *Nimble*, only to be picked up a fortnight later by a fishing-boat off Mousehole, trailing fourteen fathoms of broken chain. It was to break loose many times during the next fifty years. On 15 September 1826, even as the revenue cutter *Dove* was re-laying the buoy after stormy weather, the Teignmouth schooner *Fanny* foundered on the reef. On 14 November 1827 the Dove laid a new buoy, anchored by stout cables sent by their Lordships of the Admiralty. Lieutenant Davy probably sailed away well satisfied, but hardly had the barnacles begun to encrust the buoy than the Dartmouth sloop *Polyblank,* flying around Land's End before a westerly gale, coal-laden from Newport, struck the reef. She sank instantly, and her crew crawled ashore at Lamorna from their capsized longboat. Occasionally the runaway buoy brought about a tragely, as on the morning of 11 March 1833 when, the buoy having been adrift for several weeks, a brig of about 150 tons, with black sides and no figurehead, struck the Stone and sank with all hands.

The *Cornish Telegraph* for the week ending 20 March 1841 reported that Lieutenant Crese of the Packet *Hope* had arrived at Falmouth with the news that the Runnelstone buoy was drifting in heavy seas, miles from its proper position. The report expressed the hope that it would be immediately replaced, but the same edition of the paper carried an account of a large derelict ship ashore at Porthgwarra, which had obviously struck the Runnelstone and drifted in. The only clues to her identity were a torn Belgian flag with an unusual armorial device, and her figurehead of a black lion. Her scattered cargo of dyewood, bags of sumach, casks of naptha, small animal skins, casks of caoutchouc gum, berries and wool, suggested that she was an Indiaman. Four days later two local men, Hall and Luke of St Leven, were brought before the magistrates on charges of wrecking.

The buoy was again reported adrift on 2 March 1877, when it was sighted off Cape Cornwall, having rounded Land's End. It had broken loose several weeks previously and been replaced by another, and was now a menace to shipping as the sound of its bell and its shifting position could easily confuse a mariner. It was proposed that the St Just Volunteer Artillery Corps should sink it by gunfire, but the success or otherwise of this doubtful enterprise is not known.

The toll of the Runnelstone continued. Many of its victims were from the myriad West Country coasting fleets; brigantines, schooners or ketches bearing names of such old-fashioned charm as the *Maid of the Mist* of Brixham, the *Carrie* of Truro, the *Louisa* of Dartmouth, the *Friends* of St Ives, the *Providence* and the *Plymouth Packet*, both of Plymouth, the *Galeed* of Salcombe and the *Emily* of Looe. Little reminder is now left of these many small wooden craft, except perhaps a shapeless cake of rust that might once have been an anchor, a few lines of small print in an early Cornish newspaper, or a long-forgotten grave in a churchyard near the coast.

Sometimes the Runnelstone wrecked large sailing ships. At dawn on 4 November 1895, the cottagers around Porthcurno awoke to find the Yankee windjammer *Granite State* rolling in the swell off the beach, with most of her canvas still set. Owned by D Marcy of Portsmouth, New Hampshire, and launched at Kittery, Maine, in 1877, she had arrived at Falmouth four days previously with wheat from the River Plate, and received orders to discharge at Swansea. She left Carrick Roads on the afternoon of the 3rd, and four o'clock next morning found her shaping up to round Land's End, under easy sail in a fresh north-east breeze. Captain Fulton handed her over to the first mate, who made a slight alteration to the course. Less than an hour later there came a heavy thud aft, and a hurried examination revealed a foot of water in the bilges. The Cardiff tug *Elliott & Jeffry* was only a mile away as her master, expecting the windjammer to need a tow around Land's End because of the east wind, had followed in her wake since she left Falmouth. His offer of help was accepted with alacrity, and the *Granite State* was hauled off Le Or. She was badly damaged and the tug just managed to nose her into the sandy shallows of Porthcurno.

Page 224: The Land's End cliffs as a shipwrecked seaman sees them; a sheer wall of rock, here confronting the trawler *Victoire Roger*, wrecked on 24 March 1964.

Captain Fulton went to Penzance in the tug to consult with his owner's agent and Lloyd's officials. When he returned to the *Granite State* several hours later, she was rapidly settling down and taking a list to port. She rolled and bumped heavily and even before high water the decks were awash. The wheat cargo began to swell and when the hatches burst under the pressure Captain Fulton and the crew abandoned ship. As darkness fell, the wind hauled southwards, freshened strongly and sent a heavy ground swell into the bay. A lot of wreckage was swept ashore and by morning it was obvious that the ship would never be refloated. She broke up soon afterwards in a winter gale.

Typical of the many small steamers wrecked on the Runnelstone in the second half of the nineteenth century was the 140-ton three-masted, iron screw *Acklington*. Unlike the master of the big Lancaster schooner *Margaret Jane*, wrecked two winters earlier, Captain Henry actually heard the muffled clang of the bell-buoy as his vessel rounded Land's End on 20 August 1887, deep-laden with steam coal from Newport to Portsmouth. But fog plays strange tricks with sound and what seemed to come from well off the port beam was actually dead ahead. The *Acklington* struck the Runnelstone and sank within ten minutes, leaving her crew to row into Penzance. Similar weather wrecked the small iron steamer *Camel* on Le Or on 7 February 1891, while bound from Garston to Plymouth. Down with her went 320 tons of best Lancashire coal, destined for the Plymouth Co-operative Society, but the crew got away in two boats. The chief officer of another small steamer, the 691 tons gross *Primrose* of West Hartlepool, Waterford for Rouen with oats, deviated from the course set by his captain, lost sight of the Longships light during a squall and steered her on to the Runnelstone. Her crew rowed into Mousehole, but the *Primrose* washed clear of the reef and appeared off Porthgwarra, starting the rumour that there had been another wreck. Slowly filling, she drifted westwards until she sank in nine fathoms off Tol-Pedn.

Not all the wrecked steamers were southbound around the Longships; the Runnelstone was just as hazardous for any crossing Mount's Bay from the Lizard. The *Harley*, in ballast from Looe to Neath, missed her bearings in thick fog on 28 May 1892 and two hours after losing sight of the Lizard light steamed straight on to the reef. She sank quickly and her crew were picked up by

N

a St Ives lugger as they rowed away out past the Wolf Rock in the firm belief that they were heading for Penzance. A much larger steamer, the 1,884-ton *Benwick*, of Newcastle, Antwerp for Barry in ballast, likewise steaming blindly from the Lizard, struck the Runnelstone at 5 am on 13 February 1903. Crippled, she drifted before the strong south-west wind, until shortly before dawn she drove ashore and was wrecked near Porthcurno.

Other vessels were lost as they groped around off Land's End in thick fog, vainly searching for the open waters of the Bristol Channel, among them several big Spanish steamers engaged in the iron-ore trade between Spain and South Wales. The 2,035-ton *Sardinero*, of and from Bilboa for Newport, struck the Runnelstone on 12 May 1906, and sank only seconds after her crew were taken off by the steamer *Valhalla* of Bergen. The Spaniards were so unnerved by their experience that it took the Norwegian crew a considerable time to calm them. On 23 May 1915, the 2,388-ton *José de Arambura* avoided the German U-boats off Scilly, only to smash her bows on to Le Or. Her crew of twenty-three pulled into Porthgwarra, leaving the 17-year-old steamer bubbling oil and debris, six fathoms deep off Tol-Pedn.

It was another ore steamer, the 1,863-ton steel screw *Febrero*, which went down with the heaviest loss of life ever known on the Runnelstone. Owned by the Bilbaina Navigation Co of Bilboa, she was launched in 1898 by the Campbelltown Shipbuilding Co, who had also built the *Sardinero*, as a schooner-rigged steamer of 1,126 tons net, powered by 172-hp compounds. She sailed from Bilboa on the evening of 18 June 1910, bound for Newport with a crew of twenty-eight, and with three men and a boy as passengers. The weather was dirty but all went well until 10 pm on the 20th, when the *Febrero*'s young cook, Roque Triarte, was roused from his bunk by a resounding crash. He rushed on deck where the crew were trying to launch the three big lifeboats, but there was no time. Triarte jumped overboard as the *Febrero* went under and swam away to avoid being sucked down. Soon he got on to a drifting hatch cover, which kept him afloat until the waves carried him ashore at daybreak in Nanjizel Bay, where he was found by a farmer sitting on the cliff-top drying out his clothes. He was the only survivor, the sunken steamer being found a week later by a fisherman, less than half a mile ENE of the Runnelstone.

Sometimes ships which struck the reef escaped with only dented plates, and though this could be serious if the weather was rough there was still a chance of reaching Newlyn or Penzance. It was not an infrequent sight for one of these cripples to lurch past Mousehole Island, almost awash, with her siren wailing and her life-jacketed crew pumping desperately to keep afloat. On 27 February 1906, the Workington coaster *Stainburn* reached Newlyn only minutes before the rising oily-black flood in her engine-room swamped the fires. The Cardiff collier *Castleford*, outward bound to Havre with coal, which struck the 'Stone' in a south-westerly gale on 29 June 1906, made the longer run to Falmouth. She arrived with twenty-one feet of water in her hold, down by the head and with her foredeck awash. Others which had less serious encounters with the reef were the steamers *Friargate* of Hull, *Speedwell* of Falmouth, the coaster *Florida*, the Newcastle steamer *David Dawson*, the coaster *Falmouth Castle*, the steamer *Dubravka* of Dubrovnik, and the well-known auxiliary coasting ketch *Tralee* of Barnstaple. One ship which sank within a mile of safety was the French steel barque *Alice Marie*. Crippled and sinking, she reached Mount's Bay, and though she came near enough to Penzance to hear the church bells ringing through the fog she could not find her way in and foundered in shallow water off St Michael's Mount.

There was no chance of reaching safety for the 177-ton Royal Fleet Auxiliary *Moorview*, which, bound from Belfast to Devonport, struck the Runnelstone at 2.30 am on 4 March 1920 in dense fog. She sank at once, but her crew of twenty-eight got clear in the boats; Captain Robinson and ten men were picked up by the Liverpool coaster *Fleswick* and the rest rowed into Sennen Cove at dawn. The *Moorview* was less than three months old, launched at Paisley for the Admiralty in December 1919. Two months and ten days after her wreck she was followed by the 1,609-ton Chicago steamer *Lake Grafton*, which struck Le Or on the night of 14 May 1920, fifteen hours out from Swansea with coal for Copenhagen. She listed heavily to starboard, and the wireless operator radioed an 'SOS' and then flashed distress signals from the deck, which attracted the coaster *Dunmore*, bound from Par to Preston with china clay. Meanwhile the crew had, with great difficulty, launched the boats, and because of the fog and heavy seas it took them half an hour to reach the *Dunmore*. She stood by until daylight, when all that could be seen of the *Lake Grafton* were her masts, funnel and forecastle head showing above the waves.

In the autumn of 1923 the Runnelstone had its fangs drawn at last; it wrecked its largest vessel and in doing so lost its granite tip which, since time immemorial, had stood just awash from the tides. The ship was the 6,173 tons gross steel screw steamer *City of Westminster*. Launched in 1916 as the *Rudelsburg* by the Flensburg Schiff S B Gest, she was taken over by the British Shipping Controller at the end of the 1914-18 war and found her way into the Ellerman Lines fleet, when her name was changed. She was bound from Belfast to Rotterdam to discharge a part cargo of South African maize, under command of Captain Ring when, at 3 pm on 8 October 1923, she hit the Runnelstone.

The weather was very thick, with drizzly rain and a strong south-west wind which sent the white caps racing past the grounded 'City's' tall sides as she rolled and bumped in the tide, which was just on the turn. Ten sailors, the captain's wife and daughter, and a lady passenger, were taken off by the Sennen lifeboat before a sudden heavy swell flung her against the steamer's side. The lifeboat's fenders took most of the blow, but the impact jerked one of her engines off its bed. The Penlee lifeboat put in a timely appearance and the rescue was able to continue, even though the *City of Westminster* was lurching even more heavily in the strongly flooding tide. A further thirty-five officers and men were taken off, and twenty-five others who had manned two of the ship's lifeboats were taken in tow by the Penzance steam drifter *Pioneer*; as dusk fell, all the shipwrecked people were landed at Newlyn. Hardly had they stepped ashore than the Penlee lifeboat put out again, after reports of a ship's siren wailing from the Runnelstone, but the mystery was soon solved. The Falmouth tugs standing by the wreck signalled to the coastguards that it was the *City of Westminster*'s own siren sounding, its lanyard having fouled some rigging.

That night the sea worsened and when dawn came the *City of Westminster* lay broken-backed, with her stern balanced over twenty fathoms, submerged at high water except for her masts, bows and funnel. She lasted an even shorter time than the *Lake Grafton*, as on the night of the 9th a ssw gale carried her off the reef into deep water. Little was salvaged from the wreck, though some

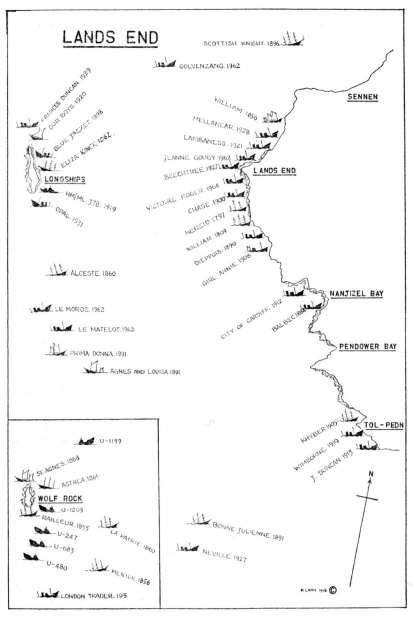

LANDS END

SCOTTISH KNIGHT. 1896

GOLVENZANG. 1962

SENNEN

FRANCES DUNCAN. 1929
OUR BOYS. 1920
BLUE JACKET. 1898
ELIZA KINCK. 1062.

LONGSHIPS

HM/ML. 378. 1919

OPAL. 1931

WILLIAM. 1856
MELLANEAR. 1928
LAMBANESS. 1921
JEANNE GOUGY. 1962
BEECHTREE. 1927
VICTOIRE ROGER. 1964
CHASE. 1900
NEREID. 1797
WILLIAM. 1809
DIEPPOIS. 1890
GIRL ANNIE. 1908

LANDS END

ALCESTE. 1860

LE MOROS. 1962

LE MATELOT. 1962

PRIMA DONNA. 1891

AGNES AND LOUISA. 1891

CITY OF CARDIFF. 1912
BALBEC.1888

NANJIZEL BAY

PENDOWER BAY

KHYBER.1905
WIMBORNE. 1910
J. DUNCAN. 1913

TOL - PEDN

N

U-1199

ST. AGNES. 1868
ASTREA. 1861

WOLF ROCK
U-1209
RAILLEUR. 1855
LA PATRIE. 1860
U-247
U-683
U-480
MENTOR. 1856

LONDON TRADER. 1915

BONNE JULIENNE. 1891

NEVILLE. 1927

R. LARN. 1968 ©

Wreck locations off Land's End and the Longships.

of her derrick booms and masts were recovered and for many years did duty as telegraph poles in the Penlee Quarries at Newlyn. Though the *City of Westminster* was a complete wreck, her loss was not in vain; the impact of her great bulk had demolished the top of the Runnelstone, so that it now lies twenty feet below the surface and is harmless to ships of less than that draught. There has been no wreck on it since.

Land's End—the very name has a remote and magical sound. But there is a great difference between the Land's End of legend and romance, the haunting beauty of the sea and sky of summer and the Land's End of stark winter reality. Then the tall cliffs face all the wild weather that the Atlantic can conjure up. Line upon line of breakers with a gale at their backs, unimpeded for a thousand miles, sweep in from the great northern ocean and race headlong into the cliffs. The impact makes the solid granite shudder, spray flies a hundred feet in the air and, caught by the wind, drives across moors and fields for a mile or more. It is then, desolate and windswept, that Land's End is at its finest, and its worst.

In this weather the ship *Nereid* of London, Henry Yeoman master, wrecked on 17 December 1797 while homeward bound from Quebec with timber and hides, was battered into almost unrecognisable fragments. Much of her cargo was recovered and sold at various auctions over the next eighteen months, including 115 pieces of 'exceeding fine' oak timber, 1,867 deer skins, 246 racoon and marten skins, 32 bear skins, 3,032 white oak pipe and hogshead staves, and six mountain cat skins. On 22 January 1809 the Demeraraman *William*, John Sinclair master, bound for the Thames with rum and sugar worth £40,000, mistook the Land's End beacon for one on the Scillies and the heavy south-west gale drove her into the cliffs. Her crew got ashore over the bowsprit, but as they crouched on the rocks the captain, mate and five men were swept away. The five survivors, one of them the owner's son, were rescued with ropes by the efforts of Lieutenant Jones, the young naval officer in command of the signalling station at Tol-Pedn. Neither the excise men nor the local wreckers were able to lay hands on anything of value as the *William* was smashed up by the sea, dissolving the sugar and shattering the rum barrels.

Only a few ships have been wrecked at Land's End and identified, though often after a storm wreckage would be found between

Tol-Pedn and the Peals. Many more sank offshore, driven under by wind and seas, or were lost on the outlying reefs. Fog and a sudden change of weather were together responsible for even more wrecks than the gales; Land's End is never safe, even in fine weather. The 848-ton early Cunarder *Balbec* was wrecked on a bright March day in 1884, when she struck a submerged object off the Longships, and had to be beached in Nanjizel Bay. She had left Liverpool the previous day on her regular run to Le Havre, loaded with hides, chemicals and Manchester goods, with a crew of twenty-nine and five saloon passengers. It was the lowest tide for years as she rounded Land's End at noon on the 28th, in calm seas and an easterly breeze. Suddenly she gave a slight shudder, but sailed on; a hasty inspection revealed water pouring in through the coal in the port side bunker. The pumps were started but could not cope, so Captain Marsh ran her ashore. No one was drowned, but the *Balbec*, which had been launched on the Clyde in 1853, was a total wreck, the fourth Cunard steamer lost on the Cornish coast since 1857. A Trinity House steamer searched for the mysterious obstruction, but found neither reef nor sunken wreck.

But it was a severe gale that caused the worst wreck of all at Land's End, the loss of the Liverpool ship *Khyber*. Towards evening on 14 March 1905, the keepers of the Wolf Rock light saw a full-rigged ship bearing up from the Scillies, running free before a freshening south-west wind, on course for the Lizard. But the glass was falling, and at dusk James Quick, coxswain of Porthleven lifeboat, saw the *Khyber* being slowly forced into Mount's Bay. Though she flew no distress signals, he sent a telegram to Falmouth for tugs and joined Chief Officer Bell at the coastguard station, watching the ship wallow in heavy seas, too far to leeward to round the Lizard. Studden Cowls, a Porthleven net-maker, saw some of her sails blown away in the rising gale, which was shifting more to the westward as darkness fell. She had still made no signal when night finally hid her, and it was thought that she must have worked seaward, or somehow scraped around the land and made for Falmouth. Even John Rowe, an aged fisherman, watching her from the cliffs above his home at Porthgwarra, thought she had got clear, though earlier he had remarked to a friend that if she kept her course and the wind increased, she would be in trouble before morning.

Through the night, darkness, rain and the storm hid the *Khyber* and her crew of twenty-six. As dawn broke, a workman engaged in building a new coastguard station at Tol-Pedn ran into Porthgwarra with the news that a ship was nearly on the rocks. John Rowe and several companions hurried to the cliffs. Seventy yards out lay the *Khyber*, crippled. One huge sea had pooped her, smashed the midships bridge and carried away the quarter boats. The other boats were broken on their skids, and aloft the mainyard had cockbilled and hardly a shred of canvas was left. A fisherman set off for Sennen Cove, but as he reached Land's End he encountered a coastguard who was patrolling southwards. They ran down into Sennen, and at 6.30 am the lifeboat and rocket brigade were called. The lifeboat could not be launched as the sea had flung boulders from the breakwater across the slipway, but the rocket cart was soon rumbling up the steep hill out of the village. Even as it took the high road to St Leven, disaster had struck at Portloe.

Shortly before seven o'clock the *Khyber* took an enormous sea. She rose to it well, her two anchor cables bar taut as her bows reared high in the air. The wave roared past, but as she sank into the trough another great breaker caught her on the port bow. She yawed to leeward, and with a grating rumble her stern dropped squarely on to the rocks. The mizzen mast collapsed, then the fore and main, flinging many of the crew into the sea; her hull suddenly parted amidships, and the waves tore into the open ends. In fifteen minutes the *Khyber* was a pile of debris, surrounded by a sea of floating wheat. Only three of her crew escaped. John Harries, an 18-year-old apprentice, jumped overboard seconds before she struck and, clinging to a piece of timber, was hauled from the surf unconscious. Able seaman Gustavus Johannsen and ship's boy Leonard Willis, after seeing seven of their shipmates swept away by a single wave, dropped from the stern on to a group of rocks and were later hauled to the clifftop by fishermen and coastguards. The Sennen rocket brigade arrived at Portloe just as their rescue had been completed, and the Penzance lifeboat appeared round Tol-Pedn an hour later, in tow of the salvage steamer *Lady of the Isles*. But it was too late for Captain Henry Rothery and twenty-two of the crew. His body and some of the others were recovered and are buried beside the tower of St Leven church.

The *Khyber*, an iron full-rigger of 1,967 tons, was launched on Merseyside in 1880 by W H Potter for the Indian trade of the Brocklebank Line. She was one of the first windjammers to carry a 'spike' or one-piece bowsprit. In 1899 she was sold to the Calgate Shipping Co (J Joyce, managers) and her last voyage began on 16 September 1904, when she sailed from Williamstown at the mouth of the River Yarra, Melbourne, bound for Queenstown, Ireland, for orders, with 3,000 tons of Victorian wheat. She was 138 days out from Melbourne, instead of the usual 100 or 110, when she passed the Wolf Rock on that fateful March afternoon.

A mile or so from Portloe, in the surf of Nanjizel Bay, lie the boilers of the Cardiff collier *City of Cardiff*, whose engines were as ineffective as the *Khyber*'s sails against the fury of a March gale. Under the command of Captain Henry Storey, she sailed from Le Havre on 6 March 1912, in water ballast for Cardiff. She bunkered at Dartmouth and at midnight on the 20th passed the Lizard in a freshening southerly gale. Dawn found her trying to round Land's End, but again and again she was beaten back, once as far as Porthcurno, when her crew glimpsed the hulk of the *South America*. At last making some headway, she passed Tol-Pedn at 9 am, though so close it was feared she would be blown ashore by the gale, which had veered wsw and increased. Close under her lee stood Carn Guthenbras, where on 7 November 1910 another Cardiff steamer, the *Wimborne*, had been wrecked in similar weather while bound from Rotterdam to Barry in ballast.

By eleven o'clock the *City of Cardiff*, now unable to make a yard of headway, came to anchor a mile south of Land's End, but less than half a mile from Carn Les-Boel, the wave-battered flank of Nanjizel Bay. Though her engines were kept full ahead to ease the strain on the cables, she slowly dragged towards the shore. Captain Storey made one last desperate attempt to get clear, but a sudden squall drove the collier to leeward and she struck the rocks 150 yards out. The flooding tide carried her ashore until she grounded broadside on. Within minutes she was reached by a rocket line fired by the Sennen brigade, which had followed her along the cliffs. Far from panicking the crew strolled calmly about the spray-swept decks, smoking and chatting, while the wives of Captain Storey and chief officer Bethke moved among them, tightening lifejacket tapes or helping the sailors on with the bulky cork and canvas garments. The two women were the first to come ashore in the breeches-buoy, followed by chief engineer Meek with Mrs Bethke's two-year-old son Fritz tied to his waist. The rest of the crew followed, and finally Captain Storey, who had refused to leave the bridge until the last moment although the funnel threatened to collapse. Hardly was the rescue over than the coast-

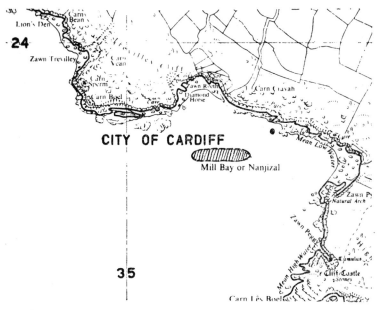

Location of the 3,089-ton collier *City of Cardiff*, wrecked beneath the Nanjizel cliffs in 1912.

guards heard the popping of rivets as the collier's hull bilged under the battering of the waves.

Within twenty-four hours the *City of Cardiff* was a broken hulk beneath the Nanjizel cliffs. She was only six years old, launched in 1906 by Ropner & Co of Stockton, as a steel screw steamer of 3,089 tons gross. Two of her sister ships were to be lost within three years of her; the *Cornish City*, destroyed by the German raider *Karlsruhe* in the south Atlantic on 21 September 1914, and the *Indian City*, sunk by *U-29* nine miles off Scilly on 12 March 1915.

In a violent gale there is no shelter off Land's End; wind and sea come booming in from the Atlantic through the narrow bottle-neck, only twenty-one miles wide, between the mainland and the Scilly Isles, building up enormous waves. When the wind veers north-west, as it usually does after a southerly gale, it combines with the fierce tides and currents to produce a heavy and confused cross sea. These storms have sunk many ships off Land's End, often unseen and unidentified. On 28 June 1845, the St Ives schooner *Ivy* was rounding Land's End in a northerly gale, when she encountered another schooner of about 100 tons burden hove-to with her crew in the rigging. She sank before the *Ivy* came within two cables length of her and none of the crew stayed afloat long enough to be picked up. Many other small coasting craft, and a good number of larger sailing ships, must have gone down over the years, unwitnessed and without trace. Only when the crew got away in the ship's boat was her name usually discovered, as in the case of the brig *Tancred* of Sunderland which sank on 23 April 1848. In 1860, the Liverpool barque *Alceste* foundered near the Longships on 5 April, and on 29 November the brig *La Patrie* of St Brieux sank off the Wolf. Others were the Boston schooner *New Unity*, cut down off Longships 29 September 1876; the schooner *Emile* of Granville, on 1 June 1882; the brigantine *Bonne Julienne* of Lorient, left derelict and sinking on 6 January 1891; two months later the schooners *Prima Donna* of Penzance and *Martha* of Caernarvon, the ketch *Agnes and Louisa* of Newquay and several others went down with all hands during the great blizzard of 9-10 March.

Less certain was the fate of the 2,066-ton Liverpool steel barque *Afon Cefnui*, which disappeared after leaving Swansea for San Francisco with general cargo on 5 January 1894. A month later wreckage bearing her name was washed up at Scilly, Penzance and Land's End; nothing was found of her crew and she was presumed to have foundered somewhere off Land's End during a heavy westerly gale a few days after she sailed. In the spring of 1905 the 1,470-ton full-rigger *Glenburn* of Greenock also disappeared with all hands. She was posted missing when three months overdue from San Francisco to Liverpool, when wreckage, including a shattered lifeboat bearing her name, was found northwards of Land's End.

The offshore sinkings did not cease with the decline of sail. On

16 April 1911, six weeks after the Plymouth schooner *Holly How* sank off Land's End, the 3,431-ton steamer *Cargo Layo*, Swansea for Mexico with coal, passed the Longships and was never seen again. Two years later, the small Glasgow steamer *Toanui*, bound from the Clyde to New Zealand with general cargo, vanished in the same place. Then, on 5 February 1915, the little steam coaster *London Trader*, on her regular run from Dublin to London, was sunk by a furious ssw gale near the Wolf Rock, with only four survivors.

The crew of the 1,084-ton Cardiff collier *Neville*, which capsized and sank in a southerly gale six miles south of Land's End on 1 April 1927, while bound from Barry to Rouen, were rescued by other steamers by little short of a miracle, but there was serious loss of life when another large Cardiff steamer went down two years later. The 2,384-ton *Frances Duncan* succumbed to a 100-mph westerly gale as she rounded Land's End on 5 December 1929, twelve hours out from Barry with coal for Bergen. As she capsized, swept by thirty-foot seas, her crew had to jump overboard; five survivors, including Captain Frederick Martin, a Cornishman from St Erth, near Hayle, were picked up by the Newcastle steamer *Alicia Marie*, but sixteen other men were lost. When the Glasgow coaster *Opal* sank a mile off the Longships on 4 September 1931, her captain and chief engineer were drowned. More recently, during a severe north-west gale on 10 January 1962, three entire crews were drowned when the trawlers *Le Moros* of Concarneau, *Le Matelot* of Lorient and *Golvenzang* of Zeebrugge went down off Land's End.

The coast of West Cornwall is particularly subject to sudden changes in the weather. A clear day can be quickly blotted out by a squall of rain, and as quickly the sun can shine again, but even more dangerous to navigation is the suddenness with which the land and sea can be hidden by thick fog. The French steamer *Dieppois* was homeward bound to Dieppe from Swansea, on her maiden voyage on 28 March 1890, when one such fog came down and she ran on to the great Armed Knight Rock. She soon broke up under the pounding of the heavy ground swell which so often accompanies a fog at Land's End. and only with difficulty was her crew able to get ashore in the ship's boats.

A Lowestoft sailing trawler, the *Girl Annie*, was wrecked a short

distance away at Pardenack on 4 May 1908, while homeward bound
for the Padstow fisheries. Her crew rowed away in the boat, but
the fog was so thick that it was ten hours before they landed in
Nanjizel Bay, bringing the first news of the wreck. But there was
plenty of help at hand when the 1,939-ton Cardiff collier *J Duncan*
ran ashore below Carn Guthenbras in the early morning of 14
August 1913. As she was under charter to the Admiralty with steam
coal for Devonport Dockyard, naval tugs and the destroyer *Liffey*
were sent to her aid, together with local lifeboats and salvage craft.
Although her stern was afloat in deep water, nothing would free
her bows from the rocks and eight days later she was abandoned
as a total loss. The *J Duncan* was launched by the Ailsa Shipbuilding Co in 1905 for the J Duncan Steamship Co of Cardiff.

Close to the tip of Land's End lie the Peal Rocks, just awash,
and here on 28 September 1921 the Swansea steamer *Lambaness*,
bound from Barry to St Malo with coal, steamed right over the
reef in thick hazy weather. She sank until only her masts and
funnel stood above the water; her crew survived, but the fifteen-
year-old *Lambaness* did not last long in such an exposed position.
Another 2,000 tons of Welsh coal strewed the seabed around the
Peals on 2 March 1927, when the 827-ton steamer *Beechtree*, of
and from Cardiff for Rouen, had a steering gear failure as she came
round Land's End late at night in thick, blustery weather. She
smashed on to the reef at full speed and her crew had to abandon
her at once, as within minutes she was listing heavily, decks awash.
By dawn, only her foremast and part of her bridge showed above
the breaking seas. Eighteen months later the same coastguards and
fishermen who had saved her crew went to the rescue again, this
time to the 438-ton Penzance coaster *Mellanear* which had run
into dense fog after passing Sennen on voyage from Cardiff to
Morlaix with coal and struck the Peals. The date was 28 September
1928 and she remained upright on the reef for several days, though
slowly settling deeper with every tide until she finally broke her
back and slipped off into deep water to join the *Lambaness* and
the *Beechtree*. The *Mellanear* was launched by J Fullerton & Co
of Paisley, in August 1921, and though registered at Penzance was
owned by Harvey's of Hayle and always known locally as a Hayle
boat, being one of the last of the once large steamer fleet of that
port.

As if gales and fogs were not enough for the mariner to contend with, a number of dangerous reefs lie off Land's End; the Shark's Fin, the Kettle's Bottom, the Fillis and, right opposite the Land's End promontory, the great Longships rocks, the name a reminder of the days when Vikings roved the Cornish seas. Though there has been a lighthouse on the Longships since 1795, it has not prevented wrecks on the reef. The Danish ship *Eliza Kinck*, Hamburg to Cardiff in ballast, was becalmed nearby in hazy weather on 29 May 1862 and the strong flood tide carried her on to the reef. Her crew stood by in their longboat until she drifted clear, and a passing steamer took the waterlogged ship in tow for Falmouth. Less fortunate were the crew of a foreign barque whose topmasts were seen sticking out of the water when the fog lifted at noon on 26 January 1873. The tremendous ground swell prevented a coastguard boat from even identifying her before she broke up, and it was assumed that all her crew had perished.

As with the *Eliza Kinck*, light airs and a strong flood tide brought about the wreck of the 850-ton Glasgow iron barque *Scottish Knight*, Chile to Leith with nitrates, which was idling up past the Wolf in a light south-westerly breeze when the current caught her and swept her ashore near the lighthouse. A steamer towed her clear, but the barque soon sank before the disappointed gaze of the crew of a Hayle tug which had been intent on salvage. Two other small wrecks on the Longships were the naval motor launch *ML 378*, lost in a December gale in 1919, and the Porthleven lugger *Our Boys* on 22 September 1920, whose crew were marooned on the rocks until, with the flood tide round their ankles, they were rescued by the Sennen lifeboat.

The most spectacular wreck on the Longships was that of the Cardiff tramp *Bluejacket*, which struck the rocks not sixty feet from the main door of the lighthouse on 9 November 1898. The wreck came at the end of a long tramping voyage which began on 4 June, under the command of Captain James Thomas, when she sailed from South Shields with coal for Venice, and ended in the course of a voyage from Danzig to Plymouth with railway sleepers.

At five o'clock on the evening of 9 November, the *Bluejacket* sailed from Plymouth Sound in ballast for Cardiff. The weather was thick, with a strong ESE wind, but shore lights were visible so she was kept at her full speed of ten knots. Before he went below at 9.30 pm, Captain Thomas told the second mate to call him when they approached Land's End. Just before midnight the captain was roused by the tramp's engines going full astern. Even as he made for the bridge there came a rending crash and the engineers were driven from the boiler room by an inrush of water. The *Bluejacket* was on the Longships and the brilliant flash of the light showed up her already listing decks. The crew, including the captain's wife, took to the boats and were picked up by the Sennen lifeboat and landed at the cove. At dawn the *Bluejacket* presented a startling sight, poised like a gigantic seesaw across the rocks, at the very foot of the lighthouse. Eight days after the wreck she was sold to Joseph Breen, shipbreaker of Penzance, who began to demolish her when weather and tide allowed. The *Bluejacket*, which had been launched in 1883 by J L Thompson of Sunderland, as an iron screw, schooner-rigged steamer of 2,205 tons gross, was owned by the Bluejacket Steamship Co of Cardiff. She was still on the Longships in January 1900, when the small tug *Chase* used by Joseph Breen dragged her anchors in a strong westerly gale and was herself wrecked beneath Land's End Hotel.

Eight miles south-west of Land's End stands the Wolf Rock, in deep water, isolated and lonely, and almost perpetually beaten by heavy seas. Its name derives from the wolf-like howl which the sea used to make as it swept into a cavernous funnel in the rock. Legend has it that wreckers, annoyed at this natural warning to ships, once rowed out and blocked up the small blow-hole, but if they did the Wolf Rock certainly did not stop howling. Over the years, there have been several schemes for placing a new warning signal on the rock. In the early 1800s an enormous wolf, designed to howl when the wind blew, was cast in bronze. It was taken out to the Wolf Rock in a boat, but heavy seas prevented it from being landed and installed, and eventually the project was abandoned. A bell buoy was next suggested, but in the end a tall post-and-cage beacon was erected. It had no light and was hard to see in bad weather, and there were still wrecks on the Wolf Rock. On 9 January 1855 the French sloop *Railleur*, Roi master, Bordeaux to Bristol with general cargo, struck and sank within minutes. Her crew of four were rescued from their boat off Penzance at dawn by the revenue cutter *Badger*. On 11 May the following year, the 220-ton Cornish brigantine *Mentor*, bound for Swansea from her home port of Devoran with copper ore, ran on to the Wolf in thick fog. She drifted clear and Captain William Pearce steered for the land, but a few hours later she sank, just after the crew had been taken off by the *George* of Truro.

Worse was to follow; the 350-ton Prussian barque *Astrea*, a few hours out from Falmouth, bound for Newry to discharge her cargo of Crimean wheat, ran into rain and fog. At 2.30 am on 16 March 1861, her lookouts sighted the Wolf, but she missed stays and drove beneath the highest and steepest side of the rock. A small boat was lowered but was swept away with only one man in it, who was later picked up off Land's End by the Newlyn lugger *Band of Hope*. Through mismanagement, they lost the longboat as well, and then took refuge in the foretop, dragging with them the captain, who had been injured when the harness cask broke loose. At 5 am the Newlyn lugger *Triumph* saw the wreck, came as close as she could and her crew hailed the Prussians to launch their boats, as she herself did not carry one. While the *Astrea*'s crew were trying to make them understand that their boats were gone, the barque slipped off the rocks and sank. Only the captain and a young sailor were picked up as they clung to wreckage; nine other men were drowned. The *Triumph* had only just rescued these two when a schooner nearly ran her down in the fog; its flying jib-boom smashed off her mizzen mast.

Three months after the wreck of the *Astrea*, on 2 July 1861, the young but celebrated constructor of lighthouses, James Douglass, arrived at Penzance with men and materials, ready to begin work on the erection of a lighthouse on the Wolf Rock. It was as well that the workmen's families accompanied them, for it was to be eight years before the lighthouse was completed and two more before the light first flashed out on 9 January 1871. Even while the tower was under construction there was a wreck, when the Cornish schooner *St Agnes* of St Agnes, Nankivell master, bound from Rio Grande to Liverpool with bone ash, failed to clear the Wolf in a south-west gale. She broke up fast and one man was swept overboard, but Captain Nankivell and the others drifted in the boat for twenty hours before a Falmouth pilot cutter picked them up.

With the completion of the lighthouse, the Wolf Rock was no longer a hazard but a signpost of the sea. Even so, there was an

unusual wreck there on 18 December 1944, when the German submarine *U-1209*, cruising around Land's End with her schnorkel but
no periscope up, managed, in that wide expanse of deep water, to
hit the Wolf Rock. In spite of her strengthened hull for deep diving,
she sank quickly, but some of her crew were picked up by naval
craft. *U-1209* was one of four submarines sent out via North Scotland to harass convoys off Land's End; two were destroyed and
only the fourth eventually limped back to base. By the end of the
war five U-boats lay on the bottom round the Wolf Rock, *U-1209*
wrecked, and *U-247*, *U-683*, *U-480* and *U-1199* sunk by Allied
warships or aircraft.

A simple lighthouse may have made the Wolf Rock safe, but
even with all the modern aids to navigation and advanced rescue
services Land's End is still deadly. Shortly before 5 am on 3
November 1962, the coastguard on watch at Cape Cornwall saw
the navigation lights of the 250-ton Dieppe trawler *Jeanne Gougy*
about two miles offshore. She was steering southwards and he was
expecting the lights to vanish behind the Land's End headlands
when she suddenly altered course towards the land and he could
see that she would pass very close to the cliffs beyond Sennen. His
warning signals brought no apparent response, but the trawler
stopped shortly afterwards, almost as if her crew had suddenly
realised their danger. The coastguard sent a colleague to investigate
and minutes later a red distress flare soared up from Land's End
and rescue services closed in on Gamper Bay, a small rocky inlet
tucked into the headland. A fresh northerly wind and frequent
sharp rain squalls buffeted the coastguards and LSA men as they
assembled on the clifftop, where the air was already heavy with
the stench of fuel oil. Below them lay the *Jeanne Gougy*, rolling
and lurching as an immense ground swell swept over her decks.
Parachute flares were fired, and in their glare five or six men could
be seen crouched in the starboard wing of the bridge balcony. A
line-carrying rocket was fired, but it fell in front of the shattered
glass of the wheelhouse windows and several arms were thrust
through the jagged shards, grabbing wildly at the line. Another
rocket was fired, but the man who tried to retrieve it was swept
overboard and the same great wave ripped away one of the wheelhouse doors and the sea poured into the superstructure. More
lines were fired, but every one fouled a wire stay which ran from

o

the foremast to a corner of the bridge. Minutes after the sixth rocket soared across, the *Jeanne Gougy* crashed over on to her port side, a tragic repetition of the wreck of the *Vert Prairial*. By dawn the *Jeanne Gougy* lay swept by the seas, a dead ship, on her side in a tangle of nets and ropes.

Hope that there might be survivors dwindled through the morning as the trawler rolled lifelessly in the surf. Sennen lifeboat picked up a body offshore and a 'Whirlwind' helicopter from RAF Chivenor recovered another, but still the watchers stayed on the cliffs. Suddenly, at eleven o'clock, a woman on holiday, who had motored over from Coverack to see the wreck, saw a hand waving weakly from the battered wheelhouse and cried, 'There's someone alive in there!'

Though the trawler had then been under water for the best part of six hours, rescue efforts were at once resumed. Another rocket line fouled the wire forestay but the LSA men were able to manœuvre it within reach of the man in the wheelhouse who secured it but was too weak to climb into the breeches-buoy which followed.

Then a second near-miracle occurred. Four bedraggled figures crawled out of the trawler's forepeak, clambered up the vertical decks and hung on to the guard rail, their faces upturned to the cliff. While they were being hauled to safety on ropes manœuvred over them by the coastguards above, the helicopter returned and hovered over the wreck. A belt was let down to the man in the wheelhouse but again he was too weak to grasp it and Flt Sgt Eric Smith was then lowered on to the deck, looped the strop over the man's shoulders and both were hauled up to the helicopter, which landed the man on the clifftop. Believing that more men might still be trapped, Flt Sgt Smith made a second descent on to the trawler and found a young boy crouched in a passage behind the bridge. He, too, was winched up and landed, after which the flight sergeant made yet a third visit to the trawler but, seeing no one and getting no reply to his shouts, he was ordered back up to the helicopter.

Eleven men, including the captain, lost their lives in the wreck, which was as inexplicable as it was tragic. The *Jeanne Gougy* had left Waterford the evening before and the weather had been rough all the way across. She ran ashore during a particularly bad squall but, like the *Vert Prairial*, she had been built to withstand far worse conditions. Flt Sgt Smith was later awarded the George Medal for his bravery. The men he saved, as well as the four others, owed their lives to their good fortune in finding an air pocket in the hull and their tenacity in keeping themselves afloat and refusing to give up hope of survival.

In less than eighteen months, the tragedy of the *Jeanne Gougy* came perilously near to being repeated. If the seas had been higher, the story of the 90-ton Ostend trawler *Victoire Roger*, which ran ashore in wet, foggy weather only 200 yards from the Dieppe trawler's wreckage on 24 March 1964, might have been very different. As it was, her crew were only saved by a brilliant and daring rescue. The Sennen Cove coxswain, manœuvring his lifeboat with extreme skill in the narrow cove, twice went alongside the trawler, the second time with keel bumping on the rocks, to take off the injured skipper.

At Land's End, and in the present, this volume ends. But the history of shipwreck, of which this is but a small part, goes on. The cliffs still stand, storms still rage and the sea does not change. Modern technology and the disappearance of commercial sail have greatly reduced the incidence of wrecks, but to err is still human and so long as men build ships and seamen sail in them there will be no end to the story.

ACKNOWLEDGMENTS

The authors gratefully acknowledge the help given by the following people and institutions: J. J. Behenna (Brixham); H. L. Douch (Curator) and R. Penhalurick (Royal Institution of Cornwall, Truro); Miss R. Beckett (Falmouth Reference Library); the staff of Camborne Public Library; the staff of the Local History section, Plymouth Central Reference Library; J. Bottrell (The *Cornishman*, Penzance); Station Officer R. Paul (HM Coastguard, Treen); P. I. Hughes (Camborne); P. Barnes (Carbis Bay); D. McGibney (Penzance); Maureen Larn (Helston) and Mrs R. D. Carter (Camborne).

Thanks are also tendered to the following for permission to reproduce photographs: K. Hancock (Falmouth); F. E. Gibson (Scilly); T. Roskrow (Truro); Richards Bros (Penzance) and *The Western Morning News* (Plymouth).

APPENDIX:

THE LAW OF WRECK AND SALVAGE

THE law of salvage and much of the law of wreck is contained in Part 9 of the Merchant Shipping Act of 1894. Unfortunately, when it was written, many circumstances and situations that arise today were not envisaged, so that interpretation of the law is difficult and produces many arguable points, especially in connection with underwater archaeology and similar diving activities. Even the apparently harmless pastime of 'beachcombing' can constitute a felony.

The term 'wreck' includes any vessel, part of a vessel, its fittings, equipment or cargo, and any aircraft or part of an aircraft; but, it also includes any object lost or abandoned at sea or in tidal waters, although the object may have no apparent connection with a vessel or aircraft. Anything 'foreign' to the sea, no matter how long ago it was lost or abandoned, whether found on the sea-bed, floating on the surface, or on the foreshore, remains the property of its lawful owner. To take such an object with the intention of permanently depriving the owner of his right of possession, even to keep it as a souvenir, is a criminal offence. Section 15, para 3, of the Larceny Act of 1916 states that every person who steals any part of any vessel in distress, wrecked, stranded or cast ashore, any goods, merchandise or articles of any kind belonging to such wrecked vessels, is guilty of felony, and upon conviction shall be liable to imprisonment for any term not exceeding fourteen years.

Since no offence can be committed if the lawful owner gives his permission for an object to be salvaged, it would appear at first sight that ownership must be established before anything can be salvaged. However, the Act of 1894 states that where there is no apparent owner, objects salvaged are to be declared and handed to a Receiver of Wreck. This is usually an officer of HM Customs and Excise or a Coastguard, appointed by the Ministry of Transport, who is empowered to receive and hold 'wreck' in a 'Queen's

245

warehouse' for a maximum period of one year, during which the Receiver attempts to establish ownership and displays a public notice to this effect. If the 'wreck' is not claimed within the year, the Receiver can sell the object, or allow the salvor to keep it in lieu of salvage expenses.

Normally, HM Receivers of Wreck are accommodating people and at the end of the year will often give a salvor the choice of the cash balance of the sale, or keeping the object in question. If the object is sold, the Receiver deducts any expenses he incurred (transport, postage, storage etc), subtracts a sum to a set scale which goes to the Crown, and the salvor receives the balance. This choice is especially useful when the object is reasonably small or of negligible value, in which case the salvor probably places more value on his 'souvenir' than his services in recovery. If the 'wreck' is of greater value, for example a quantity of scrap metal, a ship's propeller, some bales of rubber etc, a sale will almost certainly be arranged, the salvor then claiming for salvage expenses, taking into account the use of a boat, fuel, wages of crew, cost of compressed air, technical skill, wear and tear on diving equipment, special equipment needed etc. If the 'wreck' is of little value or is of a perishable nature, the Receiver can dispose of it immediately, but the proceeds must then be held for a period of one year after which a settlement will be made.

Even if a salvor has the permission of the owner of 'wreck', or the owner carries out his own salvage, they must both declare everything they land to the Receiver under penalty of a fine not exceeding one hundred pounds. There are various reasons for this formality; the objects salvaged may be subject to some duty or restriction—two examples being spirits and gold—or a counter claim may later be made by a third party, and the Receiver must then be in a position to carry out immediate enquiries.

A receipt, known as a 'salvor's warrant' is issued by a Receiver for all objects handed over to him. This states the nature of the 'wreck', name of salvor, etc., and is returned to the Receiver at the end of the year upon final settlement.

It is illegal to salvage any 'wreck' within the territorial waters of the United Kingdom, and then to dispose or attempt to dispose of it in a foreign port. In the same way it is an offence to bring into the United Kingdom any 'wreck' salvaged from outside the territorial waters without declaring it to the Receiver of Wreck. Failure to comply with any of the requirements of declaration or delivery of 'wreck' to a Receiver is punishable by a fine not exceeding one hundred pounds. In the case of a conviction where it is proved that the salvor was not the lawful owner of the 'wreck', that person forfeits all claim to salvage expenses and is liable to reimburse the owner double the value of the goods stolen.

Two other points worth special mention concern trespass and salvage claims. Whilst it is commonsense not to venture on or near a wreck actually being salvaged, it is not an offence, and a diver can go down and take photographs or measurements as he pleases, provided nothing is removed or disturbed in any way. The second point covers the situation where a salvor recovers an item of 'wreck', declares it to the Receiver, and the owner then appears. The salvor may have gone to endless trouble to salvage the particular item, and even some expense, but his actions were completely voluntary. Therefore, the owner can claim the 'wreck' and is under no obligation to the salvor; he can also make the salvor return the 'wreck' from whence it came, at the salvor's expense! Ownership of a wreck is a financial investment, and the owner may have a very good reason for not wanting anything salvaged. He may be awaiting an increase in the price of a particular scrap metal, the wreck may be for sale awaiting survey by a buyer, or the wreck and its contents may even constitute a surety for some obligation. Would-be salvors are therefore strongly advised to follow the correct procedure, though it is to be hoped, in view of the widespread development of underwater exploration, that there may soon be some much-needed changes in the law of wreck and salvage.

Every wrecked ship belongs to someone, and if ownership can not be traced then it becomes vested in the Crown, provided the wreck is within territorial waters. Ships usually carry heavy insurance, borne by one or more underwriters. When such a ship sinks, the underwriters have to meet the claim and the ownership of the wreck becomes vested in the insurers. If the wreck is valuable, they are usually deluged with offers of purchase or salvage within hours of the wreck, and it may change hands again. But if the wreck is of little value, it may never be sold, or may be auctioned off on some lonely beach for as little as £5. As time passes, ownership of the wreck may change many times, and there is no requirement for this exchange to be made public. There is no central authority who knows exactly which wreck is owned by whom; one can only start enquiries at the office of the underwriters and work from there, provided the underwriters are still in business! Where the ownership is vested in an individual, when that person dies the title passes to the heirs. If the owner dies intestate, the title reverts to the Crown, but in this case, although the Crown technically 'owns' the wreck, they may not sell it to anyone else. This also applies to a foreign vessel wrecked in UK waters; ownership lies with the Crown but they cannot sell it or give salvage rights to it.

Research into wreck ownership requires endless patience and correspondence, and one can spend a whole year in research and letter writing and still be no nearer the goal. It is not until one attempts to trace back the ownership of a fifty-year-old wreck that one realises how many people go abroad to live, change their names, change addresses, re-marry, die intestate, appoint executors in other countries, have heirs that live in Australia or Chile, or just disappear from the face of the earth. Nevertheless, it is possible to establish ownership of even the most obscure wreck and there is a great sense of achievement in bringing such an investigation to a successful conclusion.

BIBLIOGRAPHY

Baring-Gould, S. *Cornish Characters and Strange Events*, Bodley Head, 1908

Blight, J. T. *A Week at the Land's End*, and *A Week at the Lizard*, Lake & Lake, Truro, 1893

Chard, C. A. *Don't Forget the Diver*, W. & R. Chambers, 1958

Coate, M. *Cornwall in the Civil War and Interregnum*, Clarendon Press, 1933

Course, Capt A. G. *Painted Ports*, Hollis & Carter, 1961

Dawson, Maj A. J. *Britain's Lifeboats*, Hodder & Stoughton, 1923

Domville-Fife, C. W. *Epics of the Square-rigged Ships*, Seeley Service, London, 1958

Elliot-Burns, L. E. *Medieval Cornwall*, Methuen, 1955

Grant, R. M. *U-Boats Destroyed*, Putnam, 1964

Greenhill, Basil. *The Merchant Schooners*, Vols I and II, David & Charles, 1968

Halliday, F. E. *Richard Carew of Antony*, Andrew Melrose, London, 1953

Hamilton Jenkin, A. K. *The Cornish Miner*, Allen & Unwin, 1927

Hamilton Jenkin, A. K. *Cornwall and its People*, Dent, 1945

Harvey, E. G. *Mullyon*, W. Lake, 1875

Hurd, A. *The Merchant Navy*, Vol II, John Murray, 1924

James, William. *The Naval History of Great Britain*, Richard Bentley, 1837

Jameson, William. *The Most Formidable Thing*, Rupert Hart-Davis, 1965

Keble Chatterton, E. *Fighting the U-Boats*, Hurst & Blackett, 1942

Le Fleming, H. M. *Warships of World War I*, Ian Allan, 1965

Lubbock, Basil. *The Last of the Windjammers*, Vols I and II, Brown, Son & Ferguson, 1963

MacMurrie, Francis E. *The World's Warships*, Sampson Low, 1944

Majdalany, Fred. *The Red Rocks of Eddystone*, Arrow Books, 1962

Marder, Arthur J. *From the Dreadnought to Scapa Flow*, Vols I to III, Oxford University Press, 1965

Mattingly, Garrett. *The Defeat of the Spanish Armada*, The Reprint Society, 1961

Page, William (Ed.). *The Victoria History of the Counties of England (Cornwall)*, Archibald Constable, 1906

Parkes, Oscar. *Ships of the Royal Navy*, Sampson Low, 1932
Pearse, Richard. *The Ports and Harbours of Cornwall*, H. E. Warne, 1964
Pearse Chope, R. (Ed.). *Early Tours in Devon and Cornwall*, David & Charles, 1967
Penaluna, W. *Survey of Cornwall*, Vols I and II, Whittaker, London, 1838
Pool, P. A. S. *Penzance, Brief History of the Town and Borough*, Penzance Old Cornwall Society, 1965
Roskill, Capt S. W. *The War At Sea*, Vols I to IV, HMSO, 1954
Tregellas, W. H. *Cornish Worthies*, Vols I and II, Elliot Stock, 1884
Trengrouse, H. *Shipwreck Investigated*, Penaluna, Helston, 1818
Walling, R. A. J. *The Story of Plymouth*, Westaway Books, 1950
Whitley, H. M. 'The Treasure Ship of Gunwalloe', *Journal of the Royal Institution of Cornwall*, No 10, part 1, 1890

NEWSPAPERS, JOURNALS, ETC

Alfred West of England Journal & General Advertiser, 1816-31
Commercial Shipping & General Advertiser for West Cornwall, from 1867
Cornish Magazine, Penpol Press, Falmouth. Various, 1960-68
Cornishman, from 1878
Cornish Telegraph, from 1851, and *Tidings*
Cornish Times and General Advertiser, from 1857
Daily Western Mercury, from 1860
Devonport Independent and Plymouth and Stonehouse Gazette, from 1833
Falmouth Packet, from 1832
Felix Farley's Bristol Journal, from 1714
Lifeboat, Journal of the Royal National Lifeboat Institution
Lloyd's Universal Register, various, 1764-1967
Mercantile Navy List and Maritime Directory, HMSO, 1939
Royal Cornwall Gazette, 1803-1952
St Austell Gazette, 1870-78
Sea Breezes, various, 1932-67
Trewman's Exeter Flying-post, from 1763
West Briton, from 1810
Western Luminary and Family Newspaper, from 1827
Western Independent
The Western Morning News, from 1860

INDEX OF SHIPS

Page references in italic type denote illustrations

Name	Wrecked	Page reference
A-1 submarine	1913	48
A-7 submarine	1914	48
Aberfoyle—see *Hansy*	1911	127
Abernyte	1898	*119*, 154
Abertay	1912	*170*, 207
Achilles	1867	153
Acklington	1887	225
Active	1853	32
Active	1881	121
Adele	1865	175
Adolf Vinnen	1923	*118*, 134
Adriana	1856	166
Affleck	1838	83
Afon Cefnui	1894	235
Afric	1917	47
Africa	1906	*126*, 186
Agnes	1911	46
Agnes	1925	210
Agnes and Louisa	1891	235
Alarm	1880	121
Albion	1872	38
Alceste	1860	235
Alexander Kennedy	1945	50
Alice Marie	1908	227
Alicia Marie	1929	236
Alkon	1966	71
Allegrity	1961	*18*, 50
Alliance	1886	178
Almond Branch	1917	47
Alpha		178
Ancona	1912	100
Andola	1895	*61, 77-9, 80*
Andromeda	1915	*35*, 44
Anemone	1903	41
Ann Elizabeth	1895	96
Anna Maria	1866	113
Anna Maria II	1881	113
Ansgir	1920	*170*, 195
Anson	1807	15, 22, *144, 145*, frontispiece
Antwerpen	1917	185
Aquilon	1891	84
Arab	1888	124
Archangelos	1929	63
Ardangorm	1940	37
Ardgarry	1962	137
Arethusa	1895	209
Argylle	1854	84
Ariel	1878	38
Arwenack	1862	151
Asama	1941	50
Astrea	1861	240
Auric	1893	125
Auspicious	1828	83
Australiabush	1917	47
Avebury	1884	197
Bacchus	1883	39
Badger	1855	239
Balbec	1884	231
Baltic	1907	193
Band of Hope	1861	240

INDEX